T0305254

Infrastructure and the Political Economy of Nation Building in Spain, 1720–2010

The Cañada Blanch / Sussex Academic Studies on Contemporary Spain

General Editor: Professor Paul Preston, London School of Economics

Germà Bel, *Infrastructure and the Political Economy of Nation Building in Spain, 1720–2010.*

Gerald Blaney Jr., *"The Three-Cornered Hat and the Tri-Colored Flag": The Civil Guard and the Second Spanish Republic, 1931–1936.*

Michael Eaude, *Triumph at Midnight in the Century: A Critical Biography of Arturo Barea.*

Soledad Fox, *Constancia de la Mora in War and Exile: International Voice for the Spanish Republic.*

Helen Graham, *The War and Its Shadow: Spain's Civil War in Europe's Long Twentieth Century.*

Angela Jackson, *'For us it was Heaven': The Passion, Grief and Fortitude of Patience Darton – From the Spanish Civil War to Mao's China.*

Gabriel Jackson, *Juan Negrín: Physiologist, Socialist, and Spanish Republican War Leader.*

Sid Lowe, *Catholicism, War and the Foundation of Francoism: The Juventud de Acción Popular in Spain, 1931–1939.*

Olivia Muñoz-Rojas, *Ashes and Granite: Destruction and Reconstruction in the Spanish Civil War and Its Aftermath.*

Linda Palfreeman, *¡SALUD!: British Volunteers in the Republican Medical Service during the Spanish Civil War, 1936–1939.*

Cristina Palomares, *The Quest for Survival after Franco: Moderate Francoism and the Slow Journey to the Polls, 1964–1977.*

David Wingeate Pike, *France Divided: The French and the Civil War in Spain.*

Isabelle Rohr, *The Spanish Right and the Jews, 1898–1945: Antisemitism and Opportunism.*

Gareth Stockey, *Gibraltar: "A Dagger in the Spine of Spain?"*

Ramon Tremosa-i-Balcells, *Catalonia – An Emerging Economy: The Most Cost-Effective Ports in the Mediterranean Sea.*

Dacia Viejo-Rose, *Reconstructing Spain: Cultural Heritage and Memory after Civil War.*

Richard Wigg, *Churchill and Spain: The Survival of the Franco Regime, 1940–1945.*

Published by the Cañada Blanch Centre for Contemporary Spanish Studies in conjunction with Routledge / Taylor & Francis

1. Francisco J. Romero Salvadó, *Spain 1914–1918: Between War and Revolution.*
2. David Wingeate Pike, *Spaniards in the Holocaust: Mauthausen, the Horror on the Danube.*
3. Herbert Rutledge Southworth, *Conspiracy and the Spanish Civil War: The Brainwashing of Francisco Franco.*
4. Angel Smith (editor), *Red Barcelona: Social Protest and Labour Mobilization in the Twentieth Century.*
5. Angela Jackson, *British Women and the Spanish Civil War.*
6. Kathleen Richmond, *Women and Spanish Fascism: The Women's Section of the Falange, 1934–1959.*
7. Chris Ealham, *Class, Culture and Conflict in Barcelona, 1898–1937.*
8. Julián Casanova, *Anarchism, the Republic and Civil War in Spain 1931–1939.*
9. Montserrat Guibernau, *Catalan Nationalism: Francoism, Transition and Democracy.*
10. Richard Baxell, *British Volunteers in the Spanish Civil War: The British Battalion in the International Brigades, 1936–1939.*
11. Hilari Raguer, *The Catholic Church and the Spanish Civil War.*
12. Richard Wigg, *Churchill and Spain: The Survival of the Franco Regime, 1940–45.*
13. Nicholas Coni, *Medicine and the Spanish Civil War.*
14. Diego Muro, *Ethnicity and Violence: The Case of Radical Basque Nationalism.*
15. Francisco J. Romero Salvadó, *Spain's Revolutionary Crisis, 1917–1923.*
16. Peter Anderson, *The Francoist Military Trials. Terror and Complicity, 1939–1945.*

To Milagros,
because she chose her own capital
To Anton,
because he is capital

Infrastructure and the Political Economy of Nation Building in Spain, 1720–2010

GERMÀ BEL

Translated by William Truini

Brighton • Portland • Toronto

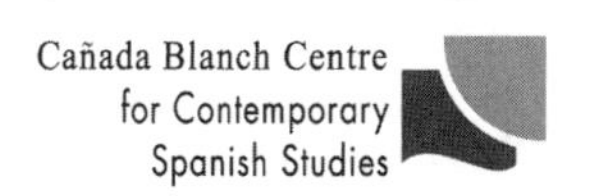

2 4 6 8 10 9 7 5 3 1

First published in Spanish by Destino in 2010 (title, España, capital París).
First published in English in Great Britain in 2012 by
SUSSEX ACADEMIC PRESS
PO Box 139, Eastbourne BN24 9BP

and in the United States of America by
SUSSEX ACADEMIC PRESS
920 NE 58th Ave Suite 300
Portland, Oregon 97213-3786

and in Canada by
SUSSEX ACADEMIC PRESS (CANADA)
90 Arnold Avenue, Thornhill, Ontario L4J 1B5

Published in collaboration with the Cañada Blanch Centre for Contemporary Spanish Studies and The Catalan Observatory, London.

British Library Cataloguing in Publication Data
A CIP catalogue record for this book is available from the British Library.

Library of Congress Cataloging-in-Publication Data
Bel i Queralt, Germa.
Infrastructure and the political economy of nation building in Spain, 1720–2010 / Germà Bel.
p. cm.
Includes bibliographical references.
ISBN 978-1-84519-507-6 (h/b : alk. paper) —
ISBN 978-1-84519-532-8 (pbk. : alk. paper)
1. Infrastructure (Economics)—Spain—Madrid (Region) 2. Madrid (Spain : Region)—Economic policy. 3. Spain—Politics and government.
I. Title.
HC387.M2B45 2012
330.946′41—dc23

2011032281

Typeset & designed by Sussex Academic Press, Brighton & Eastbourne.
Printed by TJ International, Padstow, Cornwall.
Printed on acid-free paper.

Contents

The Cañada Blanch Centre for Contemporary Spanish Studies

In the 1960s, the most important initiative in the cultural and academic relations between Spain and the United Kingdom was launched by a Valencian fruit importer in London. The creation by Vicente Cañada Blanch of the Anglo-Spanish Cultural Foundation has subsequently benefited large numbers of Spanish and British scholars at various levels. Thanks to the generosity of Vicente Cañada Blanch, thousands of Spanish schoolchildren have been educated at the secondary school in West London that bears his name. At the same time, many British and Spanish university students have benefited from the exchange scholarships which fostered cultural and scientific exchanges between the two countries. Some of the most important historical, artistic and literary work on Spanish topics to be produced in Great Britain was initially made possible by Cañada Blanch scholarships.

Vicente Cañada Blanch was, by inclination, a conservative. When his Foundation was created, the Franco regime was still in the plenitude of its power. Nevertheless, the keynote of the Foundation's activities was always a complete open-mindedness on political issues. This was reflected in the diversity of research projects supported by the Foundation, many of which, in Francoist Spain, would have been regarded as subversive. When the Dictator died, Don Vicente was in his seventy-fifth year. In the two decades following the death of the Dictator, although apparently indestructible, Don Vicente was obliged to husband his energies. Increasingly, the work of the Foundation was carried forward by Miguel Dols whose tireless and imaginative work in London was matched in Spain by that of José María Coll Comín. They were united in the Foundation's spirit of open-minded commitment to fostering research of high quality in pursuit of better Anglo-Spanish cultural relations. Throughout the 1990s, thanks to them, the role of the Foundation grew considerably.

In 1994, in collaboration with the London School of Economics, the Foundation established the Príncipe de Asturias Chair of Contemporary Spanish History and the Cañada Blanch Centre for Contemporary Spanish Studies. It is the particular task of the Cañada Blanch Centre for Contemporary Spanish Studies to promote the understanding of twentieth-century Spain through research and teaching of contemporary Spanish history, politics, economy, sociology and culture. The Centre possesses a valuable library and archival centre for specialists in contemporary Spain. This work is carried on through the publications of the doctoral and post-doctoral researchers at the Centre itself and through the many seminars and lectures held at the London School of Economics. While the seminars are the province of the researchers, the lecture cycles have been the forum in which Spanish politicians have been able to address audiences in the United Kingdom.

Since 1998, the Cañada Blanch Centre has published a substantial number of books in collaboration with several different publishers on the subject of contemporary Spanish history and politics. A fruitful partnership with Sussex Academic Press began in 2004 with the publication of Christina Palomares's fascinating work on the origins of the Partido Popular in Spain, *The Quest for Survival after Franco. Moderate Francoism and the Slow Journey to the Polls, 1964–1977*. This was followed in 2007 by Soledad Fox's deeply moving biography of one of the most intriguing women of 1930s Spain, *Constancia de la Mora in War and Exile: International Voice for the Spanish Republic* and Isabel Rohr's path-breaking study of anti-Semitism in Spain, *The Spanish Right and the Jews, 1898–1945: Antisemitism and Opportunism.* 2008 saw the publication of a revised edition of Richard Wigg's penetrating study of Anglo-Spanish relations during the Second World War, *Churchill and Spain: The Survival of the Franco Regime, 1940–1945* together with *Triumph at Midnight of the Century: A Critical Biography of Arturo Barea*, Michael Eaude's fascinating revaluation of the great Spanish author of *The Forging of a Rebel.*

Our collaboration in 2009 was inaugurated by Gareth Stockey's incisive account of another crucial element in Anglo-Spanish relations, *Gibraltar. A Dagger in the Spine of Spain*. We were especially proud that it was continued by the most distinguished American historian of the Spanish Civil War, Gabriel Jackson. His pioneering work *The Spanish Republic and the Civil War*, first published 1965 and still in print, quickly became a classic. The Sussex Academic Press/Cañada Blanch series was greatly privileged to be associated with Professor Jackson's biography of the great Republican war leader, Juan Negrín.

2011 took the series to new heights. Two remarkable and complementary works, Olivia Muñoz Rojas, *Ashes and Granite: Destruction and Reconstruction in the Spanish Civil War and its Aftermath* and Dacia Viejo-Rose, *Reconstructing Spain: Cultural Heritage and Memory after Civil War*, opened up an entirely new dimension of the study of the early Franco regime and its internal conflicts. They were followed by Richard Purkiss's analysis of the Valencian anarchist movement during the revolutionary period from 1918 to 1923, the military dictatorship of General Primo de Rivera and the Second Republic. It is a fascinating work which sheds entirely new light both on the breakdown of political coexistence during the Republic and on the origins of the violence that was to explode after the military coup of July 1936. The year ended with the publication of *France Divided: The French and the Civil War in Spain* by David Wingeate Pike. It made available in a thoroughly updated edition, and in English for the first time, one of the classics of the historiography of the Spanish Civil War.

An extremely rich programme for 2012 is opened with Germà Bel's remarkable *Infrastructure and the Political Economy of Nation Building in Spain*. This startlingly original work exposes the damage done to the Spanish economy by the country's asymmetrical and dysfunctional transport and communications model. It will be followed later in the year by several important titles on the Spanish Civil War beginning with *The War and Its Shadow: Spain's Civil War in Europe's Long Twentieth Century*, by Helen Graham.

PAUL PRESTON
Series Editor
London School of Economics

Series Editor's Preface

The centralism that underlies the approach to infrastructure in Spain is a legacy of policies that have remained common for almost three hundred years. In present-day terms, this is reflected in a particular enthusiasm for high-speed passenger train lines that radiate out from the capital to the detriment of other parts of the country and which have failed to relate to commercial needs. Spanish governments are proud of the fact that the country is a European leader in terms of high-speed lines but this is not reflected in economic stability. The same centralist model can be seen in policies regarding airports and in significant regional asymmetry in the financing of motorways. *Infrastructure and the Political Economy of Nation Building in Spain* is a remarkably original work that sets out to examine how this dysfunctional model has come into being.

Madrid inevitably plays a crucial role in Germà Bel's account. Long since Spain's political capital, governmental engineering has converted it into the nation's economic capital as well over the last three or four decades. As the author puts it, Madrid has finally attained the status of 'the Paris of Spain', the goal of the Bourbon Kings in the eighteenth century.

Part of the explanation for this resides in the geographic location of Madrid in the geometric centre of the Iberian Peninsula. This advantageous situation in terms of its political and administrative control constituted a serious disadvantage in logistical terms. Madrid is at the furthest point from any access to the sea, which made its own sustenance extremely expensive and, to a large extent, dictated the damaging infrastructural policies of the monarchy. The disadvantages to the national economy were further augmented by government policies over centuries of deliberately developing a radial model first of road, then of rail and later still of air transport and communications.

The combination of these factors has clearly been advantageous for Madrid but the central issue addressed by Professor Bel is the extent to which they have been detrimental for the rest of Spain and why that has happened. To do so, he examines three centuries of infrastructural policies in Spain. His fascinating story begins on 23 April 1720 when the first Bourbon King Felipe V literally changed the map of Spain by designating six 'royal routes' (*carreras reales*) which radiated out from Madrid like the spokes of a wheel and have remained the communications spine of the country. His successor Fernando VI was determined to modernize communications in his Kingdom and upgraded the routes to 'the highways of the King' (*carreteras del Rey*). Since the municipalities along the way were reluctant to meet the cost, he decreed in 1747 that the six royal highways be financed from the royal treasury. The consequences of this decision were cast in stone when his successor, Carlos III, decreed in 1761 that the state funds would continue to meet the costs of the six highways while 'delegating' finance for all other roads on whomsoever was interested in their creation.

In contrast, the same principle of the initiative being left to those it stood to benefit saw mid-nineteenth century railway construction responding to commercial necessity and, with few exceptions, privately financed. The consequent fears that Madrid would be left isolated saw the introduction in 1855 of a law giving preference to five radial lines to connect Madrid to key ports and borders. These lines absorbed the lion's share of public funding for railway construction and, in 1870, legislation was passed for the state funding of the extension of railway links from Madrid to every provincial capital.

Professor Bel's conclusion is that the transport infrastructure established in the eighteenth and nineteenth centuries saw state resources used in order to consolidate the political and economic necessities of the Crown and its capital – a policy executed without consideration of economic priorities and the need for links between the key nuclei of economic production. These centres were systematically excluded from state priorities and the distribution of state resources. The consequence was an economically dysfunctional structure, separating for instance, major centres of industry and raw materials such as Bilbao and Barcelona in what Professor Bel summarises as 'a radial state in a transversal market'.

The stark conclusion of this perceptive study is that, over the last three centuries, the priority given in Spain to administrative and political objectives has severely undermined the efficiency of transport in terms of its potential contribution to economic productivity. This historic pattern has continued to be applied in modern times to infrastructural policies with regard to motorways, high-speed rail links and airport development. The solution proposed by Professor Bel is simple but hardly likely to be welcomed by centralist governments. It requires recognition by the Madrid government not only that a fundamentally radial policy flies in the face of the dynamics of economic activity but also that it brings in its wake the need for uneconomic subsidies. Radial policies have little economic rationale but merely respond to a historic pattern, the quest to make Spain like France, with a capital like Paris. Professor Bel thus explains why Spanish infrastructural policy is so different and so much more inefficient than that of its neighbours.

Author's Preface

> "To help resolve political problems, I don't think it is entirely a waste of time to distance oneself from them for a moment or two, placing them in historical perspective. From this virtual distance, things seem to clarify themselves on their own and spontaneously adopt the posture that best reveals their underlying reality." (José Ortega y Gasset, España invertebrada, 1921, p. 29)

'Connecting the dots' could have been an alternative subtitle to this book. The book's origins lie in the curiosity – in fact, the need – to understand the very special characteristics of infrastructure policy in Spain: an enthusiasm for high-speed rail that has made Spain Europe's leaders in this form of transportation, with the goal of connecting Madrid to all of the provincial capitals and yet, at the same time, freight railway is ignored; a centralized and integrated model of management of airports that is unique among comparable countries; a mixed model (tolls, yes or no?) and great territorial asymmetry in financing motorways . . . These questions began to occur to me as I went about my academic and political activities at the end of the 1990s and early 2000s.

One fact made me think it was possible that some historical regularity existed at the base of such policies: the observation of certain striking parallels between models of development and financing of motorways in the second half of the 20th century – after my own research in this area[1] – and railways in the latter half of the 19th century – gleaned from the doctoral thesis of professor Alfonso Herranz Loncán,[2] whose committee I formed a part of in 2003. Few economists, unfortunately, take an interest in history; but almost all of us become excited by regularities. That's why it seemed to me like an excellent idea to distance myself from current political problems, in order to try and understand them by placing them in historical perspective. My periods as visiting professor at Cornell University in 2004–2005 and as a visiting researcher at Harvard University in 2005–2006 certainly helped me to get some distance. The pieces of this project were already in place by 2007, and only the fortunate insistence of Emili Rosales and Ramon Perelló, at Destino, kept me from putting off organizing them into book form until 2012, which was my original plan. The result is what the reader now holds in his hands.

To acquire historical perspective, this book invites the reader to take a journey through the history of Spain over the last three centuries. Our starting point is the Madrid of 1561, designated by Philip II as the permanent capital of the Hapsburg court. The journey, properly speaking, begins in 1720, on the post roads established by Philip V, who changed by decree – literally speaking – Spain's map of communications. We continue on the radial roads thought up by Ferdinand VI and promoted by Charles III. We shall travel along these until reaching the Spain of the railway, in the mid-19th century. The conventional railway will take us to the motorways of the 20th century, the next milestone on our journey, which races along at ever-greater speeds in present-day Spain, characterized by the high-speed train and air transportation.

And, just as Ortega y Gasset predicted, glimpsed from a distance events seem to clarify themselves on their own, spontaneously adopting the posture that best reveals their underlying reality.

Madrid occupies a central position in this tale, for indeed, it couldn't be otherwise. The capital of Spain has acquired the status of economic capital in recent decades, which, combined with its position as political capital has made it into a total capital. A 'Paris of Spain', as desired by the first Bourbon monarchs – of French origin – up to the illustrious reformers of contemporary Spain. In the romantic words of Santos Juliá: "Paris is again, and always will be, the mirror in which the people of Madrid, travellers like Mesonero, exiles like Fernando de los Ríos, or scholars broadening their studies like Azaña, contemplate their city and which forces them to change their gaze."[3]

It is necessary to point out that some of the ideas expressed and documented in this book are good, but not new. The idea that Madrid owes its condition of economic capital to its location, to its status as political and administrative capital and to the radial system of transportation and communications has already been expressed – and very graphically, by the way – by authors such as professor José Luis García Delgado, professor of Applied Economics at the Universidad Complutense of Madrid. The citation is long, but its value is unquestionable: "There are three factors that together explain the importance achieved by Madrid's economy [. . .]. The first of these elements is nothing other than the *geographic location* of Madrid at the geometric centre of the peninsular territory [. . .] The *status of political-administrative capital* constitutes the second explicatory factor of what Madrid's economy has become [. . .] Madrid's election as the capital of public bureaucracy with powers reaching throughout the national territory is decisive for its economy [. . .]. The two above-mentioned expedients of Madrid's destiny will end up determining the third, already suggested factor: the interior *radial system of transportation and communications,* to which the postal routes, railway and roads (and later, regular air traffic) basically correspond."[4] The effects of these combined factors have certainly been decisive in configuring the Paris of Spain, as can be deduced from the conclusion drawn by professor García Delgado: "Still more: location, the status of political-administrative capital and the radial structure of transportation and communications generate through their multiple interactions other advantageous conditions for Madrid's economy [. . .]. The die is thus definitively cast: Madrid, economic capital of Spain, in the fullest sense and strictest terms."[5] That is to say, total capital, and irreversibly so.

With the *what* and the factors explaining it confirmed, the primary challenge is to understand the *why*. To this end, some perhaps novel ideas, which I furthermore hope are good ones, will be proposed in this study:

Firstly, the idea that the radial policies of transportation infrastructure, by responding primarily to political and administrative goals, could not be supported by the dynamic of economic activity. For this reason, their implementation demanded an intense allocation of budgetary resources in the form of subsidies and aid that made possible what the legislation on its own couldn't achieve. This was how it was, and how it continues to be.

Secondly, these policies correspond to a regular and continuous historical pattern in Spanish politics, beginning with the arrival to the throne of the Bourbon dynasty in the early 18th century; they put into practice the project of building a country like France, with a capital like Paris.

Thirdly, the constant validity of this historical pattern makes it possible to understand why the infrastructure policies of present-day Spain are so singular and different from those of other countries in Spain's vicinity.

I believe my aim of understanding – and contributing to an understanding – of the nature of infrastructure policy in Spain has been fulfilled in a sufficiently satisfactory way, through its contextualization within a more general political project of the country: to achieve a Spain like France, with a capital like Paris. Of course, and as the theological canons demand, a great distance separates understanding from comprehending. And when understanding isn't sufficient for comprehension, the act of faith becomes essential. I leave to the reader's discretion such an act of faith, something quite alien to my – rather non-confessional – character in respect to public policies.

A clarification here is necessary to avoid misunderstandings. This is an explicatory and interpretive study. It doesn't have, however, a propositional purpose. There are various reasons for this. Firstly, to keep from boring the reader more than is strictly necessary; for this reason, I don't think it is necessary to repeat proposals for public policy in this area, which I have already published on other occasions, some quite recently and which interested readers can easily find.[6]

Secondly, and more importantly: because no relevant demand exists for alternatives to the current policy of infrastructures in Spain. This is the only area in which systematic agreements exist between the governing party and the principal party of the opposition (and the only real alternative to the governing one). The reform of the Law of National Ports, negotiated in the parliament in 2010, was agreed to by PSOE and PP, making manifest the similarity of their positions. Likewise, in practice, the agreement on the model of management and financing of airports is wide, as will be documented in Chapter 6. In the same way, PSOE and PP coincide in their railway model, with the present government having assumed the priorities established by their PP predecessors in respect to freight railway routes and their connection to the European network,[7] and in the extension of the high-speed railway network. In sum, no discrepancies exist in the territorial nature of the infrastructure models.

Stated in countable terms: 323 of the members of the 2008–11 Congress, from the *Socialist* and *Popular* groups, along with UPyD (Union, Progress and Democracy [Spanish: Unión Progreso y Democracia]), coincide with the fundamental aspects of the applied policy of infrastructures. This number represents 92% of the Congress, and totals 85% of the votes cast in the last legislative elections of 2008. Of course, this doesn't necessarily imply that each and every one of the 323 members of parliament support such policy in its entirety; but this is a nuance that lacks practical relevance in an electoral and parliamentary system such as the one in Spain. It's what there is, and no alternatives are on the horizon. This is why formulating such alternatives, which may be of certain intellectual interest, lacks any practical relevance.

In his magnificent analysis of the geographical and territorial features of present-day Spanish politics, Enric Juliana questions where that "vigorous and disoriented country" known as Spain is heading.[8] In my opinion, in the realm of territorial policy, for some time now we have been in a period in which a sense of direction is being recovered, much more so than disorientation. A return to the historical pattern, to the project of making a Spain like France, now that the capital is indeed like Paris; a project that has enjoyed majority support in Spain for the past three centuries. The parenthesis of the Transition and the first years of the democracy have ended and the waters have now returned to their original course. A course, by the way, that infrastructure policy has never truly abandoned.

And so we come to our journey's end, the final point in this history. In the final pages of this book, written in a much more speculative tone, I take the liberty of hazarding a guess as to the directions some debates on public policy may take in a future that has already begun. As is well known, we economists tend to be mistaken when we make predictions, and once the future has arrived we must explain why we erred in our predictions of it. I sincerely hope that this will be the case on this occasion.

Acknowledgements

This book has been encouraged and supported by a good many friends and colleagues from different disciplines. Although it is impossible to mention them all, it would be frankly unforgivable to overlook some of them.

With my friends from the research group, *Governs i Mercats (Governments and Markets)*, at the Universitat de Barcelona, I have shared many conversations on these (and many other) subjects, which have helped me organize my ideas. The interaction has been most intense with those with whom I jointly did research on transportation and communications: Joan Calzada and, particularly, Daniel Albalate in land transportation, and Xavier Fageda in air transportation. The bibliographical reference is irrefutable proof of this. I am grateful to Marta González Aregall for her enthusiastic research assistance. Also at my university, Alfonso Herranz has given me great help, especially valuable as he is one of the finest Spanish experts on the historical analysis of the railway. And I must recognize the influence teachers have had on the way I have thought through these subjects: Jordi Nadal, because he taught me that without passion there is no enterprise; to Ernest Lluch, for conveying important views and lessons of a career and experience stupidly interrupted; and to Antón Costas, my mentor, in the literal sense of the term.

The long, but in fact too short, discussions with Ángel de la Fuente have helped germinate a friendship that stands the test of inconsistencies concerning the subjects of this work. Alain Cuenca, an *aragonés* friend with a French education and an important position in the absolute capital, has given me his friendship and, furthermore, substantial commentaries after a methodical reading of the first chapter. Carlos Álvarez Nogal provided me with information and suggestions on regional level economic growth in the 17th and 18th centuries. With Harvard's Jack Donahue I have had the opportunity of commenting on the importance of trust within organizations and the dissolving effect its loss brings.

Political activity has allowed me to enhance my reflections through conversations with colleagues during that period – which now seems so distant – when we shared seats in the Congress of Deputies. Among them, it seems fair that I make special mention of Jesús Caldera, Carme Miralles and José Segura, with whom I agreed – and also differed – on infrastructure policy, always with sincerity and affection. Pere Macías very kindly directed my attention to the sessions of the Comisión Olózaga in 1850, and Montserrat Palma provided me with a copy of the acts of the Comisión de Infraestructuras of the PP of September of 1997. Finally, I must mention that various conversations with the presidents Pasqual Maragall and Jordi Pujol have given me firsthand knowledge of crucial viewpoints concerning the deeper questions underlying this book, in addition to being a true honour for me. They deserve recognition for everything they have achieved. And also for what they have attempted without success. In the final analysis, it was perhaps an impossible mission.

The Documentation Centre of the Ministerio de Fomento has very kindly attended to my requests for information, which has saved me from making some undesired trips. The suggestions and tips that Domingo Cuellar Villar gave me concerning infrastructure activity at the end of the 19th century were of great use. Salvador Guillermo directed my attention to parliamentary information of 1876, which was very illustrative of the debates over subsidies to the railway. I have been enriched by the debates in the Observatory on infrastructures and the environment of the Cercle d'Economía, led by Pilar de Torres and Ángel Simón. I have been similarly enriched by the experiences shared by Toni Brunet and Jordi Valls from the perspective of those who operate large transportation infrastructures and facilities, the reflections of Josep Maria Ureta, astute analyst of the economy, and the careful attention and comments to the chapters on railways provided by José Manuel Grijalvo.

Emili Rosales and Ramón Perelló, at Destino, are responsible for this project not having had to wait until 2012 to appear, as was my initial intention. Fortunately, they convinced me that it made no sense to let more time pass before carrying it out. I am indebted to Ramon Aymerich and Manel Pérez for allowing some of my ideas to appear in the Economy section of *La Vanguardia*. William Truini has made a great job translating the original text into English.

I leave for last my special thanks to Milagros, for having accompanied me on my own journey and for demonstrating that it is not only possible to live with complexity on a daily basis, but also enriching. And to Anton, whose future is the true course.

"When high roads, bridges, canals, etc. are in this manner made and supported by the commerce which is carried on by means of them, they can be made only where that commerce requires them, and consequently where it is proper to make them."

Adam Smith, *The Wealth of Nations*

1

A Madrid Like Paris?

The principal idea maintained in this book is that Madrid has become the *absolute capital* of Spain, having acquired a function similar to that of Paris in respect to France.

Madrid acquired the status of administrative capital of the Hapsburg monarchy in 1561, when Philip II designated the city as the permanent seat of the court. A century and a half later, following the War of the Spanish Succession that ended in 1714 and the Nueva Planta decrees, Madrid acquired the status of political capital of Spain, extending its power to the territories of the former Crown of Aragon as a result of the suppression of the political constitutions of those territories, and of the centralization of political power. Much more recently, at the end of the 20th century, Madrid has acquired the status of economic capital of Spain. The result of the concentration of political capital status and economic capital status is the transformation of Madrid into an absolute capital, into the Paris of Spain.

This process corresponds to a political plan set in motion in the 18th century, following the Bourbon dynasty's arrival to the throne. The dynasty's French origins and the fact that France was a great power of the time – if not the great power – and Paris a great capital – if not the great capital – were decisive in adopting the French model as the standard for Spain to follow. It was logical: Spain at the end of the 17th century was in decline, more acutely so after the Battle of Rocroi on 19 May 1643, precisely against the French armies. The battle marked the first defeat in the open field by the Spanish armies since the beginning of Spain's imperial period and symbolizes the fall of the military system that had sustained Spain.[1] When the War of the Spanish Succession ended in 1714, the new dynasty sought to overcome Spain's decadence through the project of building a country like France, with a capital like Paris.

Such a project has been an intrinsic part of Spanish politics since the beginning of the 18th century. It is a tendency with strong underpinnings that has experienced occasional ups and downs, the last of which being the recent democratic transition and the first years of democracy. The ever-renewing validity of this project to organize the country and system of power can only be understood if one considers that it has enjoyed broad and continuous majority support from the elites and the population of Spain. This explains why, after periodic ups and downs, the waters always return to their course.

With greater or lesser intensity, this underlying current has been decisive in the formulation and application of diverse public policies. Notable among these is the policy of infrastructres and transportation, of great importance to the organization of the territory and, because of this, with great potential in determining the organization of political power. At the same time, the existence of this underlying logic – of this standard – in the history of infrastructure policy makes it possible to understand why this policy has such unique features in Spain when compared to the policies found in the countries of her geographic and economic vicinity.

The policies of transportation in neighbouring countries have tended to give priority to the contribution of infrastructures to productivity and to economic activity. In the case of Spain, in contrast, territorial organization has been dominated by the desire to fit it within the framework of a specific preference for the organization of political power – centralization. These considerations will be illustrated over the course of this chapter and discussed within the context of the principal aspects of recent infrastructure policies.

Spain Is Different (?)

This phrase made a fortune in the 1960s and 70s as the country opened itself economically to the outside world and was visited by a growing and increasingly European tourism. The phrase 'Spain is different' reflected the survival of a dictatorial regime in a setting – Western Europe – presided over by political liberties and democracy. Such a burden imposed a heavy yoke on the spheres of civil liberties, the economy, culture and social relations. For this reason, with the return of democracy, as much during the political transition as in the years afterwards, one of the objectives that garnered the greatest political and social consensus was precisely to cease being different. That is to say, to become more like our European neighbours – and more recently, partners. An important milestone on this path was the entry in 1986 into the European Union– then known as the Community. Viewed in perspective, the result is indisputable: we have been successful. Spain is – and, in general, looks like – any another European country. It has its special characteristics, like all countries. But fundamentally, Spain is one more component of the social, economic and political model of Europe. We wanted this and we got it.

Spain is no longer *different* . . . but some of its characteristics are still quite striking. In the area of infrastructure and transportation policy Spain is so exceptional, so unique in so many respects, that this area has become one of the last vestiges of traditional character and difference in respect to our partners. For indeed, no other country has made the 'idea' of connecting all – *all* – of the provincial capitals with the political capital by high-speed rail a national objective. And then there's the fact that we have a mixed system of financing motorways (combining tolls and public budget) that is unique in Europe. And we have a centralized model of management of airports that is unique among countries of a certain size, population and air market in the developed world. And . . . But let us proceed step by step.

A guiding principle of the infrastructure policies of all Spanish governments during the entire first decade of the 2000s was to establish in Spain the world's longest high-speed railway network (explicitly stated so by the president of the government, José Luis Rodríguez Zapatero). And, in effect, we already are the European champions of high-speed rail (which is no small

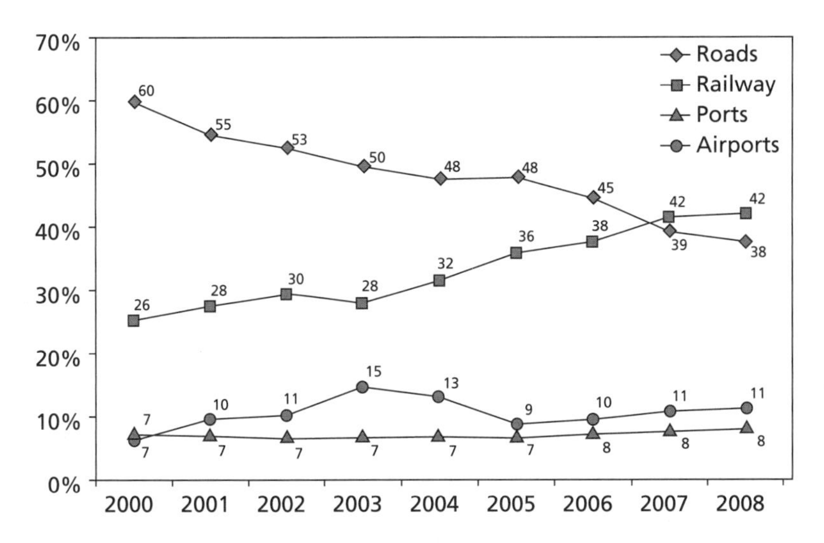

Note: Not including urban transportation or gas pipe transporation.
Source: Based on information concerning spending from the annual reports of the Ministry of Fomento (various years).

Graph 1.1 Evolution of interurban infrastructure spending 2000–2008. Share (%) of each mode out of the total.

feat: who can compete with China?). We surpass even Japan and France, pioneering countries in the development of high-speed rail. To achieve this, the Spanish State since 2007 has spent more on railways than any other means of transportation, as indicated by Graph 1.1.[2] This is a true milestone in infrastructure policy, after many decades of motorway domination. And, of course, investment in the railway in Spain has become the highest in the European Union, in relative terms to Spain's wealth. Or, as economists say, 'in terms of GDP' (Gross Domestic Product).

This has involved – and involves – a significant portion of the national budget, given that the rate of recouping the investment in railway infrastructure through payment by users is extraordinarily low, in contrast to what occurs with other modes of transportation, such as airports. Although still not common knowledge, it is necessary to keep in mind that the investment costs in railway lines (including those of the high-speed AVE) are financed almost entirely by State budgets, while the investment costs in airports are generally financed by users – through taxes of various types – and don't receive significant contributions from national budgets (at least until now).

It is quite paradoxical, however, that despite such significant budgetary strain, freight by railway in Spain has steadily lost its market share. Between 2000 and 2008 the percentage of goods transported by train has declined from more than 7% to less than 4%. Railway's share has thus fallen well over 40%. This decline is much greater than that of the EU as a whole, where the railway's share fell 10%, and where trains continue to transport almost a fifth of all goods.[3] And, unfortunately, it is not possible to affirm that the railway's share in passenger transportation has compensated for this development. The figures for 2008, with the latest lines of the AVE functioning, suggest that the railway's share in passengers grew between three and four tenths in the last year (at great economic cost) and maintained the same levels it had at the start of the decade. A similar growth was achieved in the EU as a whole, but at much lower economic cost.

The degradation of the railway as a means of freight transportation in Spain, in addition to being paradoxical, is very worrying: the primary economic and social contribution of the railway to interurban mobility is the transportation of goods. A good offer of this type of safe and reliable transportation avoids congestion on the roads and reduces negative environmental impacts and accidents. In contrast, the economic and social impact of the high-speed train is much less, as will be more broadly discussed in Chapter 5. The significant investment in the railway in Spain (let's not forget: the highest in the EU in percentage of GDP) has resulted in a lower contribution to productivity and social well-being.

What is the reason for this? Perhaps, after all, it isn't so paradoxical. Despite the enormous investment made, attention hasn't been focused on the needs of freight trains in Spain; instead, almost all efforts and material and human resources have been dedicated to the passenger AVE. This is why, for example, serious deficiencies exist in the connections between Spain's large peninsular ports and the railway system. They are serious because the inter-modal connection between maritime transportation and railway transportation is essential to increasing the efficacy of the railway. But this is not all; it is highly surprising that the government in 2003 prioritized the Algeciras–Madrid–Zaragoza–Pyrenees–France line in the trans-European network of railway freight.

Spain is unique in the sense that no other countries exist with as much coastline where the priorities of railway freight are located more than 300 kilometres from the principal ports in terms of volume of shipping. Why wasn't priority given to the Mediterranean corridor on the Algeciras to France connection? This is, by far, the corridor with the greatest volume of freight traffic in Spain, even more so if we consider the freight that is *directed toward* and *comes from* the rest of Europe. To give only one figure, when these decisions were made in the early 2000s, almost 40% of Spanish exports originated in Mediterranean regions (excluding Andalusia).[4] But their railway network still has inexplicable deficiencies, such as the absence of a connection between Almería and Murcia, the very deficient connection from Murcia northward, or the existence of a single track between Vandellòs and Tarragona.[5] All of this, in the context of the need for a general modernization of the entire Mediterranean corridor. In accordance with the positions expressed by the European Commission and by the French government, the Spanish government solicited in June 2010 the inclusion of the Mediterranean corridor to likewise be given priority in the trans-European network. Will the commission accept the existence of two priorities in the case of Spain? What will the option be should it be necessary to make a choice? To learn the answers to these questions, it will be necessary to wait until the European Union will make its final decisions on this subject.

Spain's peculiarity is also evident in respect to its financing of high-capacity roads: dual carriageways, main roads and toll-free motorways and toll motorways. Tolls are present in approximately 20% of the total number of motorways in Spain. This percentage rises to 25% in the case of the network of motorways overseen by the central government, all of which are subjected to exploitation through concession to private companies.[6] The remaining motorways are toll-free.

Spain's mixed system is unique. Among the countries of the European Union, some have a motorway financing model based fundamentally on tolls, which cover almost the entire network and are distributed at regular intervals throughout their territory: France, Italy, Portugal, Greece and Slovenia. In the rest of the countries of the European Union, the presence of direct tolls is not very significant (Austria and Finland), marginal or null.[7] In the case of Austria (since 2004) and Germany (since 2005), tolls for heavy vehicles have recently been introduced throughout the entire network of motorways.

We have, therefore, a mixed system of motorway financing that is quite peculiar in the context of the European Union and one, furthermore, with a distinguishing feature of an even more exceptional character: the considerable inter-territorial variability in the price of the tolls. These characteristics confer great singularity on the Spanish model of motorway financing within the framework of the European Union. In Chapter 4, an analysis will be made of the superposition of road infrastructure policies that has led to this situation.

Spain's system of airport management, however, is even more special. Practically all of Spain's commercial airports are managed by the State organization Aeropuertos Españoles y Navegación Aérea (AENA) dependent on the Ministry of Fomento (the Spanish ministry of public works, which also manages air traffic control). The only exceptions – more anecdotal than anything else in terms of their size – are the airports of Ciudad Real, of mixed private-public (regional) ownership, which entered into service on 18 December 2008, and the Lleida-Alguaire (of autonomous public ownership), whose first commercial flight took place on 5 February 2010. Furthermore, operations are slated to begin soon at the Región de Murcia airport and the Castellón airport, promoted both by territorial governments. In all, the 47 airports managed by AENA moved more than 193 million passengers in 2010, more than 99.9% of the total.

The case of Spain is unique among comparable countries – in terms of area, city structures and size of the air market – in the European Union (and the OECD) in that a centralized, public company globally manages the country's commercial airports, in contrast to what occurs in Germany, Australia, Canada, the United States, France, Italy, Japan and the United Kingdom.[8] Among countries of a relatively comparable size and population, only Romania (although with a much smaller air market) has a management system similar to Spain's. At present, Spanish airports are undergoing a process of (relative) reform, the fundamental feature of which is the separation of air traffic control (which generally is centrally managed) and management of the airports. Nonetheless, the fundamental bases of this system (fixing taxes, spending decisions, and assigning the timetables for flight operations) will be kept under strict centralized control. Why is the centralized system of management of Spanish airports being obstinately maintained, in contrast to what the norm is among our neighbouring countries? Chapter 6 will more broadly address this question.

Why Are We So Special?

How can a series of characteristics as peculiar as those just related be understood? How to explain the exceptional characteristics of infrastructure policy in Spain? One way of dealing with a response to these questions would be to assume the attitude held by a great power, such as the United States, during its period of greatest self-sufficiency (for example, during the recent presidency of George W. Bush). In this sense, it would be fitting to ask, why is the rest of the world different from us? But doing so doesn't seem to me an appropriate strategy for analyzing a medium-sized country such as Spain (nor is it perhaps for the United States).

I believe it is more appropriate to ask the following question: why are we so different from the rest of the world? Answering this question is the primary purpose of this book. And the answer is the following: the Spanish case is an extreme example of the use of infrastructure policy in the service of territorial hierarchical structuring and the organization of power in Spain. Achieving this objective has been of much greater importance in Spain than servicing the priority needs of transportation, as much in terms of the industrial system as daily interurban mobility, which constitute the primordial purposes of infrastructure and transportation policy in the countries around us.

In sum, the explanation I propose is that infrastructure policy in Spain has been in the service of an objective that was formulated over the course of the 18th century and which ever since then has been in the background of Spanish politics: to create a country like France, with a capital like Paris. Chapter 2 of this book reviews this question.

Needless to say, the intensity by which this goal has been pursued has depended on the political and economic circumstances of the recent history of Spain. Different periods have either emphasized or ignored it. But the underlying tendency has been maintained in the same direction. In my judgement, at the start of the 21st century, it is difficult to affirm that Spain has managed to become a country like France. Nonetheless, I think it is reasonable to state that the political capital, Madrid, has managed to achieve a status in Spain similar to what Paris has in France.

The matter seems to me relevant and current because a distinctive characteristic of recent Spain has been how the process of Madrid's transformation into Paris has become irreversible. As mentioned earlier, Madrid, administrative capital since the mid-16th century, achieved the status of true political capital over the rest of Spain in the 18th century. The status of administrative and political capital, however, had not been combined with the status of economic capital . . . until recently.

In the past two decades, Madrid has acquired the status of economic capital of Spain.[9] The Community of Madrid is the Spanish region with the largest per capita gross domestic product; in 2009, its GDP per capita was 38% higher than that of Spain as a whole.[10] The great majority of Spanish multinational companies have their headquarters here; the region attracts a very high percentage of foreign investment; sectors with significant added value have been developed such as the audiovisual sector, and it counts with a considerable share of the activity related to high-tech and knowledge.

As a consequence of all this, more than 30% of the 5,000 principal Spanish companies have their headquarters in Madrid, and these companies generate at present more than half of the total income of those 5,000. Catalonia occupies second place, with 23% of the companies having their headquarters there, which generate 18% of the income. The Valèncian Community, Andalusia, and the Basque Country follow, with a range of between 6% and 8% of the headquarters, and between 4% and 6% of the income generated.[11]

In terms of economic power, the location of the headquarters of the country's largest companies provides very relevant information. More than legal headquarters, which have unquestionable fiscal repercussions, it is pertinent to look at the operational headquarters (that is to say, the main operational office, which can be different from the legal headquarters per se). In the case of Spain, for example, the headquarters of the Banco de Santander is in Santander, those of BBVA and Iberdrola are in Bilbao, and that of Iberdrola Renovables (of which Iberdrola has an 80% capital stake) in València. This has great importance in terms of satisfying fiscal obligations. But what is truly relevant from the point of view of the economic impact of the headquarters and the classification and concentration of economic power is the location of the operational headquarters.

In this sense, the process of concentration of operational headquarters in the political capital that has taken place over the last two decades in Spain has no equal among comparable countries and has been the result of a combination of processes of privatization and business mergers between large financial companies and of public services. The result is that in comparison with other countries we have an exceptional degree of difference between (fiscal) headquarters and (real) operational headquarters.

Table 1.1 shows the operational headquarters[12] of the ten top companies

Table 1.1 Ten companies with the largest market capitalization in their national exchanges, and operational headquarters

	United Kingdom		France		Spain		Italy		Germany	
Ranking	Company	Operational headquarters	Company	Operational headquarters	Company	Operational headquarters	Company	Operational headquarters	Company	Operational headquarters
1	HSBC Holdings	Londres	Total SA	París	Banco Santander	Madrid	ENI	Roma	Siemens	Múnich
2	British Petroleum	Londres	Sanofi-Aventis	París	Telefonica	Madrid	Unicredit	Roma	E.ON	Düsseldorf
3	Vodafone	Newbury-Berk.	GDF Suez	París	BBVA	Madrid	Intesa Sanpaolo	Turín	Deutsche Telekom	Bonn
4	GlaxoSmithKline	Londres	BNP Paribas	París	Iberdrola	Madrid	Enel	Roma	BAYER	Leverkusen
5	British A. Tobacco	Londres	L'Oreal	París	Inditex	Arteixo-A Coruña	Assicurazioni Gen.	Trieste	SAP	Walldorf-Frankfurt
6	Rio Tinto	Londres	France Telecom	París	Endesa	Madrid	Telecom Italia	Milán	BASF	Ludwigshafen
7	BHP Billiton	Londres	Lvmh Moet	París	Repsol YPF	Madrid	Saipem	Milán	RWE	Essen
8	Astrazeneca	Londres	AXA	París	Iberdrola Renovables	Madrid	Snam Rete Gas	Milán	Allianz	Múnich
9	BG Group	Reading-Berk.	Société Générale	París	Gas Natural	Barcelona	Fiat	Turín	Daimler	Stuttgart
10	Tesco (BC)	Londres	Danone	París	Criteria Caixacorp	Barcelona	UBI Banca	Bérgamo	Deutsche Bank	Frankfurt

Sources: The ranking of the companies has been made based on their market capitalization (France, Germany and Spain) and floating capital in the market (the United Kingdom and Italy), 12 February 2010. Companies whose headquarters are not in the country have been excluded. The operational headquarters have been obtained through the web pages of the corresponding companies.

with headquarters in their own countries, in the five largest economies of the European Union: the United Kingdom, France, Spain, Italy and Germany. From the information included in this table one can see that the ranking of the location of the largest companies in Spain is much more similar to the pattern observed in the United Kingdom and France (countries where headquarters have long been concentrated in the capital) than that of Italy and Germany.

In effect, each and every one of the operational headquarters of the ten largest French companies in terms of market capitalization is located in the capital, Paris. In the case of the United Kingdom, eight of the largest companies have their operational headquarters in London; the remaining two are in Berkshire (a county contiguous to Greater London and which in fact forms part of its real metropolitan area). In the case of Spain, seven of the ten largest companies have their operational headquarters in Madrid.

The cases of Italy and Germany are substantially different. In the former, only three of the largest companies have their headquarters in Rome (another three are in Milan, two in Turin, one in Trieste and one in Bergamo). And in Germany, the dispersion is extreme; none of the largest companies in terms of market capitalization have their operational headquarters in the federal capital, Berlin: two companies are in Munich, two in the Frankfurt area, and the rest in different cities.

With Madrid's evolution over the past few decades, its status as administrative and political capital has been reinforced by its having become the

Table 1.2 Demographic and economic figures of the metropolitan agglomeration of the capital, and comparison with the country's largest agglomeration, excluding the capital. Year: 2008

	London Metro-area	Paris – Ille de France	Madrid	Rome	Berlin
Population (millions)	14.9	11.6	6.1	3.8	3.4
% Population country	24.4%	18.8%	13.5%	6.5%	4.1%
Population (Capital/Alter)	5.81	6.02	1.14	0.99	0.80
GDP (million Euros)	616,508	468,978	144,796	111,504	79,033
% GDP country	32.3%	28.9%	17.8%	8.7%	3.5%
GDP per capita ppa (EU27 = 100)	157	174	132	135	96
GDP per capita (Capital/Alter)	1.45	1.55	1.13	0.85	0.58

Notes: «Alter» indicates the most densely populated metropolitan agglomeration in the country, besides the political capital. They are, respectively, Great Manchester (United Kingdom), Marseille-Bouches du Rhône (France), Barcelona (Spain), Milan (Italy), and Munich-Oberbayern (Germany).

GDP per capita ppa: GDP per capita in purchasing power parity.

Source: Author, based on data obtained from Cambridge Econometrics. *European Regional Database* (Cambridge: Cambridge Econometrics, 2008).

economic capital. Madrid has come closer to resembling what the two great European metropolises, Paris and London, represent to their respective countries, and to the role that both cities have as city-headquarters of the financial sector, of large public service networks (such as telecommunications or energy), and of communications media . . . although in other respects there is considerably less similarity. Table 1.2 compares some indicators related to the political capital status of – once again – the principal countries of the European Union: the United Kingdom, France, Spain, Italy and Germany. For London and Paris, their functioning metropolitan areas are used as references, while for Madrid, Rome and Berlin the equivalent of the province is used as a reference, an area somewhat larger than the functioning metropolitan area.

The position of the metropolitan areas of London and Paris-Ille-de-France in the demographic and economic structure of their respective countries is very similar: their demographic weight is almost 25% in the case of London and almost 20% in that of Paris. Both agglomerations have a population six times larger than that of the second metropolitan area (Greater Manchester in the United Kingdom and Marseille-Bouches du Rhône in France). Both concentrate 30% of the GDP of their countries. Their per capita GDP is much higher than the European Union average (between 50% and 75% more) and about 50% higher than the secondary areas of their respective countries.

The case of Italy is different. Rome has a more moderate weight in Italy's overall population, its population is similar (99%) to that of the other large Italian agglomeration – Milan – and the per capita GDP of the latter city is even somewhat higher than that of Rome. The case of Berlin is much closer to that of Rome than that of London and Paris; nonetheless, its per capita GDP is lower than the German average, given the confluence in the area of zones of the former East Germany, which situates it a good deal below Munich-Oberbayern.

Lastly, the case of Madrid/Spain in terms of demographic and economic position is located relatively near that of Rome/Italy, although in Spain the demographic and economic weight of the political capital is somewhat greater than that of the second agglomeration, Barcelona; in contrast, Milan has a slightly greater weight in Italy than Rome. Clearly, the absolute and relative position of Madrid in terms of demography and the creation of wealth in Spain is far from that of London in the United Kingdom and Paris in France.

Taken altogether, Madrid's success in having become the economic capital is undeniable and makes it possible to defuse one of the traditional tensions that has dominated Spanish territorial policy for a long time: the contradiction between political power and economic power. Madrid's position is now similar to that of Paris: it is a total capital. What Santos Juliá[13] considered the "age-old aspiration of *madrileño* reformers, to make Madrid into, with Madrid, something similar to what Paris had been made into," has been fulfilled.

Logically, some territorial type tensions will continue,[14] although on increasingly smaller scales of intensity and reach. After all, Spain is not wholly similar to France, as the systemized information in the previous table and a superficial examination of its territorial and urban structure reveals. Nonetheless, the new scenario confers a self-causative characteristic on Madrid's status of total capital, in the sense that its present entity has become its cause.[15] Or, as Willard van Orman Quine would say,[16] *what there is.*

The Logic of Kilometre 0

> "The greater part of such public works may easily be so managed, as to afford a particular revenue sufficient for defraying their own expense, without bringing and burden upon the general revenue of the society [. . .] When high roads [. . .] are in this manner made and supported by the commerce which is carried on by means of them, they can be made only where that commerce requires them, and consequently where it is proper to make them. Their expense too, their grandeur and magnificence, must be suited to what that commerce can afford to pay. They must be made consequently as it is proper to make them. A magnificent high road cannot be made though a desert country where there is little or no commerce, or merely because it happens to lead to the country villa of the intendant of the province, or to that of some great lord to whom the intendant finds it convenient to make his court" (Adam Smith, *The Wealth of Nations*, 1776).[17]

Madrid's rise to the position of total capital is due as much to its own merits as to the boost it has received from certain public policies. The city's merits, unquestionably deserving of recognition,[18] are not the subject of this study. Attention will be focused, however, on the boost given by public policies to that rise, and more specifically by the central policy of transportation infrastructures. To illustrate the nature of this impetus, an examination will be made of some of the aspects of the policy followed during different historical periods in respect to different modes of transportation.

Firstly, the reordering of the roads and their financing in the 18th century. Secondly, the implantation of the railway infrastructures in Spain during the second half of the 19th century. Thirdly, the major modernization of the road networks in Spain carried out over the last four decades of the 20th century. Fourthly, the second 'modernization' of the railway system, with the implantation of the high-speed train with international rail widths (the high-speed train in Spain is known as the *Alta Velocidad Española* – AVE), beginning in the last decade of the 20th century. And lastly, at a time when management and knowledge are progressively displacing the importance of cement, the management model of airports of in Spain.

It is interesting to observe that the development of the conventional railway network and the development of the motorway network followed processes dominated by a shared dynamic. The initial development of both systems was fundamentally carried out through financing from users. This made the possibilities of financing the infrastructure with its own income (which crucially depends on the volume of freight and passenger traffic) into an essential factor when determining the priorities of the investment. In both cases, therefore, the first railway lines and the first (toll) motorways were implanted on the principal railway and road trajectories. In a second stage, the financing of the investment and service was essentially assumed by the national budget, and the respective networks were radialized with all corridors converging on Madrid, which became the kilometre 0 of interurban transportation infrastructures. This process configured the largely radial physiognomy of Spain's present, ground-based infrastructure networks.

The fourth episode, the implantation of the high-speed rail network, is the first major modernization of a transportation infrastructure network in the last two centuries to be financed almost entirely by the national budget. And, also for the first time, the development of the network has, from its origins, radial characteristics, extending itself in all directions from kilometre 0.

The fifth episode, centred on airports, presents a few different features. Despite the insistence by the political and bureaucratic authorities responsible for airport management in Spain on speaking about an 'airport network', the concept of network is technically inapplicable to airports, given that – in contrast to railways and roads – these are single facilities that strengthen point to point operation. Operating air networks are characteristics of the conventional airlines that offer connections, above and beyond the characteristics of airports. In this case, therefore, it is the management itself of the airport facility that provides control over the strategic decisions that condition connectivity in terms of available infrastructure. This explains why the preservation of a centralized and integrated management model is the suitable instrument for applying a logic based on territorial policy, rather than a logic based on transportation needs.

The infrastructure policies applied in the last two decades have been deeply influenced by this territorial logic. Eminent figures of Spanish politics have explicitly and very clearly recognized this to be so. We shall illustrate this point further on. First, however, it is appropriate to analyze the contribution made by transportation infrastructures to the industrial system and social welfare.

Infrastructures and Productivity

Understanding the way in which infrastructures contribute to improving economic productivity makes it possible to comprehend the basic criterion infrastructure policy has followed in many of the countries in Spain's vicinity. For this reason, I believe it is fitting to discuss here how, why and under what conditions the impacts of infrastructures on economic activity are produced. This will provide us with an interpretive framework that will make it possible to judge the motivations that, as we shall see in later sections, have presided over infrastructure policy in recent years.

Economists have long been interested in the impact of infrastructures and the transportation system on the organization of the industrial system and, therefore, on economic productivity and growth. Indeed, the question was already present in the seminal study of economics, *The Wealth of Nations*, which appeared in 1776 and which it is appropriate to quote here for the second time. In this work, Adam Smith very precisely states the relationship between transportation and the organization of the industrial system:

> "As by means of water-carriage a more extensive market is opened to every sort of industry than what land-carriage alone can afford it . . . A broad wheeled wagon . . . in about six weeks time carries and brings back between London and Edinburgh near four ton weight of goods. In about the same time, a ship navigated by six or eight men . . . frequently carries and brings back two hundred tons of weight goods. Where there was no other communication between these two places, therefore, but by land-carriage, as no goods could be transported . . . except such whose price was very considerable . . . they could carry on but a small part of that commerce which at present subsists between them, and consequently could give but a small part of that encouragement which they at present mutually afford to each other's industry". (Adam Smith, *The Wealth of Nations*, 1776)[19]

The citation is long, clearly, but it would be difficult to describe the impact of infrastructures and transportation services on productivity with greater clarity. In essence, efficiency in providing transportation benefits the industrial system, which is manifested primarily in two ways: (1) reduction of distribution costs of the products of the industrial sectors; and (2) expansion of the product and the market area, which facilitates the emergence of economies of scale in production.

However, this classical view of the effects of the transportation system, and thus of infrastructures, on the economy, was ignored for many years in favour of more macro-economic approaches. In this view, the impact of infrastructures on economic activity is analyzed with the emphasis placed on the effects of public spending. Thus, spending is seen above all as a 'shock' of *demand* on the economy. This shock of demand increases economic activity and has positive effects on the creation of employment – above all if it occurs during an economic crisis – in addition to other macroeconomic type effects that are not necessary to either detail or discuss here. This is a legacy left to economists by the efforts of John Maynard Keynes, among whose works *The General Theory of Employment, Interest and Money*, published in 1936, is especially well-known and influential. One thing necessary to mention is that these effects are produced in the short-term and derive from the process itself of carrying out the spending. Once construction has ended, its effect becomes progressively diluted over time until eventually vanishing altogether. For this reason, if spending is made on infrastructures of little use, not much is achieved.

Only towards the end of the 1980s was emphasis once again placed on the impact of infrastructures on the costs of the industrial system. Recent economic analysis gives much greater importance to the long-term effects of infrastructures. This implies a different perspective (although not an opposing or exclusive one), to the extent that the spending of public capital is seen as a shock *offer* to the economy.

Its most important characteristics are the following: (1) the relevant activity is the use of the infrastructure, once this has begun functioning; (2) the entering into service of the – new – infrastructure makes it possible to transport people and goods. The entering into service of the – improved/enlarged – infrastructure makes it possible to reduce the temporal costs of transporting people and goods; (3) in terms of the monetary costs of the transportation, the size of the reduction of these costs depend on how the infrastructure is financed. Is it financed by the national budget or through the payment of tolls and fees?

Notable among the effects are the following:

1. The use of the infrastructure implies a decrease in the costs of distribution (and of production) in the economy. The reduction in costs above all affects the private sector, which produces the goods and services.
2. The decrease in the costs of the private sector implies an increase in the general productivity of the economy, because: (a) more activities can be done at the same costs: more production. Or (b) the same activities can be done at lower costs. The saving in costs in realized activities makes it possible to do more new ones: more production.
3. The increase in productivity will translate into a combination of increase in company profits, real increase in salaries and increase in employment. The fiscal bases of the economy increase. Tax collection increases (from profits, from income, etc.).

We can, therefore, sum up the effects of infrastructure improvement in the following way: (1) an increase in the general productivity of the economy; (2) an increase in economic activity and a decrease in unemployment over the long-term; (3) an increase in the potential of tax revenue collection for the public administration. The most notable aspect of these effects is that they are long-term and derive from the use of the infrastructures. They last as long as the infrastructures are in good, serviceable condition.

These types of effects can be specified by simple examples, such as the transport of citrus fruits by road from València. Before a motorway existed between València and Madrid, it could take a lorry considerably longer than ten hours to make a round trip journey on the old N-III road. This made only one trip per day possible, the payment of ten more hours in salary to the driver, and a certain level of fuel consumption. The entering into service of the A-III motorway shortened the journey to around eight hours. This made a more intensive use of the lorry possible, the reduction by almost a third of the salary costs of the trip, and fuel savings given the greater energy efficiency of travelling by motorway at speeds in the range of 90–100 km/hour. In sum, the motorway made it possible to lower the costs of transporting citrus fruits from València to Madrid or, alternatively, to gain greater distribution if the previous quantitative level of costs (monetary and temporal) were maintained.

A critical factor must be taken into account for this sequence of results to function adequately: the improvement of the infrastructure has to serve to prevent or resolve an existing or expected bottleneck. Thus, the effect will be greatest when the capacity of a congested infrastructure is enlarged and, in contrast, it will be least when the capacity of an infrastructure with low-intensity of use is enlarged. In this sense, it is appropriate to warn against the excessive expectations that are often generated by an improvement, as if by the sole fact of increasing quality a large increase in use will result. In the final analysis, the demand for transport depends on a large variety of factors, and not only or primarily on the offer of the infrastructure. Indeed, a dozen airports managed by AENA have always had very low passenger traffic (below 100,000 passengers a year) and some cases are simply marginal.

In sum, the effects analyzed above explain the importance of infrastructures to a territory's competitiveness. This is so as much in terms of their impact on the productivity of the economy as on the possibilities of enlarging markets and, therefore, of spaces of economic, social and cultural inter-connection.

The Political Rationale of Infrastructures in Spain

> "It is essential, therefore, that we become accustomed to understanding all national unity not as an internal coexistence but rather as a dynamic system. Central force is as necessary to its continuation as is the force of dispersion [. . .] to keep from weakening, the unifying, central, totalizing energy – call it what you like – needs the centrifugal force, that of dispersion, the centrifugal drive that lives on in the groups. Without this stimulus, cohesion atrophies, national unity dissolves, the parts fall apart and float isolated and each must go back to existing as an independent whole." (José Ortega y Gasset, *España invertebrada*, 1921)[20]

The restoration of democracy in Spain and the political transition gave rise to a process of decentralization that implied a measure of change in the territorial distribution of political power. The centralized structures inherited from the Franco regime were replaced by the autonomous system. Some policies that demand the use of large amounts of public resources, such as health and education, are managed on a regional level, although their basic organization and their financing are decided centrally. While a range of opinions exists on the true political depth of the process of decentralization in Spain, it is undeniable that this process generated logical tensions; all processes of redistribution of power give rise to such tensions. Over the course of the first half of the 1990s, these tensions increased in the context of a process of bitter political confrontation that ended with the Partido Popular replacing the Partido Socialista Obrero Español in the central government in 1996.

Apparently, the leaders of the new government hadn't read Ortega y Gasset. The transportation infrastructure policy encouraged by the Ministerio de Fomento[21] was a clear example of the new focus of the territorial policy that was adopted. On 29 September 1997, the public works minister, Rafael Arias-Salgado, met with the Comisión Nacional de Infraestructuras para las Comunicaciones of the Partido Popular. Various news media, such as *El País* (22 February and 3 March 1998) and *La Vanguardia* (25 February), among others, gave a full account of the content of the minister's speech, which was reproduced in the minutes of that meeting. These are the sources used here to refer to the minister's talk.

Arias-Salgado stated that the government's infrastructure policy was focused on "the intention of strengthening the centre of the peninsula". And he straightforwardly declared his view of the evolution of Spain's territorial organization: "I believe that over the past 30 years the country has been tilting toward the Mediterranean, and this, while not being of decisive importance in the short-term, may end up having established political importance." From there, with the aim of "rebalancing the Spanish map of infrastructures," the minister stated the core priority of his ministry's policy: "To set in motion a series of investments that keep in mind what we might call the 200 kilometres around Madrid and the connection of certain regions of Spain with the centre of the peninsula."

Clearly Arias Salgado hadn't read Ortega y Gasset, but he was most likely familiar with the Act promoted by the minister of Fomento (Public Works), Miguel de Reinoso, from December of 1851, which proposed the construction by the State of four *first class* railway lines, from Madrid to Andalusia, Castile, La Mancha and Aragon, that would connect Madrid with territories located at a distance of 200 and 300 kilometres. Where these lines ended, the *second class lines* or branch lines would continue, beginning from where the first class lines terminated and running to the sea and the country's borders.[22] In Chapter 3 we shall return to the origins of the Spanish railway system.

It's true that a single flower does not make a spring. But it's also true that after spring comes summer. Perhaps for this reason, the president of the government, José María Aznar, in his investiture speech given on 25 April 2000, after having won an absolute parliamentary majority in the March elections of that year, stated his priorities in infrastructure spending, notably mentioning "a high-speed railway system that, in ten years, will locate all of the provincial capitals within four hours distance from the centre of the peninsula."[23] It was understood that the president was referring here to the peninsular provincial capitals, and the timeframe of ten years turned out to be overly optimistic. Although it should be pointed out that it also took more than ten years to realize the goal of connecting all of the provincial capitals with Madrid when the Spanish railway network was initially begun, a wish first expressed in 1864.[24] As for the rest, the practical realization of the directives that the previous minister of Fomento had put forward in September of 1997 took on greater relevance and has constituted the core of transportation infrastructure policy up to the present.

In effect, the priorities defined in the final years of the 1990s have maintained their validity, as if the directives of that government had maintained a hegemony – even if implicit – despite the arrival of a different political party to government. It is difficult to offer a better interpretation of the content of the speech by the president of the government, José Luis Rodríguez Zapatero, at the Teatro Real in Madrid on 1 February 2007, on the occasion of the celebration of the 100th edition of the magazine *La Aventura de la Historia*: 'The increase and bringing up to date of the powers of self-government of the Autonomous Communities that has occurred in recent years goes hand in hand, on the one hand, with the strengthening of the State's muscles, in terms of what we may consider its essential pillars; and, on the other, *with an increase in cohesion arising from infrastructure policy*."[25] This is why, according to the president Rodríguez Zapatero, the planning of infrastructures and transportation has precedence in the less developed zones. Such policy objectives are reminiscent of those made by the government that formulated the Railways Act of 1870, which emphasized the need to include the "disinherited provinces" within the system and to overcome the "scandalous inequality" affecting the different provinces.[26]

Solidarity, territorial cohesion as the goal of transportation policy, gains emphasis in this less essentialist but perhaps more state-centred approach. The State is instituted as the guarantor of a policy of transportation whose fundamental declared goal is territorial cohesion, much more so than the needs of the industrial system, or the contribution of infrastructures to productivity. Above and beyond intentions, however, the practical results are very similar. The aim is to bring the AVE to all areas of Spain to reinforce – so the claim goes – territorial cohesion and connectivity. As the minister of Fomento, José Blanco, clearly stated in his speech before 'Ágora' of the newspaper *El Economista* on 1 June 2010, "with the high-speed lines now built we have already greatly advanced connectivity between most of the Autonomous Communities. Thus, to ensure territorial cohesion, we need to advance, above all, the country's main lines that have yet to be completed. Finishing those lines will bring all of the Communities within three and a half hours reach of the centre of the peninsula from the furthest point." One hundred and forty years after 1870, territorial cohesion in Spain continues to mean being connected to Madrid.

Following the same logic, centralized control has been maintained over the strategic decisions that affect the sea ports considered of general interest, whose numbers in Spain are very high, even keeping in mind the geographic characteristics of the peninsula and the archipelagos. The management of airports is kept under centralized control to – it's claimed – guarantee the viability of the smallest airports that wouldn't otherwise be able to maintain themselves on their own. To what extent does reality correspond to this rhetoric? This question will be answered over the course of this study.

What Has Happened in Spain over the Past 40 Years? Regional Economy and Demography

Has Arias-Salgado's view, which formed the basis of the policy of 'strengthening the centre of the peninsula' (sic) promoted by Aznar, corresponded to the real evolution of Spain's economy and demography since the 1960s? In

Table 1.3 Public infrastructures, Gross Domestic Product, and population between 1964 and 2004

	% Public infrastructures			% Gross Domestic Product			% Population		
	1964	2004	Change in pp.	1965	2004	Change in pp.	1970	2001	Change in pp.
Madrid	8.02	11.41	3.39	13.92	17.71	3.79	11.09	13.32	2.23
Valencia C.	6.60	8.99	2.39	9.01	9.71	0.70	9.08	10.23	1.15
Canary Islands	2.57	3.83	1.26	2.47	4.08	1.61	3.32	4.16	0.84
Andalusia	14.17	15.26	1.09	12.69	13.73	1.04	17.66	18.07	0.41
Basque Country	4.86	5.61	0.75	7.73	6.14	–1.59	5.51	5.12	–0.39
Catalonia	13.01	13.63	0.62	19.93	18.82	–1.11	15.06	15.58	0.52
Murcia	1.62	2.21	0.59	1.97	2.52	0.55	2.45	2.94	0.49
Asturias	3.33	3.50	0.17	3.24	2.15	–1.09	3.10	2.61	–0.49
Cantabria	1.49	1.64	0.15	1.59	1.26	–0.33	1.38	1.31	–0.07
La Rioja	0.94	0.88	–0.06	0.83	0.74	–0.09	0.69	0.68	–0.01
Balearic Islands	1.70	1.53	–0.17	1.97	2.50	0.53	1.57	2.07	0.50
Navarra	2.34	1.58	–0.76	1.58	1.71	0.13	1.38	1.37	–0.01
Galicia	7.05	6.09	–0.96	5.90	5.06	–0.84	7.89	6.62	–1.27
Castile-La Mancha	6.73	5.28	–1.45	3.94	3.36	–0.58	5.11	4.32	–0.78
Extremadura	4.40	2.79	–1.61	2.20	1.66	–0.54	3.45	2.60	–0.85
Aragón	7.25	4.92	–2.33	3.62	3.09	–0.53	3.40	2.96	–0.44
Castile and León	13.03	7.89	–5.14	7.22	5.41	–1.81	7.87	6.03	–1.83

Note: Change in pp. = Change in percentage points.
Source: For infrastructures and GDP, Matilde Mas Ivars, Francisco Pérez García y Ezequiel Uriel Jiménez (dirs.). *El stock y los servicios del capital en España y su distribución territorial (1964–2005). Nueva metodología* (Bilbao: Fundación BBVA, 2007), pp. 138–143. For population, I am using data on census compiled in Francisco Goerlich Gisbert, Matilde Mas Ivars, (dirs.); Joaquín Azagra Ros y Pilar Chorén Rodríguez, *La localización de la población española sobre el territorio, un siglo de cambios; un estudio basado en series homogéneas (1900–2001)* (Bilbao: Fundación BBVA, 2006), pp. 65–66.

2007, the BBVA foundation published the study *El stock y los servicios del capital en España y su distribución territorial (1964–2005). Nueva metodología*, directed by Matilde Mas, Francisco Pérez and Ezequiel Uriel, which provided regional figures for infrastructure policy, gross domestic product and population in the first half of the 1960s and in 2004, figures that have been used to create Table 1.3.

From the figures compiled in this table, one can see that of the five regions in which participation in their public infrastructure most increased in Spain as a whole, only one – the Valèncian Community – is located entirely on the Mediterranean corridor. The weight of infrastructure also increases in the Mediterranean provinces of Andalusia. Nonetheless, the region that undergoes the greatest increase in its quota of public infrastructure is Madrid (+ 3.39 percentage points [pp.], which likewise enjoys the greatest increase in gross domestic product (+ 3.79 pp.) and in population (+2.23 pp.).

In fact, the increase in the weight of the Mediterranean area in the Spanish GDP is very moderate, with the growth of the Valèncian Community, Murcia and the Balearic Islands (+1.78 pp.) practically compensated for by the loss of weight of Catalonia (–1.11 pp.), and the population increase of this last region is surpassed by that of Madrid, the Valèncian Community and the Canary Islands. Because of all this, it seems a bit precarious to attribute to the Mediterranean area responsibility for the loss of weight of the regions of the interior *meseta*, except for the Madrid region, which leads – by far – the level of improvements in each and every one of the observed registers.

Is It Solidarity or Centralization?

Economic analysis has increasingly focused on studying the factors that explain the regional distribution of public spending on infrastructures. Following pioneering works that centred on the contradiction (trade-off) between efficiency and equity,[27] studies have been developed that extend the analysis to include the role of political factors as determiners of public spending on infrastructures.[28] In these studies, it is customary to consider the spending in the least wealthy regions as an indicator of equity (an expression of 'solidarity').

However, is it really possible to consider the multi-million euro investment in the AVE line in the province of Guadalajara, whose station is located more than eight kilometres from the city and has no connections with the station of regional trains, as 'solidarity'? Does this expenditure truly serve the province of Guadalajara, considering that in 2010 an average of about 19 passengers a day used the AVE, in contrast to the more than 10,000 who daily used the regional train line and station? It seems that what is meant by solidarity can occasionally be confused. In this specific case (and it isn't the only one), it turns out that the high-speed rail line between Madrid and Barcelona, had to pass through the province of Guadalajara, where it doesn't provide any significant service. For this reason, it is misleading to compute the amount of the expenditure in Guadalajara as inter-territorial solidarity because of the simple fact that it is a province with a relatively lower income.

Let us look at the case of Spain in more general terms to illustrate this idea.[29] Table 1.4 shows the different ratios of spending on infrastructure by the central government in each region of peninsular Spain from 1991 to 2004, in respect to the gross domestic product of the region: (1) total spending; (2) spending on roads; and (3) spending on railway. The table includes a column that shows the average distance between Madrid and the provincial capitals of each region. The table doesn't include the regions where the territorial governments have exclusive power – or almost so – over ground transportation: the Canary Islands, the Balearic Islands, the Basque Country and Navarra.

When examining the total spending (column 2), no systematic relationship is visible between the ratio of spending/regional GDP (in %) and

Table 1.4 Spending by the central government on surface infrastructures (1991–2004)

Region	Average distance in Km from Madrid (1)	Total investment (%GDP) (2)	Investment in roads (%GDP) (3)	Investment in railways (%GDP) (4)
Castile-La Mancha	146	1.9	1.0	0.5
Castile and León	210	1.7	1.0	0.4
La Rioja	321	0.9	0.6	0
Aragón	330	2.5	0.9	1.2
Extremadura	351	2.3	1.2	0.1
Cantabria	387	2.1	1.6	0
Murcia	387	1.3	0.5	0.1
Valencian C.	393	0.9	0.4	0.2
Asturias	435	2.3	1.3	0.3
Andalusia	498	1.4	0.6	0.2
Galicia	550	1.6	1.0	0.2
Catalonia	563	0.7	0.2	0.2
Spain (aggregated)	–	1.1	0.5	0.2

Source: Data on investment has been obtained from Esther Sànchez, «La inversió de l'Estat en infraestuctures per comunitats autònomes», *Nota d'economia. Revista d'economia catalana i de sector public* (2006), 83/84, 51–67. Data on distances between Madrid and provincial capitals have been obtained from the Ministry of Fomento and the Campsa Guide (shortest route).

the distance from Madrid. Nonetheless, the picture is quite different when looking at the roads (column 3). In this case, each and every one of the six regions closest to Madrid presents higher ratios than the aggregate for Spain as a whole. In the case of the regions furthest from Madrid, we find a greater diversity of ratios. Something similar occurs when we look at the spending on railways (column 4): the regions closest to Madrid have greater ratios of spending/regional GDP, and the opposite is true for the regions located on the periphery.

The cases of Castile-La Mancha and Castile and León are especially interesting. These two regions are the ones surrounding the Community of Madrid: the first, toward the south, southeast and southwest; the second, toward the north, northeast and northwest. Both regions present ratios of spending/regional GDP that are more than double the Spanish aggregate in ground transportation (road and railway). And both regions have per capita GDP lower than the per capita GDP of Spain as a whole.

The key question here is: Did these regions receive a relatively high investment because they were relatively poor, or because they necessarily had to be crossed by infrastructures that have as their objective the development of a radial network? Of course, both motives are theoretically compatible. But very good reasons exist for thinking that the policy of

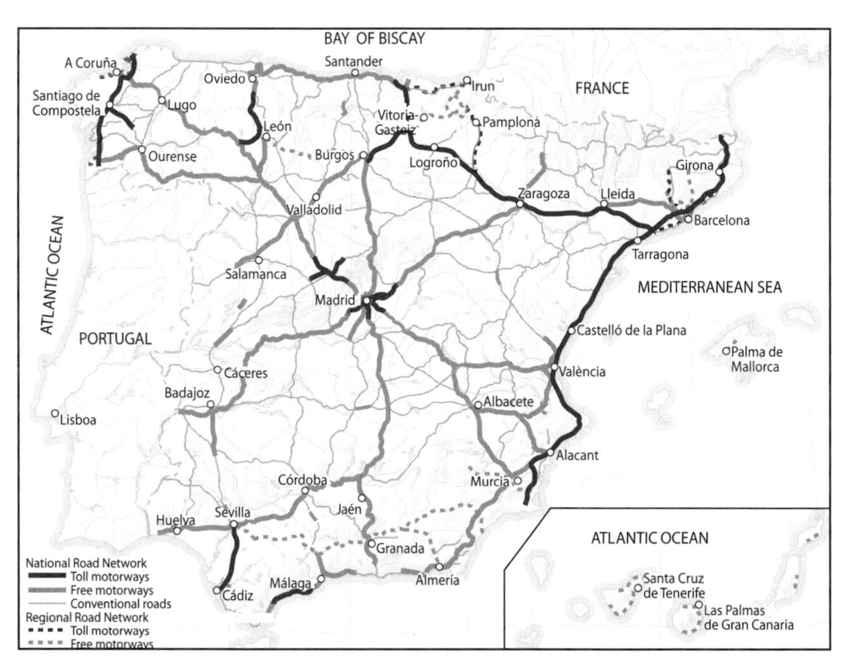

Map 1.1 Structure of the Road System in 2004

centralization has played a very important role in determining this type of regional distribution of spending on infrastructure.

Map 1.1 shows the situation of the national motorway system in 2004, the year when the time period included in Table 1 ends. The map offers a clear view of the significance of this type of radial system of ground transportation infrastructure. The primary motorways of Spain's national network converge on the capital city. The two most important exceptions are the Mediterranean corridor and the valley of the Ebro (and some trajectories of lesser significance). Note that these exceptions are toll motorways, whose investment was essentially financed by private capital, while those that converge on Madrid are toll-free motorways financed by public money, except for the Villalba-Adanero section in the Madrid-Northwest corridor (additionally, some toll radial accesses to Madrid began service in early 2004). For the high-speed rail network, the view is even more expeditious: there is no exception to the centre-periphery radial lines.

Spending on airports, decided in Spain by the central government, has been empirically analyzed in a work by Germà Bel and Xavier Fageda. Their results show– in addition to factors of political identity existing between central and regional governments – that the distribution of airport spending on a regional level has been positively related to the per capita GDP of the region and with the demand for air transportation.[30]

Of course, redistribution or equity hasn't been the principal factor guiding spending on airports in Spain. It is appropriate to add here that the existence of motives of efficiency (perhaps not very well applied) doesn't mean that centralization hasn't also been a goal of airport policy. Graph 1.2 shows the percentage of spending in each region out of the total spending in airports in the 1985–2008 period (the last year data was available); note that this period of 24 years amply surpasses a cycle of normal spending on an airport and in some cases even includes two reforms. Thus, for example, in terms of the Barcelona-El Prat airport, this period includes expenditures prior to the Olympic Games of 1992 and practically the entire enlargement begun in 2002 and completed in June of 2009.

The graph reveals that the region of Madrid has received a disproportionately large share of the total spending during the 1985–2008 period, 44.5%, almost double the capital's share of total air passenger traffic, 22.2%. The spending in Catalonia also reveals a measure of 'excess', although considerably more moderate in size (20.2% of the spending and 15.3% of the traffic). The rest of the regions with relevant airport traffic present a 'deficit' of spending – relative to passengers –, which is especially accented in the case of the island regions. In respect to the regions with the least traffic and airports, there is no systematic pattern; in some, spending

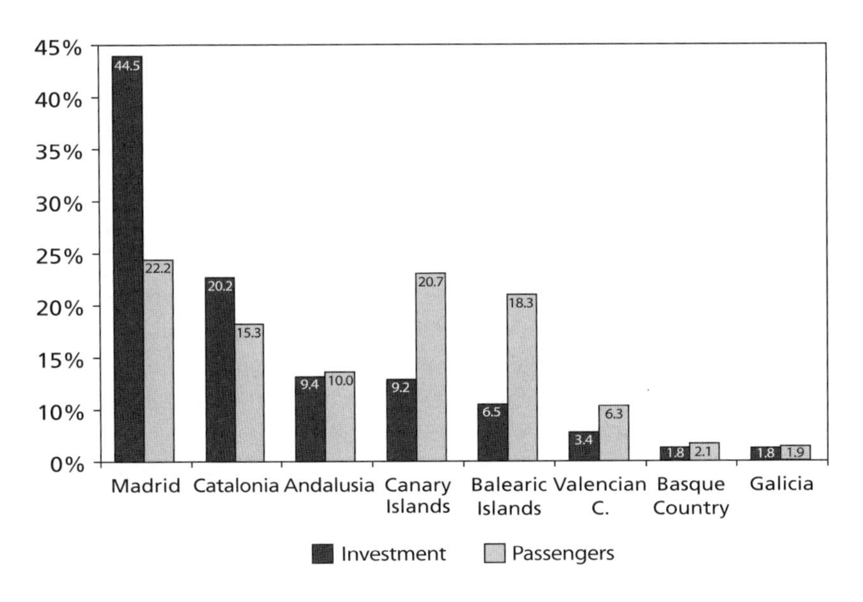

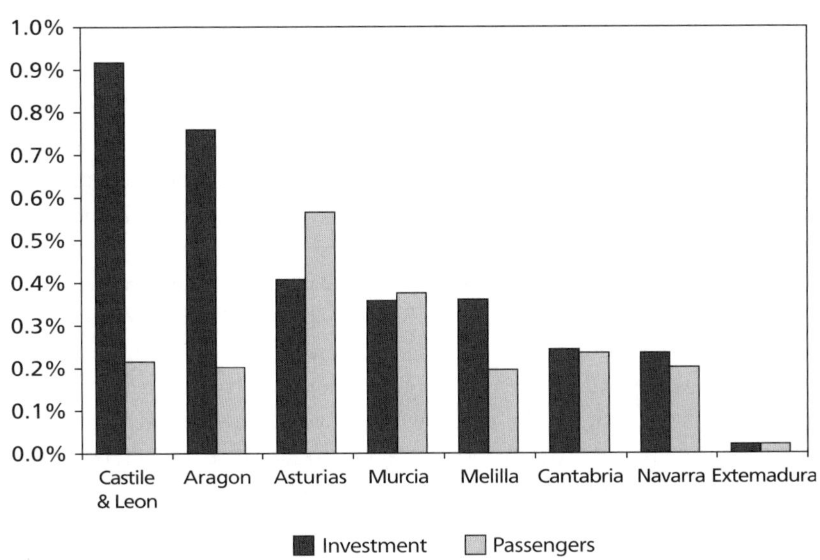

Note: At present, the airports of Albacete and Logroño are also functioning, but the regions of Castile-La Mancha and La Rioja are not included because those airports were not in service during the entire period. Both airports represent a very small quantity in terms of both spending and passengers.
Source: Figures from the Ministry of Fomento for spending, and from AENA for passengers. Factors for the CPI obtained from National Statistic Institute (INE).

Graph 1.2 Share of each region in the spending on airports (1985–2008, euros of 2008) and passengers (1985–2008) surpasses traffic (above all in Castile and León and in Aragón), while in others the opposite is true.

Centralization is also served by maintaining the totally centralized system of management of Spanish airports, a unique arrangement among developed countries of comparable size, urban structure and air market size.

In fact, the case of airports offers a very illustrative example of the use – with barely any foundation – of the solidarity argument to justify maintaining the centralized structures of control over spending and management. Since the start of the 2000s, the debate over reforming the management model of airports in Spain has grown increasingly intense, fuelled by proposals to shift from a centralized model to one of individual management on the level of each airport.

At the start of that debate, the then minister of Fomento, Francisco Álvarez Cascos, declared on 4 June 2002, that if the 12 most important Spanish airports were separated, the remaining 33 would cause losses for the State, "and someone has to explain how they would be financed."[31] From there, it followed that solidarity with the secondary airports made it necessary to maintain the centralized system. Much more recently, on 16 December 2008, during a parliamentary debate on reforming the management of the airports, the spokesman for the Socialist parliamentary group, Salvador de la Encina, sustained that "except for the airports of Madrid, Barcelona, Malaga and Palma, the rest of the Spanish airports are loss-making. How could a socialist government not maintain solidarity and equity in light of this situation?"[32]

The Socialist spokesman's appraisal of the number of airports without a deficit was overly pessimistic. At the Comisión de Fomento held on 12 January 2010, the minister José Blanco provided the figures for individual airports corresponding to 2009.[33] According to the information provided,[34] the number of airports with positive balances was nine . . . but the two principal Spanish airports were not among these. In fact, of the 433 million euros of operating deficit of the combined airports managed by AENA, a deficit of 42 million (9.7%) corresponded to Barcelona-El Prat, and a deficit of 301 million (69.5%) corresponded to the airport of Madrid-Barajas. This contradicts the results of the largest European airports, which are generally positive, and speaks quite poorly of the efficiency of the Spanish system. Above all, however, it blatantly gives the lie to the hackneyed argument that the centralized system of management is used to finance the deficit of the smallest airports. For the two largest Spanish airports to be the primary beneficiaries of solidarity – with the objective of financing their recent enlargements – is quite a uniquely practical application of such an otherwise respectable concept.

In sum, economic analysis of the distribution of spending on infrastructures has shown that efficiency and redistribution are important factors behind the decisions central governments make in respect to spending. Political factors relating to the electoral strength of the party of the government in each region and the identity of the parties in the (central and regional) government also play important roles.

Additionally, it is necessary to pay attention to factors related to metapolitical objectives that the central government may pursue through specific policies such as those pertaining to infrastructure. The case of Spain illustrates that centralization can be a decisive factor in the distribution of spending on ground transportation infrastructure. On some occasions, it may very well be the case that what is taken for redistribution or solidarity is in fact the city-capital (the geographic centre in the case of Spain) connection with peripheral regions, because this connection must necessarily pass through relatively poor regions.

'Inter-territorial solidarity' has been one of the primary, age-old slogans used by the central power to argue its territorial policy. Spanish society is very equalitarian in terms of inter-territoriality. In fact, more concern is paid to equality between territories than to equality between people within those territories. This explains why 'guaranteeing' equality between territories has served as an effective glue and an element of social legitimization of centralized power in Spain. In practice, however, rather than solidarity what has very often been carried out is centralization. This is unquestionably one of the major boosts that public policy has provided to the process of transforming Madrid into Paris.

2

From Administrative Capital to Political Capital

Prior to the first half of the 17th century, Madrid was one of the more populated cities of Castile, although it was far from being the most populous. According to figures recompiled by David Ringrose,[1] the population of Madrid in 1530 numbered about 20,000 inhabitants, a good deal less than the 30,000 of Valladolid, or the 28,000 of Toledo, and very similar to the 19,000 of Medina del Campo. The seat of the royal court was itinerant at that time and Philip II decided to move it from Toledo to Madrid in 1561. This decision ended up making the city the permanent seat of the court and, therefore, the administrative capital of the monarchy.

After the War of the Spanish Succession, which ended in 1714, the Bourbon dynasty – from France – adopted the French model as the reference for territorial organization and the exercising of power. As a result of this change in orientation of royal power, the Crown acquired full political jurisdiction over the territories of Spain. Thus, Madrid added the condition of full political capital to that of administrative capital. Over the course of the 18th century, different public policies were developed to carry out the projects of the successive monarchs, and among these policies, public works for ground transportation occupied a prominent place.

Ground transportation became a fundamental feature on which to base the political and economic position of Madrid, given that the city was the only Western European capital – because of its geographical location – without direct maritime access or communication with the sea via a navigable route. The problem of provisioning Madrid appeared as soon as the capital was designated as administrative capital and grew continuously in pace with the capital's demographic growth. For this reason, it was a decisive factor in the public policies developed since the 18th century.

Madrid, Permanent Seat of the Court

During the entire reign of Charles I, until 1556, the court had moved from city to city, a situation that continued during the first years of the reign of his successor, Philip II. In 1561, the court was moved from Toledo to Madrid. At first, this change was perhaps not considered to be definitive.[2] In fact, Philip III, who succeeded Philip II in 1598, briefly established the court in Valladolid from 1601 to 1606. But the seat of the court returned to Madrid after this parenthesis and from then on the city became the permanent capital.

No motive unanimously accepted as fundamental exists for the decision of establishing the capital in Madrid. Certainly, it seems clear that only the cities of Castile were among the options on the menu. As Alfredo Alvar Ezquerra points out, "it would have been inconceivable to establish the court outside of Castile, *abroad* – for indeed, the Castilian was as much a foreigner in Aragon or Portugal as the Aragones or Portuguese was in Castile."[3] One of the most commonly alleged reasons is the city's central geographic position in the peninsula.[4] But this factor doesn't seem to explain why Toledo wasn't preferable, given that this city occupies a location as central as Madrid, and was larger than it prior to 1561, and had a longer tradition as seat of the court. In fact, the argument of Madrid's geographic centrality was only put forward later, and in comparison with Valladolid (clearly more distant from the centre), in the controversy concerning the location of the seat of the court unleashed between 1601 and 1606,[5] period during which the court was located in Valladolid.

The defensive safety offered by a location of this type has also been put forward as a favourable factor for choosing Madrid,[6] but this wouldn't have excluded other cities of the *meseta* such as Toledo and Valladolid. Or even Seville, at a distance from the coast but connected to the sea by a navigable river. It is difficult to imagine that the military safety of the court of the principal Western military empire of the 16th century would have been a fundamental restriction for designating a city as permanent seat of the court.

It is interesting, on the other hand, to entertain Cristina Segura's suggestion[7] that rather than Madrid's central position being a decisive factor, much greater weight may have instead been given to the fact that it was a relatively new city, with many fewer established powers – whether noble or ecclesiastical – and that it offered an important asset in the form of an important administrative apparatus dedicated to the local government.

Whatever the reasons may have been for designating Madrid as the permanent seat of the court, its condition as capital was consolidated in the

17th century. From its initial designation in 1561, Madrid underwent great growth, and over the course of only 70 years, between 1560 and 1630, the city went from occupying a secondary position in the urban network hierarchy based around Toledo, to having a pre-eminent position as the largest city in Spain.[8] Towards the middle of the 17th century, in 1646, the population of Madrid reached 150,000 inhabitants, almost eight times more than a century earlier. This figure was ten times that of Toledo and more than eleven times that of Valladolid, although both cities had had larger populations than Madrid only a century before.[9] In fact, the combined population of the eight principal Castilian cities (Toledo, Valladolid, Segovia, Salamanca, Burgos, Palencia, Ávila and Medina del Campo) declined abruptly and dramatically in the first half of the 17th century: from 207,000 inhabitants in 1594 to 88,500 in 1646, during which time Madrid grew from 65,000 to 150,000. The capital's growth was nourished by people arriving from the rest of the Castilian cities, as well as from rural zones.

Madrid's growth developed almost exclusively around its functions as seat of the court. The expression '*sólo Madrid es Corte*' ('only Madrid is the court', but with the double implication that 'Madrid is only the court') has been a great hit in the historiography of the capital, with its suggestion of a double reality: on the one hand, Madrid was the only court of an immense empire; on the other, almost all of the city's social and economic activity depended on the presence of that court.[10] Without the court, Madrid would have continued being a city of modest importance.[11]

The 17th century was a century of general decline, especially so in economic terms. The decline was much more intense in the regions of the Spanish meseta: in Extremadura and the two Castiles the output per inhabitant decreased more acutely. The economic function carried out by Madrid led to the collapse of the commercial economy of Spain's interior.[12] In the words of Gil Novales, a large portion of the responsibility resides in the double economic and social polarization of Madrid, "centre of the empire, [whose] upper, administrative and parasitical classes maintain a quality economy, in contact with the productions of peripheral Spain and those of the empire, while the lower classes make do with the impoverished economy of the surrounding area of Castile; what is more, the double condition of Madrid forces the Castilian economy toward underdevelopment."[13] In sum, the administration of an empire demanded a capital, and the imperial grandness of Spain imposed as a price "a collective social subsidy for Madrid".[14]

In contrast to the territories of the *meseta*, the output per inhabitant grew in the 17th century in peripheral regions such as Andalusia, Murcia,

Catalonia and Galicia.[15] The effect of absorption exercised by Madrid was limited to its hinterland of Castile. Not in vain, "the administrative ties between Madrid and 'Spain' were extremely tenuous" in this period.[16] Furthermore, Madrid was an eminently administrative capital as seat of the monarchy's apparatus, although its political jurisdiction was more limited, especially in respect to the regions making up the Crown of Aragon (Aragon, the Balearic Islands, Catalonia and València), which had their own political, economic, taxation and judicial institutions. This situation, however, would undergo a profound change in the 18th century.

Political Capital Status

In 1700, Charles II died, the last of the Hapsburg kings, and was succeed by Philippe de Bourbon (referred to here as Philip V), duke of Anjou and grandson of Louis XIV – the Sun King – who reigned in France until 1715. Philip V arrived in Madrid in 1701 and reorganized the court according to the characteristics of the French court. As Elliot points out,[17] the government was also subjected to a general reorganization, adopting the guidelines of the French ministries and with positions of great importance in the government given to figures arriving from France with the new king.

Very shortly after Philip V's arrival to power, the War of the Spanish Succession broke out in 1702 when the Austrian empire demanded rights of succession in Spain. This war began as an international conflict, and also acquired an internal dimension, given that the territories of the Crown of Castile and Navarre aligned with the French side, while those of the Crown of Aragon gave their support to the Austrian side. The war, which inside Spain "acquired the form of a Bourbon conquest of Catalonia, Aragon and València",[18] ended in 1714, and from this moment onwards the new Bourbon dynasty consolidated its control over all of Spain.

During the course of the war, a Nueva Planta ('New Judicial Districts') decree was promulgated in June of 1707, which suppressed the native institutions of the kingdoms of València and Aragon, and reorganized the judicial system. Shortly after the war's end new decrees were published in November of 1715 and January of 1716, which had identical effects, respectively, for the Balearic Islands and Catalonia. Through this series of decrees, the Castilian language was compulsorily imposed as the administrative language. Elsewhere, the territories of the Crown of Aragon were subjected to the taxing powers of the Spanish king, the most important factor in improving the health of the treasury of the Spanish Kingdom, along with being freed from expenditures following the loss of Italy and the

Netherlands through the Treaty of Utrecht in 1713.[19] In the institutional arena, as Ringrose points out, the local parliaments were abolished, the Crown began to sell the posts of councillor in the municipal councils, the judicial courts were incorporated into the Castilian system and the chief magistrates were named from Madrid. In this way, royal authority was not only strengthened within Castile, but Castilian practices were extended to the Crown of Aragon.[20] Spain was transformed, in fact and deed, into a centralized State.[21]

The centralized and Castilianized orientation of the new dynasty, which had become apparent as soon as Philip V arrived to the throne, was further accented after the war. The new dynasty was from France and, logically, adopted the French model as a reference for the organization of power. After all, France was the principal European power and its capital, Paris, was the principal European city of that period. Like Paris in France, Madrid became a political capital in a State where political power was monopolized by central institutions.

The project of transforming Spain into a country like France, and Madrid into a capital like Paris, began at that time. As Álvarez Junco explains, given the state of decline the new Bourbon dynasty found in Spain, this new dynasty embarked on a series of reform projects: "At first, the adopted program didn't seem very problematic: it was a question of imitating the French model, so brilliantly successful under Louis XIV. This meant rebuilding the navy, centralizing the administration, improving the roads, building canals [. . .] What was good for the monarchy was good for Spain. And what had strengthened France could only benefit Spain."[22]

The new project faced barely any opposition;[23] it won the support of the Spanish elites for whom following the French cultural and administrative model was seen as a way of strengthening the political organization of the monarchy and overcoming Spain's decline.[24] In this sense, as Borja de Riquer indicates, the political elites opted to unify and centralize as a means to nationalize.[25] In sum, the Bourbon reform was the adaptation of the French model to Spain,[26] with the result that French influence was omnipresent. This was very evident in the case of prominent enlightened reformers, such as the Marquis of La Ensenada.

The model to imitate was established as Paris. A very interesting example is demonstrated by Ignacio de Luzán, secretary of the Spanish embassy in Paris from 1747 to 1750, who jotted down his impressions of the French capital in *Memorias literarias de París*. Luzán saw in Paris "the centre of science and art, of fine arts, of erudition, of refinement and good taste."[27] It was, therefore, the model that Spain should follow to reverse its decline.

The drive to transform Madrid into a European capital, following the model of Paris, received an important boost under the reign of Charles III (1759–1788), which earned him the title of being 'the best mayor of Madrid'. Enlightened reform in Spain enjoyed its greatest influence during this king's reign. In his efforts to modernize Madrid, Charles III encouraged the creation of urban avenues and promenades, the improvement of street lighting and sanitation, and promoted the construction of monuments such as the Puerta de Alcalá (1778) and the Museo del Prado (begun in 1786). Similarly, he promoted the construction of radial roads from Madrid to different points of the Iberian Peninsula, a subject we shall discuss later in greater detail.

Charles III died in 1788, only one year before the French Revolution. It was precisely this historical event that marked the reign of his successor, Charles IV, and spelled the end of enlightened reform. France ceased to be an example to follow for the Bourbon dynasty in Spain. The Napoleonic invasion in 1808 and the subsequent War of Independence until 1814 dug an emotional trench between Spain and France, but French influence was too strong to disappear as a result of these historical events. Thus, for example, the Constitution of Cádiz of 1812, upon declaring in its article 3° that 'Sovereignty essentially resides in the Spanish nation', reproduces literally an article from the French constitution of 1791.[28] In the same direction, it may be noted that the most intense debate during the drawing up of the Constitution was probably over what form the *Cortes* should have. Should the parliamentary body have two houses, as in the United Kingdom and the United States? Or only one, as in France?[29] Emulation of France was also the decisive criteria in this area and only one house was chosen.

Initially, Napoleon's defeat in Spain meant the defeat of the defenders of the Enlightenment – 'the *afrancesados*' – whose core members in the War of Independence had been politicians from the period of Charles III.[30] The disappearance of Enlightenment reform, however, didn't mean the disappearance of the centralizing project of the French model. It is important to point out here that some Spanish Enlightenment thinkers in the past – and in the present – have tended to confuse Enlightenment with centralization. The Enlightenment was – is – synonymous with freedom of thought and a critical attitude toward political power, with having the courage to serve reason, according to the formulation by Emmanuel Kant. It also took root – and with greater force – in many non-centralized countries.

In Spain, after Enlightenment reform disappeared, centralization persisted, as much during the absolutist reign of Ferdinand VII as during later periods. In the 19th century, the idea was consolidated that in order for the political-administrative construction of the modern Spanish State to be achieved, "it all had to be planned, organized and supervised from a nerve centre, a capital, a seat of government."[31] The first challenge facing political-administrative development based on the French model was judicial and territorial homogenization. Territorial homogeneity was the product of a nationalist viewpoint, in that it followed the "non-explicit (and possibly unconscious, as much as they believed in the reality of the nation) goal of giving a 'single image' to the social body."[32] That is to say, the attainment of a compact and homogenous nation, which is the principal ideological basis of any nationalism.

The practical consequence of the nationalistic emulation of France's territorial organization was the copying of the French system of prefectures or departments. This model had been implanted in France at the end of the 1770s by the finance minister, Jacques Necker, and had already wielded a measure of influence in the Spain of that time.[33] The process reached its principal milestone with the establishment of the provinces by Javier de Burgos in 1833.[34] The provincial county councils, or *Diputaciones*, were established shortly afterward in 1836. The provinces became, in the words of Vicens Vives, "the quintessence of centralized liberalism."[35] In the following decade, that of the 1840s, an effective State was established controlled by centralized interests in Madrid,[36] a capital where "liberalism had to become the backbone of a centralized governing machinery."[37]

The transposition of the models of administrative, civil, mercantile and penal organization implanted in France was a constant over the course of the 19th century. Thus, during the reign of Ferdinand VII the Mercantile Code was introduced; the Penal Code during the reign of Isabel II; the Civil and Criminal Laws during the *Sexenio Democrático*, and the Civil Code at the end of the century, during the Restoration. Unquestionably, France has been the permanent and constant model, whose influence has survived regimes and governments, which is a good indication of the strong and diverse support the idea of making Spain into a country like France has enjoyed.[38]

The Origin of the Radial State

The road system of Hapsburg Spain had its origins in the system of Roman roads dating from the 3rd to 4th centuries, and possessed the basic characteristics of a mesh, forming a decentralized network,[39] whose density was much lower in the northwest corner of the peninsula (Galicia and Asturias) and in the southwest of the *meseta*, as can be observed in Map 2.1, based on the *Repertorio de caminos* by Juan Villuga, published in Medina del Campo in 1546. The network was characterized by east to west routes that ran

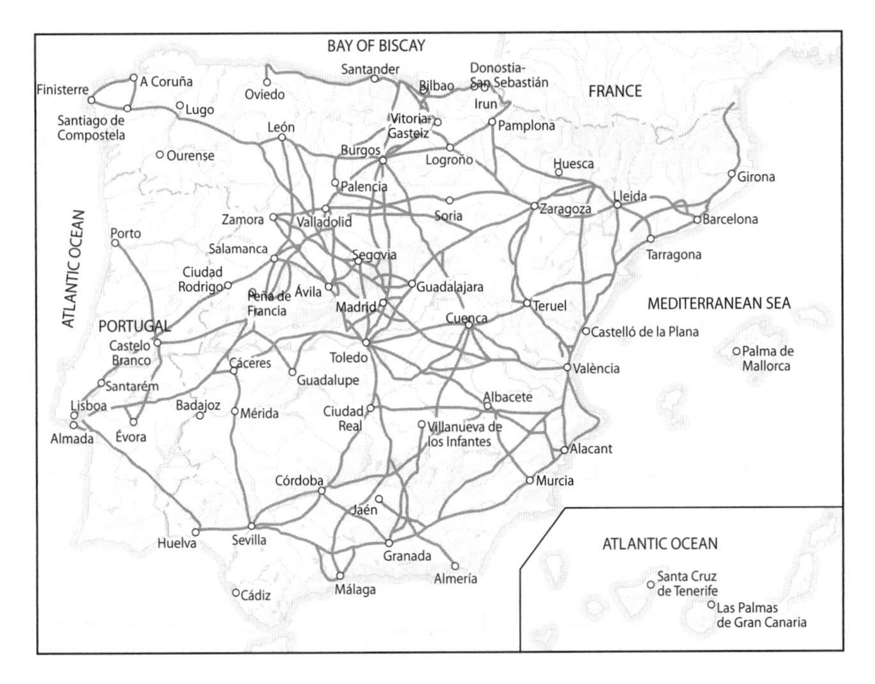

Map 2.1 Roads in 1546

through the valleys of the large rivers, north to south routes linked up to the east–west ones, and some diagonal routes that also connected to the previously mentioned ones.[40] In effect, this is the map of roads the Bourbon dynasty inherited in the early 18th century:

After consolidating its political power, the new dynasty set about reforming the postal service, which since the 16th century had been licensed out to successive private interests. Philip V internalized the service, which from then on was directly administered by the Crown in a definitive way beginning in 1716. Similarly, "as a consequence of the centralizing policy of the Bourbons [. . .] the Crown assumed responsibility for building Spain's modern road system."[41]

The legal basis for this process was laid out in the *Reglamento General para la Dirección y Gobierno de los Oficios de Correo Mayor y Postas de España, en los viajes que se hicieren* ('General Regulation for the Management and Governing of the Postal and Stage Services of Spain, in Journeys Made') issued on 23 April 1720. Among other matters, the regulation established the 'Relation of the Postal Stage Routes', with indications for the origin and destination of each route. The relation configures a radial network centralized at Madrid,[42] extending to (1) Bayonne, by way of Irún and Pamplona; (2)

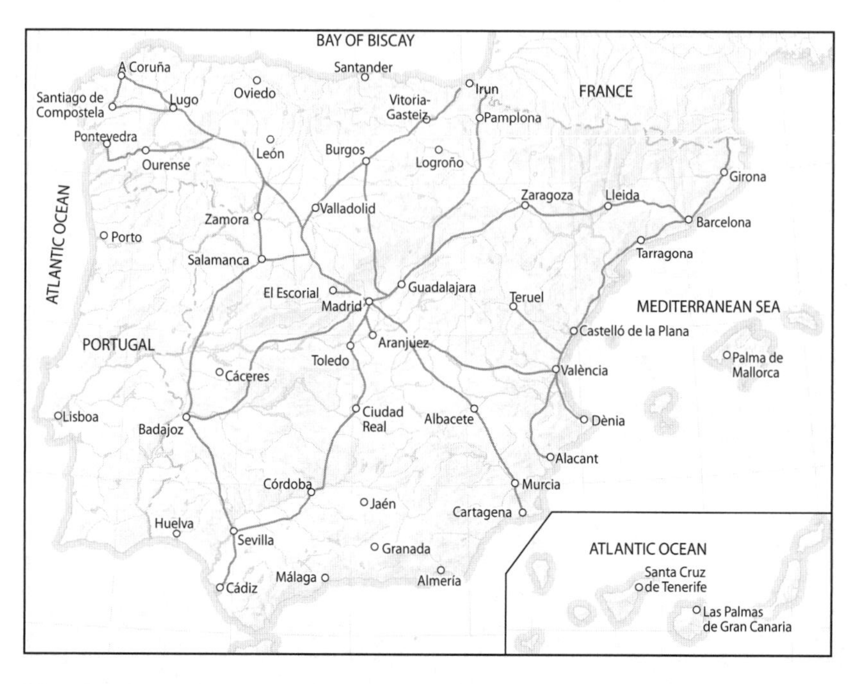

Map 2.2 Postal stage routes of 1720

Barcelona and the French border; (3) València; (4) Murcia and Cartagena; (5) Cádiz by way of Seville; (6) Badajoz; and (7) Galicia by way of Medina del Campo (with a branch to Salamanca). The network was completed by a road running parallel to the Mediterranean between Barcelona and Alacant (with a branch to Teruel), another one running parallel to the Portuguese border, between Benavente and Seville, and the connection between Burgos and Medina del Campo through Valladolid. Map 2.2 presents these routes.

The layout of the network of postal routes fundamentally served the government of the monarchy, and had as its mission the facilitating of the sending of orders from the court and the receiving of information at the capital. And it established a radial network whose characteristics have remained unchanged up to the present. Following the tradition established in earlier centuries, the creation and upkeep of the roads was the function of the municipalities, which had to assume their costs, in a process that was authorized by the Crown and supervised by the chief magistrates. This financing formula wasn't very effective at achieving the improvements desired by the Crown in respect to the postal stage routes. Because of this, in 1747, during the reign of Ferdinand VI, a royal document (*Cédula Real*) was issued that for the first time presented the possibility of building royal

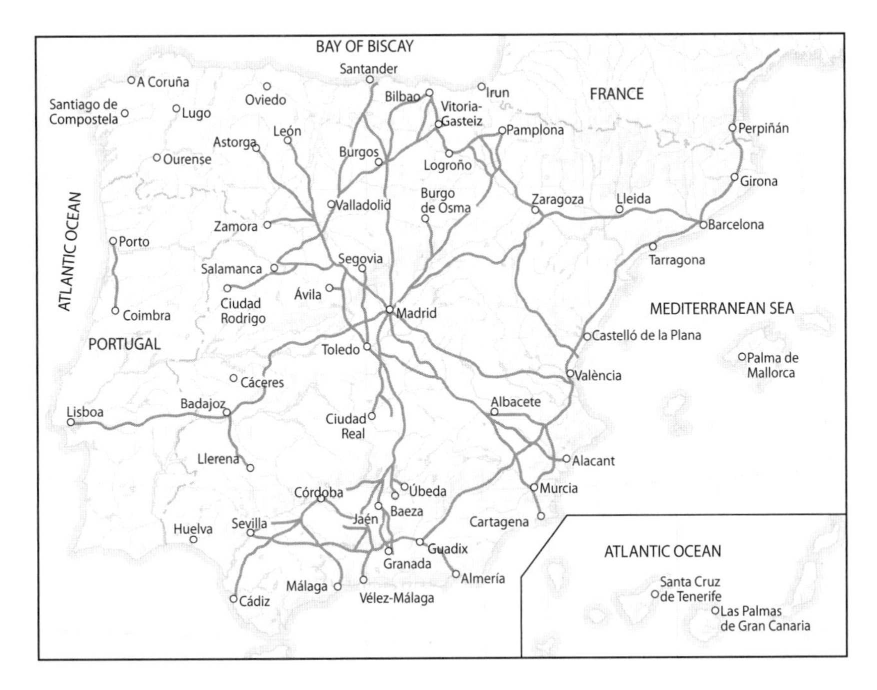

Map 2.3 Carriage roads in 1758

roads – those of the primary postal stage routes – paid for by the royal treasury (that is to say, by what we nowadays call the national budget). For the first time in the history of Spain, therefore, the State directly assumed financial responsibility for building roads, in this case, the Royal ones.[43]

In the mid-18th century, the carriage roads of Spain reproduced in the *Tratado legal y político de caminos públicos* by Thomas Manuel Fernández de Mesa (València, 1755), and in *Caminos de ruedas en 1758*, by José Escribano, already reflected – in the opinion of G. Menéndez Pidal – "the centralist criteria that the new Bourbon dynasty was imprinting on all aspects of Spanish life."[44] Escribano's routes, considered the best work, are shown in Map 2.3.

It had been postulated in the *Tratado* by Fernández de Mesa that the costs of building the royal roads be assumed by the Crown, and that the rest of the roads – the non-radial ones – be financed by those who would gain profits from them, above all the municipalities.[45] The possibility of financing roads by way of the Royal Treasury, a resource that until then had been used in an incipient and limited way, was employed with greater intensity in the reign of Charles III, which began in 1759. It is perhaps significant to point out the historical coincidence of this policy with the work of Adam Smith in his *Wealth of Nations* of 1776. As has been shown in the previous chapter, Smith warned that when roads didn't have to be financed by the fruits of commerce (by economic activity, in other words), but rather by general budgets, they could be directed principally to communicate the court and the residence of the administrative apparatus of the government. Was Adam Smith aware of the Spanish experience in radial royal roads when he prepared his magnum opus?

In effect, in 1761, a general plan of roads was initiated, inspired by the recommendations of Bernardo Ward after a request made by the Crown, completed in 1760 and published shortly afterwards (1762) with the title *Proyecto Económico*.[46] Ward's work proposed six basic radial roads, coinciding with the radial postal routes of the 1720 Regulation:

> "Spain needs six large roads, from Madrid to La Coruña, to Badajoz, to Cádiz, to Alacant, and to the French border, both to Bayonne and Perpignan, and at the same time these must also extend to various sea ports and other principal cities: one at La Coruña by Santander, which is the most essential and urgent at the moment, another by Zamora to Ciudad Rodrigo; that of Cádiz, another for Granada, and in this way, all of the others." (Bernando Ward, 1762)[47]

Ward insisted on the need to construct these roads at the expense of the Treasury, and with the participation of users in bearing the costs of their upkeep by way of tolls. Ward's proposals – already known prior to their publication – were reflected in the Decree of 10 June 1761, which included specific assignations from the funds of the Treasury for the roads to Andalusia, Catalonia, Galicia and València.[48] To finance these roads, a tax of two *reales* on each *fanega* (1.58 bushels) of salt was created, which was to be in effect for twenty years, but in fact was extended successively until 1801.[49] This was the basic financing mechanism for the radial road system proposed by Ward, with the exception of the Álava, Guipúzcoa, Vizcaya and Navarra sections, financed by the local treasuries, which in that period enjoyed a situation as unique as they do in the present day, having preserved their privileges thanks to their alignment with the Bourbon cause, triumphant in the War of the Spanish Succession.

In sum, the map of the postal routes of Philip V was definitively established as the radial map of roads in Spain through the Decree of 1761, which fixed the six main routes with their six general roads. The basic motives that led to this design have been expressed with precision and clarity by Gómez Mendoza: "Through a network of these characteristics, the Bourbon legislators aimed to satisfy goals of an administrative (mail and information), military and public order (supplies for Madrid) type. They left aside questions of a purely economic nature, such as the cheapness and regularity of the haulage."[50] Clearly, questions related to transportation efficiency and the contribution to the productivity of the economic system were ignored in favour of objectives of an administrative and political type, which were given higher priority,[51] thereby establishing the bases for a pattern that would become permanent in Spain.

Finally, it is interesting to state here that on 16 January 1769, a Royal Resolution was issued that established that the distances for all routes were to be counted from Madrid, and from the gate closest to the line of each route,[52] which constitutes the historical origin of what would become the concept – of practical use – of the kilometre zero.

The amount of spending on roads paid for out of the general budget during the reign of Charles III was very significant, and above all benefited the territories of the hinterland of Madrid, where the State financed construction. Such a policy could have made a significant contribution to the economic growth of Castilla la Nueva. This region, which, apart from the capital, had experienced acute economic decline in the 17th century, led the list of regions in terms of the growth in output per person in the 18th century.[53]

This type of policy sparked significant opposition, such as the one by Jovellanos in 1795 (*Informe sobre la Ley Agraria*), who postulated that before interconnecting the provinces, it was preferable to give priority to the internal structuring of these provinces, and "for no more money to be spent on main roads, but rather on local ones and he asks (with good sense) for the little available money to be spent with a utilitarian criteria and not with views to ostentation."[54] Such considerations are no different from ones made ever more frequently in present-day Spain concerning the impressive amount of spending on high-speed rail; we shall return later to this matter.

A Crucial and Persistent Problem: Supplying the Capital

The problem of supplying Madrid was a major determiner of public policies from the very moment in which the city was designated as permanent seat of the court in the second half of the 16th century,[55] and became more acute as time went by and the capital underwent urban growth. One factor is fundamental to understanding the restrictions imposed by the provisioning of Madrid: it is the only capital of Western Europe with no maritime communication, neither directly nor by a navigable route. All other European capitals, as much those that were already capitals when Madrid was so designated, as those that later acquired that status over the following three centuries, didn't face the problem of lacking maritime/river traffic.

In the 18th century, the capital grew as its political power increased and the Crown displayed a much greater interventionist bent in economic matters. According to estimations by Ringrose,[56] in the decade of the 1750s the Crown maintained some five thousand families, considered together as the *Casa Real* (the Royal House) and the bureaucracy. These families received incomes that the Crown collected from all of the territories subjected to its jurisdiction. Logically, these incomes had a very important impact on the economy of the city. This became even more accented in the period of Charles III, with his decided efforts in the pursuit of transforming Madrid into a city *à la* Paris. At the end of the 18th century, between 15% and 20% of the Crown's budget was spent in Madrid,[57] although the population of the capital barely amounted to more than 1.5% of the total population of Spain at that time. In fact, for a long time, the administrative apparatus was, with domestic service, the only sector of the active population that enjoyed constant growth; the percentage of the active population of Madrid dependent on the State grew from 7.1% to 11% over the second half of the 18th century, and would continue to grow up to 12.5% in 1857.[58]

The tensions caused by the growing needs of supplying Madrid, aggravated by the scarcity of productive activities in the capital, were coupled with other transportation needs, such as military ones or the distribution of products of the public monopoly, such as salt and tobacco. The result was a massive intervention by the Crown in the functioning of the systems of provisioning and transportation. The central government – rather than the local one – assumed responsibility for providing for the capital's transportation needs, in contrast to what the case was in the rest of the cities of the country, where local authorities continued to be responsible for that service. The result was that the government became responsible for a substantial part of the transportation demand in Castile.[59]

The Crown's assumption of responsibility for supplying Madrid had some notable consequences. In terms of the functioning of the supply system, it is interesting to note that the capital's enjoyed two very important privileges: (a) the agents of provisioning the Crown had the right of first offer at livestock auctions; and (b) reserves of fodder were available on the roads for the herds being led to Madrid from the cities of the livestock fairs, a privilege that didn't exist for other cities.[60] The incentives for concentrating in Madrid the national market of provisions was, therefore, irresistible.

In general, the volume of transportation *to the capital* was large in size and asymmetrical, given that there was practically no transportation of goods *from the capital*, a situation that would continue until well into the 20th century.[61] Although some manufacturing was carried out in Madrid, such as textile production for military provisioning, supplying manufactured goods and luxury products to the capital was counted among the needs of the city's provisioning. In this sense, it is very illustrating to look at the information provided by an inventory from 1789, analyzed by Ringrose,[62] that reveals imports to the capital at a value of 433 million *reales*, while exports from Madrid amounted to only 6.5 million *reales*, that is, 1.5% of the imports.

From this one can deduce that Madrid's economy depended crucially on some political and economic structures not oriented by market forces. On the one hand, the capital didn't provide commercial or industrial services to its hinterland (nor beyond it) that would permit it to finance its commercial deficit; on the contrary, the basic factor to defray that commercial deficit was the capacity of the government and the upper urban class to come to the capital and spend taxes, incomes and tithes there.

On the other hand, the collective subsidy to provisioning Madrid was the final factor that made it possible to sustain the capital's growth. To respond to the demands of the government and to supply Madrid as administrative and political capital, official subsidies were established for the transportation sector, especially cart drivers, in the capital and all of Castile. This caused significant growth in this sector, but ill-disposed them toward offering their services to the private economy. As Ringrose explains,[63] Madrid vitally depended on aid from the government, and without its intervention in the transportation system the city wouldn't have been able to grow as it did. In this way, the government, through its policy of subsidizing transportation, distributed around the entire country a portion of the costs of supplying the capital.

The constraints that provisioning the capital imposed on its hinterland and on the entire country have been clearly summed up by Gómez Mendoza:[64] "First, it is clear that Madrid bled its hinterland by imposing a burdensome servitude on it for three centuries. Second, provisioning Madrid absorbed large quantities of economic resources due to the low productivity of the forms of ground transportation in the ancien régime. Third, the key to explaining why such a rudimentary system managed to survive over time is found in the combination of two factors. On the one hand, a complex system of subsidies lowered the cost of transportation, with artificially fixed prices for the cart drivers . . . "

In sum, the Crown's subsidies to the transportation services supplying Madrid were combined with legal measures that determined the priority routes of land transportation, and with the decision to likewise finance the construction of the radial roads corresponding to those routes with the general incomes of the State.

The Bigger the Problem, the Bigger the Solution: Laws, Spending and Subsidies

Legal measures, State spending on infrastructures, and running spending on State subsidies for transportation formed a powerful combination to guarantee the vitality of the political capital, a combination that has left a permanent imprint on Spanish politics.

The transformation of Madrid into administrative capital in 1561 caused a first boost to the city's growth, whose primary motor were the demands of the Crown and the court, and the administrative apparatus of the monarchy. Its most important effect was the suction into Madrid of the economic activity and population of its Castilian hinterland, which suffered significant decline in the 17th century. In the 18th century, after the War of the Spanish Succession, Madrid acquired the status of political capital, in a context of growing interventionism by the Crown, now in the hands of the Bourbon dynasty, in respect to economic matters. The project of creating a Spain like France, with a Madrid like Paris, is fully assumed at this time.

The needs of the capital grew parallel to the growth of its political functions, in that it became the sole centre of power of the entire monarchy. For this reason, the Royal Treasury needed a growing availability of resources that it managed to acquire thanks to (1) the reduction of costs after the loss of Italy and the Netherlands as a consequence of the Treaty of Utrecht in 1713, and (2) the subjection of the territories of the Crown of Aragon to royal taxes after the Nueva Planta decrees.

Among the public policies applied in the 18th century, that of transportation infrastructures and services clearly illustrates how legal measures and State budgets (through spending and subsidies) are articulated to organize political power and satisfy the needs of the Crown and of its capital, independently of the needs of the economic system and the relations between centres of economic production – which were left out of the priorities established and financed by State incomes.

Transportation efficiency and its contribution to economic productivity were systematically subordinated to administrative and political objectives, which were given higher priority. Over time, this became a regular pattern in the development of transportation infrastructures in Spain. We shall now see how this was the case in the establishment and development of the railways.

3

Transversal Market, Radial State (I): The First Railways

In the decade of the 1830s, during the same period that Spain's provinces were established, a massive transformation was underway that would revolutionize communication systems: the appearance of the railway. After the inauguration in England of the first railway line between Darlington and Stockton, on 27 June 1825,[1] projects for implanting railways appeared in many European countries. Later, such projects also reached Spain, and on 28 October 1848, the first peninsular line entered into service, between Barcelona and Mataró.

The opening of this route was the culmination of a process marked by a succession of projects, beginning in 1829, that were never realized. A brief presentation of these antecedents is pertinent. Afterwards, a review is made of the beginnings of the railway networks in the principal European countries. Placed within this context, the development of the Spanish system is considered in its different stages: first, the initial routes built up until 1855; later, the large expansion that occurred after the approval of the Ley General de Ferrocarriles (General Railway Law) of 1855, which introduced very important doses of support from public resources; and, lastly, the second stage of large expansion that occurred after the law of 1870, backed by ever greater support from the national budget.

The most notable results obtained from the analysis of the successive stages of expansion of the railways in Spain are the following. In the first stage, characterized by private venture capital and erratic support from the national budget, the expansion of the railway was very limited and took place in different areas of the Iberian Peninsula. The second stage, begun in 1855, is characterized by the definition of a general plan based on a series of radial routes departing from Madrid, which received the systematic and important financial support of the State. The third stage culminated the radial nature of the development of the network, extending Madrid's connections to all of the provincial capitals and, secondarily, introducing some routes of a non-radial character. Support from the national budget grew. In sum, the definition of a general plan and the assignation of national budgetary funds reproduced the radial pattern introduced in the 18th century with the road system. Lacking an accelerated development that might have been financed by the market – which presented transversal characteristics, albeit limited ones – a typical intervention by the radial State occurred.

Antecedents to the Implantation of the Railway in Spain

The first concession to build a railway line was granted in 1829 to José Díaz Imbrechts, for a route from Jerez de la Frontera to El Portal (Cádiz), with the aim of transporting wine to a seaport to export this product to Great Britain.[2] But the subscription of capital to realize the project was a failure, and the Town Council of Jerez, which had been asked in 1830 to take part in the stock subscription, refused to commit public funds to the project, which was never executed.

Almost at the same time, in March of 1830, a concession was granted for the construction of a railway between Jerez de la Frontera, El Puerto de Santa María, Rota and Sanlúcar de Barrameda, promoted by Marcelino Calero y Portocarrero.[3] The project was submitted to the Town Council of Jerez for financial support immediately after the concession, even somewhat before that of the Jerez–El Portal line, and fared no better than it (the concession was transferred in 1834 to Francisco Fasio).

Shortly afterwards, in 1831 and 1832, the Diputación of Vizcaya set in motion a project for the construction of a railway from Bilbao to Burgos. This was the first project promoted by a public administration that – being a *foral* government, or in other words, a regional one that had preserved its privileges – had enough resources to commit to spending on transportation, unlike most other regional governments. To build the entire route, the collaboration of the Council of Burgos was necessary in order to complete the section of the line that reached to that city.[4] However, the large amount of resources required and the unrest after 1833 caused by the First Carlist War shut down the project, on which work was never begun.

In that same year, 1833, a concession was granted to Francisco Fasio for the construction of a line between Reus and Tarragona. The political instability of the time and the lack of active interest on the part of public authorities once again impeded the implementation of the project. This concession, along with those of the Jerez-El Puerto de Santa María-Rota-Sanlúcar (which Fasio had acquired in 1834) and the Jerez-El Portal lines expired in 1838, shortly after the first railway line in Spanish territory, albeit in America, began service.

Indeed, Calero y Portocarrero, who had failed in his attempt to build a railway between Jerez and Sanlúcar, eventually managed to carry out his project on the island of Cuba. The railway line between Havana and Güines, some 90 kilometres long, had been approved in 1831. Given the scarcity of available private capital for implementing the project, financial support from the Junta de Fomento (Public Works Board)[5] was worked out and on 10 November 1837, the 26-kilometre section between Havana and Bejucal entered into service.

The successful implantation of the railway in Cuba had no counterpart in Spain. It is interesting to highlight the fact that all of the attempted projects were located on the periphery, were initiated with private capital – except for the case of Vizcaya –, and aimed at connecting a port (in Cádiz, Vizcaya or Tarragona) with centres of production or consumption, on routes with relatively intense commercial activity at that time. Thus, the demands of economic activity were crucial factors in those first projects, but the lack of sufficient available private capital, the high costs, the lack of defined public policy guidelines and the political instability of the time doomed them to failure. It would be more than ten years before the first peninsular railway line was opened for service, in the province of Barcelona. But in other European countries, the development of the railway was already acquiring practical relevance.

Surrounding References: The Beginnings of the Railway System in the Principal Countries of Europe

The second quarter of the 19th century saw the development of railway networks in many European countries. The inauguration of the first English line in 1825 marked a milestone that precipitated projects in the principal economies of the continent. Belgium was especially active in developing the railway, and by the end of the 1860s it had the densest railway network in relation to its population and area among continental countries.[6] The two large continental powers, Germany and France, also followed in the British wake and built a large number of lines before the middle of the century. These experiences, along with that of another large European country, the yet to be unified Italy, deserve review.

Great Britain

The first functioning steam locomotive was invented by the Englishman Richard Trevithick, and its first journey on rails took place in 1804.[7] Nonetheless, the appearance of the railway has always been more associated with George Stephenson, who improved the design of the locomotive and built the railway line between Darlington and Stockton. This was an 18-kilometre line in the county of Durham, near Newcastle, in northeast England. The primary objective of the project was to carry coals from Darlington to the sea for maritime transportation; it was opened for service on 27 June 1825.

Five years later, in 1830, the definitive milestone in the early years of the railway came with the inauguration of the line between Liverpool and Manchester, populous cities in northwest England, some 50 kilometres apart, which formed the industrial cradle of English capitalism. Until that moment, their commercial traffic was served by the navigable Bridgewater canal, and satisfying the growing demand for raw materials by industries located in Manchester was the primary goal of the railway line, which could transport both goods and passengers.

Most of the branch lines of the English railway system were built in the following two decades,[8] so that by 1850 the country already had 10,000 km of rail tracks.[9] The development of the network followed the needs of economic activity. Over the course of the 1850s, the Grand Northern network was developed, and much later the Grand Central network. In this way, the British system evolved until resembling a spider web connecting all of the significant population centres, and became the most extensive network in Europe, as well as the densest up until the 1860s, when the Belgian network surpassed it.[10] The development of the network was promoted by private initiative, and the role played by the State was secondary.[11]

Belgium

The country that proved most agile in following in the British wake in railway development was Belgium. A law of 1834 established the creation of a network in the form of a cross, whose central point was at the Flemish city of Mechelen, between Brussels and Antwerp, located about 30 kilometres from either. The first line was the Mechelen–Brussels one, inaugurated in 1835, which, shortly after entering into service, transported more passengers than all of the English lines opened up until that moment.[12]

The Belgian railway system extended from Mechelen northward to the sea at Antwerp, eastward toward Prussia, westward toward Bruges and Ostend, and southward toward Mons and France. It reached an extension of 854 km in 1850, and by the 1860s was the densest in Europe. The primary junctions in the network were the cities of Mechelen and Ghent.

During the first stage of the expansion, between 1835 and 1843, only the State built lines. Between 1850 and 1860, private companies took up the initiative and after 1870 State capital regained prominence.[13] The development of the network was driven by the needs of the Belgian economy, as demonstrated by the choice of the central junction as well as by the characteristics of its expansion over time.

Germany

The development of the railway in Germany had its origins in the project for a line between Nuremberg and Fürth, in Bavaria. Prior to the culmination of this project, the economist and politician Friedrich List, in favour of transforming Germany into a centralized power, published in 1833 a pamphlet titled: 'Concerning a Saxony Railway System as the Basis for a General System of Railway Communications in Germany'.[14] List proposed locating the nerve centre of the network in Berlin, from where six lines would extend in a radial formation.[15] The proposal was rejected upon being considered to correspond much more to political motivations rather than to economic ones, given that its primary objective was the centralized unification of Germany.

At the end of 1835, the six-kilometre line between Nuremberg and Fürth was inaugurated, the first in Germany. The core of the railway system was based on the construction of branch lines between the primary commercial cities beginning in 1836,[16] given that the private companies, guided by criteria of potential demand, gave preference to the densely populated industrial zones, such as Saxony (in the east, bordering the Czech Republic and Poland) and North Rhine–Westphalia (in the northwest, bordering Holland and Belgium).[17] The first completed branch line, between Leipzig and Dresden (Saxony), entered into service progressively between 1837 and 1839, and reached Magdeburg in 1840. The network developed at great speed and by 1850 had an extension of 5,856 km, the most extensive in continental Europe.

The development of the railway system suited the needs of economic activity, whereas the design of a network with centralizing purposes was openly rejected. The German railway began life in peripheral States such as Saxony, North Rhine-Westphalia and Bavaria. In some territories, such as Prussia and Saxony, the initiative was eminently private. In other cases it was public: Hannover, Brunswick, Baden, and Württemberg. In all, the leap toward what would become an articulated network can be attributed primarily to the efforts of private enterprise, in a context in which the first railways were self-financed even in the short-term.[18]

France

The first railway project in France was the connection between Saint-Étienne and Andrézieux-Bouthéon (in the Rhône-Alpes region), inaugurated in 1827 and dedicated exclusively to transporting coal from the mines to the banks of the Loire.[19] The first railway route suitable for passenger travel was the line between Saint-Étienne and Lyon, 56 kilometres long, and inaugurated in 1832. This line was followed by projects developed in Alsace, a region in the east bordering Germany.

Shortly after these initial executions, the French parliament debated in 1838 a project that called for the construction by the State of branch lines emanating from Paris, but the project was rejected.[20] Thus, the construction of lines up until the end of the 1840s was carried out through concessions for operating specific lines as assigned by the State, and which were obtained by those companies that proposed the shortest period of time for getting the railway built and running. Finally, the Law of 11 June 1842 decreed the creation of various main lines that totalled 3,600 km, without defining their specific routes. The main lines joined Paris with Belgium and Germany; there was a line from Paris to Lyon and Marseille; a line to the Spanish border by Tours; a transversal connection between Marseille/Montpellier, Lyon, Dijon and Mulhouse; and a transversal connection between Bordeaux (on the Atlantic) and Marseille (on the Mediterranean) through Toulouse.[21] Thus, the priorities established combined border connections, connections between Paris and the Atlantic/Spain and the Mediterranean, and transversal connections in the west and south of France.

In 1850, France had 2,915 km of railway lines, half those of Germany. As a result of the application of the Law of 1842, a good number of the lines were located in the Paris area and in the industrial north, although there were also many sections in other zones of France with intense economic activity.

The expansion of the French system was given a definitive boost in 1850 with the designation of six '*grands commandements industriels*' (large industrial commandments), to which concessions were granted for building new lines grouped in regional monopolies ceded to the companies of the North, East, West, Paris–Orleans, Paris–Lyon–Mediterranean and *Midi* (the southernmost part of the country, between the Garonne and the Pyrenees).[22] The initiative was always private, with financial support from the State, until the Freycinet Plan of 1879, at which time the State began to build lines.

Italy

The development of the railway in Italy occurred later than in the previously mentioned countries. The first railway line was a short section of eight kilometres between Naples and Portici, inaugurated in 1839. During the 1840s and 1850s, the first regional networks were implanted in Tuscany (around 200 km connecting Livorno, Pisa, Siena and Florence) and Piedmont (some 200 km between Turin and Asti, and extending along the Valley of the Po).[23]

In 1850, Italy had 620 km of railway lines and during that decade, prior to the country's unification in 1861, another 1,500 km were built, primarily in the north. The Piedmontese network was the longest, with 800 km, and the Milan–Venice line was completed with its extension to Piedmont, the Tyrol and eastern Italy.[24] At the end of the 1850s, the railway extended to Emilia-Romagna, and on 16 April 1859, the first line was opened in the region of Lazio, between Rome and Civitavecchia, the seaport some 80 km from the city that was to be designated as the capital of Italy in twelve years.

The expansion of the railway in Italy had begun two decades prior to the country's political unification, and the main concern was to fulfil the needs of economic activity, which explains the great importance given to the northern regions, Piedmont and Lombardy, as well as to the region of Tuscany, located halfway between the north and the south of the country. Private companies played the leading role in the creation of the railway, although later, after 1885, public ownership began widespread.

Summary: Lessons from International Experience

The general rule followed in the principal European countries in respect to the expansion of their railway networks was to give priority to satisfying the needs of the industrial system. This was the case regardless of whatever public-private combination was chosen, as shown by the extreme cases of Great Britain, where private initiative was predominant and public intervention had the least presence, and Belgium, where the railway was built solely by the State during the first decade of its development.

The cases of Germany and France were mixed in respect to the public-private question. In Germany, the proposals to build a system of the radial type were rejected because of their centralizing objectives. In states with greater industrial activity (Saxony, North Rhine-Westphalia) the initiative was private, while elsewhere the State assumed responsibility for building the railways. At any rate, satisfying the needs of economic activity was the primary factor for the development of the network. In France, after some isolated initiatives were carried out in areas with mining and industrial activity, the parliament debated and rejected in 1838 a project for a radial design that aimed to create branch lines emanating from Paris. Later, six large regional areas were defined that formed the basis for completing the French system, in which private companies with significant State support created and developed the railway. The companies that developed the railway in Italy were likewise private and gave priority to the west-east connections in northern Italy and to the internal articulation of Tuscany; in short, the areas with the strongest economic and industrial activity in Italy.

Compared to the experience of the countries reviewed above, the expansion of the railway in Spain was insignificant. In 1850, only 28 kilometres of line had been built, the Barcelona-Mataró line, and some short stretches were under construction, such as the Madrid–Aranjuez line, and a section for mining use between Sama de Langreo and Gijón. At the start of the 1850s, new concessions were granted within a context in which an attempt was by now underway to create a general legislation. This process opened the definitive stage for the creation of the railway system, whose crucial milestone was the Ley General de Ferrocarriles of 1855 (General Railway Law of 1855).

The Implantation of the Railway in Spain: Preliminary Experiences

After the practical failures of the first railway projects in 1829 and during the 1830s, the first railway concession to be successfully completed was the one granted in 1843 for a 28.5 km line between Barcelona and Mataró, promoted by private interests that anticipated freight, much more than passenger traffic, to make up the most significant demand for the line.[25] Shortly afterwards, in 1845, a concession was granted to José de Salamanca y Mayol, later designated Marquis of Salamanca, to build a line between Madrid and Aranjuez, stretching 49 km. In fact, work on this line began in May of 1846,[26] even before work had started on the Barcelona-Mataró line. This latter went through numerous and varied ups and downs, notably in terms of the expropriation of lands, and so the building works did not start until early 1847.

After work finally got underway on the Barcelona–Mataró line, construction on the Madrid–Aranjuez line fell off because of insufficient funds. In this context, in 1847, the government issued a Royal Order for the Banco de San Fernando to accept security shares of the Aranjuez railway company, with the Public Treasury as guarantor.[27] This arrangement was not unrelated to the fact that the Treasury minister, the Marquis of Salamanca, also happened to be simultaneously the promoter of the benefiting railway, the Madrid–Aranjuez line. In fact, the private promoters of the Barcelona–Mataró line solicited the government for analogous assistance in June and November of 1847, but on both occasions they were denied such aid.[28] At any rate, work on the Madrid–Aranjuez came to a halt at the end of 1847. Construction on the Barcelona–Mataró line, however, continued and was completed even without any financial backing from the State. The line entered into service on 28 October 1848, becoming the first operating railway in Spain.

The political vicissitudes sparked by the scandal of the self-backing received by the Marquis de Salamanca ended with the Marquis being sent into a short exile, until 1849. Upon his return to Spain, work was resumed on the Madrid–Aranjuez line and in 1850 the Marquis of Salamanca received new aid from the State, which guaranteed the interest on the invested capital.[29] Released from economic uncertainties, the company continued its work, construction was finished, and on 9 February 1851 the line was officially inaugurated. After the line entered into service, it became clear that the costs of running it were very high, for which reason the Marquis of Salamanca proposed that the State purchase it. The State acquisition occurred in 1852,[30] a transaction that was linked to the concession of funds from the main national budget for the enlargement of the Almansa line, and for the Almansa-Alacant section.[31] Clearly, the Marquis of Salamanca deserved the honour of having his name designate the most affluent district in Madrid, promoted by him in the 19th century. It is also understandable that similar distinctions weren't bestowed upon him by other Spanish cities.

There were other railway lines built in those early years. The next was the mining line of Sama de Langreo to Gijón, whose first section, the Gijón-Pinzales, was inaugurated in August of 1852. The Company received a subsidy from the government guaranteeing profitability. This section was followed by others until the completion of the line at Sama de Langreo in 1856. The València–Xàtiva line, 57 km long, work on which had begun in 1851, was inaugurated in December of 1854. The expansion of the railway in Catalonia was especially active during this period, with the construction of the Barcelona–Granollers and Barcelona–Molins de Rei (and its later

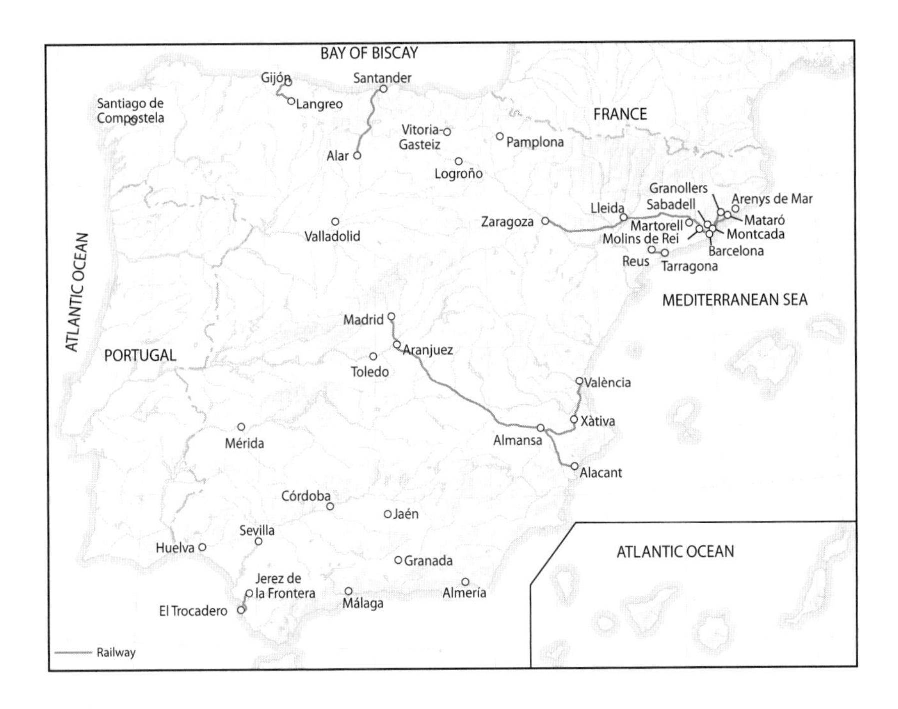

Map 3.1 Concessions prior to 1855 that were effectively built

extension to Martorell) lines, and the section of the Sabadell to Montcada line (which linked up with the Barcelona–Granollers line, forming part of the Barcelona to Zaragoza line through Lleida).[32]

Map 3.1 shows the concessions granted before 1855 that were effectively built and opened for service.[33] Most of these first lines "corresponded to a real interest in making use of traffic flows on existing roads",[34] with some exceptions, such as the Madrid to Aranjuez and Albacete, which had been assumed by the State, contravening the current legislation of the time. According to the information supplied by Miguel Artola,[35] the Madrid–València road by way of Cuenca had greater volume of traffic. Other sections with more road traffic were the Almansa-Alacant, conceded, and the Valladolid–Miranda–Santander area, in which the Alar–Santander section, likewise conceded, was located.

The Genesis of the Radial Railway in Spain: The Parliamentary Commission of 1850

In the mid-19th century, the government increased its involvement in the expansion of the railway. In 1847, Bravo Murillo, minister of Commerce, Education and Public Works, had already drawn up a first plan for a General Railway Law. The government's intention was to set in motion a study of four radial lines from Madrid to the port of Cádiz, to one of the nearest ports on the Mediterranean, and to the borders of France and Portugal, all with the corresponding budgetary allocation.[36] The text, however, was never debated in the Cortes, because it was presented after the legislature had terminated.

The formulation of a General Law was taken up again in 1850 by the then minister Seijas Lozano, whose plan was studied that same year by a congressional commission, the so-called Comisión Olózaga, after the name of the MP presiding over it. The fundamental factor for establishing a plan of the principal network was the goal of uniting the political capital with the maritime periphery, according to Mateo del Peral, because:

> "the members of the commission, *residents in the capital*, saw secondary railways emerge with partial routes, that aimed to communicate nearby centres of production, often within the same provincial area, while Madrid remained relatively isolated and in danger of that isolation increasing."[37]

Well-known military men, engineers and financiers were called upon to appear before this commission, and the content of those appearances[38] offers valuable information about the criteria on which the decisions to develop the railway were based. In fact, although the plan of 1850 wasn't formally approved, the commission's proposals formed the essential basis for the General Railway Law that was eventually passed in 1855.

The Comisión Olózaga centred its discussions around four thematic blocks: (1) the formulas of concession and the creation of concessionary companies; (2) the technical criteria for granting concessions; (3) questions related to safety and defence; and (4) determining the form of the network and the preferential lines. While each and every one of these blocks is of unquestionable interest, the most relevant to the subject matter we are examining is the one that aimed to determine the form of the network and preferential lines, which was quite closely linked to questions of safety and defence. The most relevant opinions declared by those appearing before the commission are transcribed below; these transcriptions are much more revealing on their own, verbatim, than any account that could have been made based on them.

The starting point were the priorities that the commission, in agreement with the government, tried to establish and subsidize with public funds, and were summarized by Salustiano Olózaga as follows:[39] "(1) from Madrid to Bayonne, with branch lines to the main points to the north and north-east, and one from Valladolid or its vicinity in the direction of Porto; (2) from Madrid to Cartagena, with branch lines to Alacant and València and vice versa, according to the farthest point indicated by studies to be preferable; (3) from Madrid to Barcelona by way of Zaragoza, or with a branch line to this point or another that is judged convenient; (4) from Madrid in the direction of Lisbon through Extremadura; and (5) from Madrid to Cádiz as a continuation of the preceding line or a branch of the Cartagena line, according to how these lines are determined by the study."

One of the first authorized opinions concerning this matter had been made in the March 6 session by the man who had been president of the government in 1835, Juan Álvarez Mendizábal. According to Mendizábal,[40] "the law to be drawn up must be broadest in respect to government authority, so that it combines and harmonizes one line out of the four main ones that are indicated from the court to the coast; two from the court to the Mediterranean, and the other two from the court to the Ocean, the Bay of Biscay and the French borders [. . .] the indicated law, which must be drawn up now, should include a budget of 10 million reales for the government to cover the costs of drawing the plans of the four lines."

The 23 April 1850 session of the Comisión de Ferrocarriles (Railway Commission) summoned various army generals to learn their viewpoints on railway priorities. Olózaga asked the generals for their opinions regarding the priorities established by the government. In this respect, General Zarco del Valle stated that "Madrid's centrality, which lends itself to being the hub of the new communication lines, is not opposed to the use these lines must be put to in military operations [. . .] Perhaps Madrid is located too far forward in the direction the French would have to march in the invasion of our territory."[41] For his part, General Manuel Concha added that "the construction of railway lines parallel and perpendicular to the coasts is of interest to Spain's independence."[42]

General O'Donnell (who would become president of the government in the second half of 1850) was the following military officer to declare his opinions and, while agreeing with the potential military uses of the railway, added, "In respect to the lines that can be established in Spain, starting from the same principle Sr. Zarco del Valle has considered, with the capital

Madrid being the centre of the circle of Spain, I also recognize the problem that, with two lost battles, it would be easy for the enemy to occupy the capital and for the invading army to reach Madrid; but I don't see any other option at this moment other than joining the circumference with the centre by way of radial lines, and these lines must start from the centre."[43] From General O'Donnell's considerations, one gets the idea that, despite the strategic problems arising in military terms from the placement of the central hub in Madrid, it was a matter of principle that the design of the network should nonetheless be radial, with the centre as the unavoidable point of departure. The future president didn't specify in his appearance why it wasn't possible to adopt any other option.

General Laureano Sanz, the next to appear and last on that day, placed greater emphasis on the relevance of supplying the political capital as a crucial factor in establishing priorities: "The lines that I consider more convenient to the country's prosperity are those that communicate the capital of the monarchy with the Ocean and the Mediterranean; that is to say, those that will allow us to bring whatever is needed to the centre of the monarchy". General Sanz added, in respect to military needs, "and taking the perimeter of the peninsula as a circle, whose centre we may assume to be Madrid, all of the railroads that we plan (for now) must be perpendicular from the centre to the circumference; leaving for better times, or for our children, the construction of those parallel to the circumference; because with the former and a few more hours of travel, trips can in any case be made."[44] Indeed, it can be conceded to this view that the route by two legs allows one to get from one end of the hypotenuse to the other. Of course, the trip is 'a bit' longer and slower.

The consultation of military men and experts was resumed in the following session, on 27 April. The first to appear, Sr. Mazarredo, agreed that the starting point of the railway lines should be Madrid, and supported this opinion because "the location of the capital of the monarchy in Madrid places it at a certain disadvantage due to the fact that many of the elements that permit a significant development of the capitals of other nations are not found here or in the vicinity. Madrid isn't a producer, but Madrid is in possession of the status of capital; and save through significant public disturbance, this fact cannot be changed [. . .] May the rest of Spain thus rectify the great advantage of not being subjugated to its capital; Madrid, as the capital, has great needs; these are not supplied by its own production; the means of transportation are thus necessary to bring here the foodstuffs and other staples so abundantly consumed."[45] This consideration introduced reasons of indisputable significance, related to those expressed by Sr. Sanz above.

Quite a different perspective was expressed by the brigadier and geologist Francisco de Luxán (Luján in the minutes): "In Spain at the moment we don't have a capital, militarily speaking; because it is a fact demonstrated by experience that the nations that have invaded our country have taken Madrid, and yet despite this haven't conquered Spain. The defence of Spain isn't at the current court, it's elsewhere [. . .] Madrid, which produces nothing, and which must be fed with everything, including even items of basic necessity, is a population centre that also demands work to approach, and from which the forces and life of the entire nation are more easily scattered than they are accumulated. In this sense, it is neither a defensible point, nor a stronghold, nor centre of operations; and by losing or winning Madrid, nothing is either lost or won." [46] At that moment, General Concha asked to be allowed to voice his differences with Luxán's positions, pointing out that "even for its defence, Sr. Luján says, and effectively it is so, that *Madrid is not for Spain what Paris is for France*; Madrid can be lost and yet this doesn't mean losing the monarchy; but keep in mind that *Madrid today is of great importance and grows more important with every passing day*"[47] (the italics are mine). Luxán replied that "I don't want to subordinate the general interests of the country to a particular matter; my wish is that the importance given to military considerations is not so great that it harms the general interests of the nation."[48]

The last person to appear that day, the brigadier Buenaga, rounded off the argument against Luxán's positions by stating that "Madrid of the year 8 is not that of the year 50; since that time, with most provincial antipathy quelled, with power centralized, with completely varied political constitutions that have provided new nourishment and vigour to the body of the State, the court has visibly gained in importance, and is and will be for a long time at least, the strategic political point."[49] In short, the definitive argument.

The substance behind the motives for a radial design with Madrid at the centre was already established. It's true that later Luxán's proposals for a transversal system were expressed: "I see three general lines in Spain: first, from Cádiz passing through Madrid to the north; second, from Barcelona through Zaragoza, Valladolid, Zamora to Oporto; third, from Alacant to Cartagena through Ciudad Real, Mérida, Badajoz to Lisbon."[50] For Luxán, the big advantage of his proposal was that a railway network of this type would complement the radial network of main roads, instead of overlapping with it, and would therefore increase connectivity and benefit economic activity. Differing from this was the contribution made by the ex-minister of the Treasury, Bertrán de Lis, who proposed a large cross between Cádiz and Irun and between València and Lisbon, in both cases passing through Madrid.[51] Or that of the ex-minister Alejandro Oliván, who proposed prioritizing only two lines, one Cádiz–Madrid–Irún, and another Madrid–Barcelona.

But the question was resolved exactly as the commission had first presented it, with only one substantive change: the elimination of the Madrid to Barcelona line through Zaragoza, which some of those appearing before the commission considered to be of very secondary importance for supplying the capital.

The proposals of the Comisión de Ferrocarriles differed from the British and Belgian precedents. On the other hand, it resembled in some respects the policy developed in France. The most important similarity with the French model was the choice of a model combining concessions to the private sector with strong backing by public funds. In practical financial terms, the lines deemed preferential would be built at the State's cost, that is to say, with full guarantees for recovering the invested capital and for profitability. But while the French parliament had rejected in 1838 the proposed plan for a radial network emanating from Paris, the Spanish congress decided to publicly fund a radial-style network starting from Madrid. Perhaps Paris in the 19th century didn't need such a major political decision in order for Paris to be Paris, in contrast to what the case was with Madrid.

The Development of the Railway: The Law of 1855, Its Application and the Laws of 1870 and 1877

The project that would become the first General Railway Law of 1855 was presented in 1854 to the congress by the then minister of Fomento (Public Works) Francisco de Luxán, precisely the most energetic defender of a transversal system before the Railway Commission of 1850. Perhaps because of this, Luxán's bill didn't establish a general plan. It limited itself to establishing some bases to distinguish between general and private service lines, which later would be classified by law. The declaration of public interest was reserved for the former. The primary motive to avoid specifying the lines' precise layouts was "to be cautious in not imposing an orientation that technical studies, statistical, economic and even strategic data might later advise against."[52]

Nonetheless, the Comisión de las Cortes Constituyentes (Commission of the Constitutional Parliament) that passed the bill retook up the priorities of the lines adopted in the Railway Commission of 1850, recovering the Madrid–Barcelona through Zaragoza line, adding a branch extension to

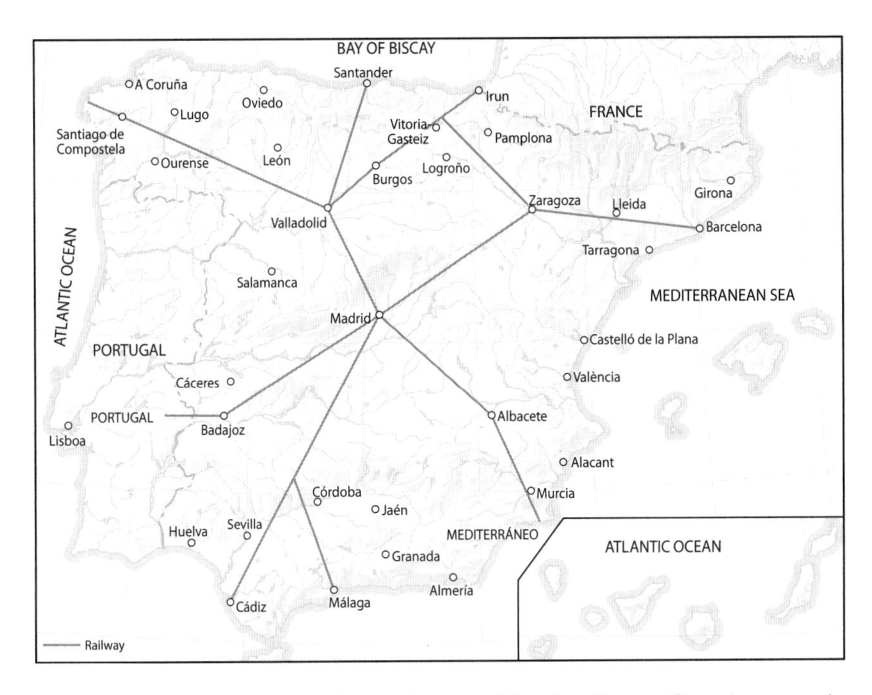

Map 3.2 Lines of the First Order Approved by the Cortes Constituyentes in 1855

Málaga on the Cádiz line, extending the line to Valladolid to the coast of Galicia, and adding a connection between Zaragoza and the Madrid–Irún line. These lines appear in Map 3.2. The radial design of the Spanish railway system was thus definitively established, in that these lines were considered the main and priority ones. And the ones, therefore, that would most intensely receive financial promotion and backing from the radial State.

After the passage of the Law of 1855, the expansion of the railway proceeded at a dizzying pace. Between this year and the end of the 1860s, almost 6,300 km of line were conceded, which, added to the 1,100 km prior to 1855, totalled 7,363 km. It is important to remember, however, that the number of kilometres conceded was higher than the number of kilometres actually being built.

In 1864, the report of the preliminary plan of a new General Plan of Railways, elaborated by a committee of engineers for the Junta Consultiva de Caminos, Canales y Puertos, proposed as the primary objective of the new plan "placing, in the best possible way and making use of already existing lines, all of the provincial capitals in communication with the capital of the monarchy."[53] This was probably the first time that the goal of connecting all of the provincial capitals with Madrid was expressed in writing, and was included a few years later in the general legislation based on this preliminary plan. José María Aznar would repeat it in 2000 (136 years later) as the crucial goal of the AVE's expansion.

Furthermore, the report positively valued the development of the network up until that moment, even "keeping in mind the large sacrifices the State has already made: One can be assured that, with a few exceptions, all of the lines that have been conceded should be built; some errors may have occurred in the order of preferences; perhaps some lines should have waited a few years; perhaps others should not have been stimulated by the powerful support of the State; but all of them respond to the real needs of the present or of the near future."[54] Passing judgment in this way on the development of the network, the report proposed distinguishing in the future between main lines, susceptible to financial support from the State, and secondary lines, which should only be conceded if entrepreneurs were disposed to build them without State support. The expansion of the proposed network was somewhat more than 3,800 km.[55] Included among the main lines were all those deemed necessary to complete the connection of all of the provincial capitals with Madrid, in addition to some non-radial exceptions. Most of the transversal connections were proposals of a secondary category.[56] Transversal market, radial State.

The Junta Consultiva de Caminos, Canales y Puertos analysed this report by the committee of engineers and modified it in respect to the southern network and its links to the one in the east, and the northern network and its links to those in the north and west. In total, the Junta Consultiva proposed expanding the network by 5,381 km of new lines.[57]

In 1865, a year after the elaboration of the above-mentioned preliminary plans, a special commission was designated to evaluate the effects of the law of 1855. The commission included among its members some of those who had most actively participated in drawing up that law. The inflation of offer induced by the public subsidies had been so great that it led the commission to conclude that the network created in Spain was much larger than what was appropriate for a country of its population, wealth and economic activity, and that it was unsustainable in terms of the available resources. Map 3.3 shows the extension of the network at the end of 1865. In the report drawn up by this commission for the new General Plan, it was pointed out that it would have been more desirable "for very few of the main service lines of the first order to have been laid; only, for example, those that connect the capital of the monarchy with neighbouring countries and with a Mediterranean port", and it added that "almost all of the railway lines have received subsidies, causing burdens to the Treasury, which weigh heavily on

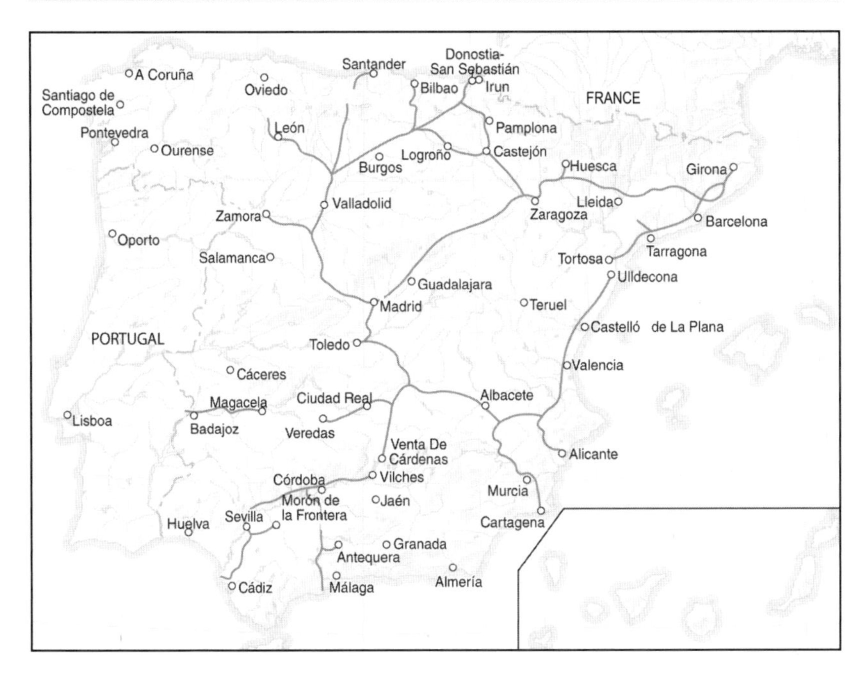

Map 3.3 State of the Railway Network at the end of 1865

the country, and causing, despite everything, the deplorable financial state in which the companies find themselves."[58]

The special commission drew up a proposal, completed in 1867, with a double objective: "In administrative and interior policy terms, Madrid linked reciprocally with all of the provincial capitals that were still separated. From the mercantile perspective, traffic tended to intensify through the connecting of productive and commercial regions, until now on the margins of the network. In this area, the transversal lines fulfilled their specific function, whose justification arose from the potential capacity of activating commerce between the primary points of export and import."[59] The length of the new lines proposed by the special commission for the expansion of the network was somewhat more than 3,300 km, and the development of these new lines was planned to take a period of ten years. But the political and economic instability that characterized the final years of the reign of Isabel II was not the most appropriate context to carry out the new planning.

In September of 1868, the Liberal Revolution brought the reign of Isabel II to an abrupt end and ushered in a more liberal government less prone to economic interventionism.[60] Even so, in the realm of public works, and the railway in particular, the new regime was very active, following Echegaray's

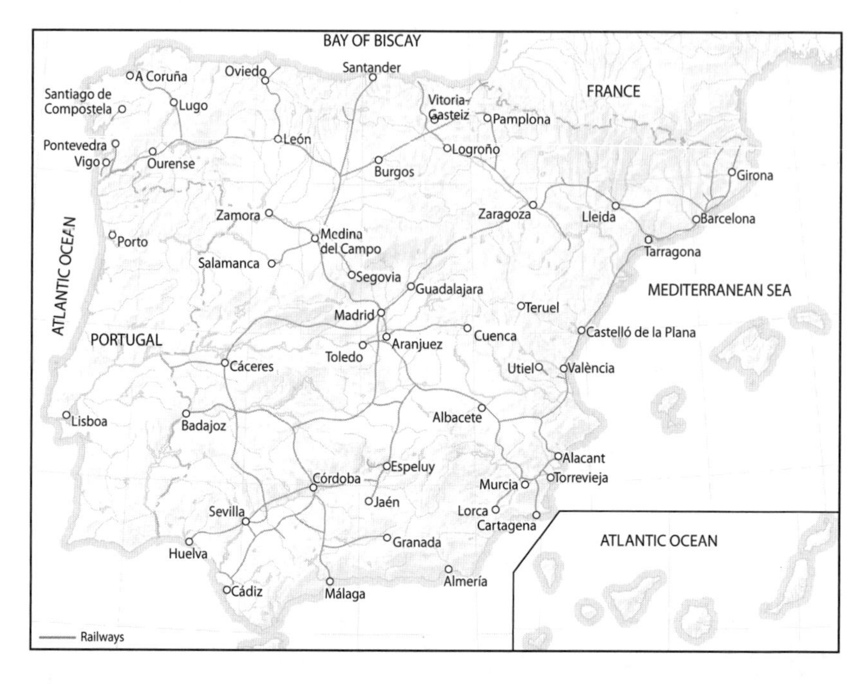

Map 3.4 State of the Railway Network at the end of 1885

maxim: "Previously, the State acted and didn't let others act; in the future, the State mustn't act, and must let others act. Until that time comes, meanwhile, the State acts and lets others act, attempting to act less and less."[61]

In 1870 the government drew up a bill that proposed 2,069 km of new lines. It placed emphasis on the need to include in the network what it termed the 'disinherited provinces' and in overcoming the 'scandalous inequality' that had affected the different provinces.[62] Nevertheless, the main objective of the bill was the connection of the provincial capitals that the actual planning hadn't foreseen communicating with the political capital (Teruel, Soria, Cáceres, Jaén, Almería, Salamanca and Pontevedra), or whose concessions were at risk of expiring without having been laid (Segovia, Cuenca, Huelva and Huesca). These plans totalled 1,284 km, the first stage of which, 761 km, had to be built in eight years. Furthermore, another 800 km of primarily transversal lines were planned, whose goal was to complete the network, and which had to be carried out within a period of 20 to 30 years. The government's plan, broadened with some amendments by the Cortes, became the Law of 1870.

In 1874, the six-year revolutionary period came to an end and the Restoration began. A few years later, in November of 1877, a new law was passed that would be in effect for a long time. The law of 1877 was created so that "the fidelity to the radial design continued with the formulation of these lines from Madrid, the most important of which was the one ending in València, passing through Cuenca and also in the direction of the Portuguese border [. . .] The Law of 1877 [. . .] didn't resolve the excessive centrality of the network."[63] Map 3.4 shows the state of the network at the end of 1885.

The Railway in Spain, Radiality and Subsidies

The general legislation on railways, inaugurated with the Law of 1855, introduced the radial and centralized design of the Spanish system and, to make it possible, significant implication by the State in the concession of aid and subsidies. These subsidies were applied with priority to the radial lines, the ones classified as being of the first order and general service,[64] which wouldn't have been developed in the way envisioned by political authorities without financial support from the State. There were three principal ways in which the State subsidized the railway companies: (1) the construction of the initial establishment paid for by the State, (2) the concession of subsidies in cash or in public obligations, and (3) the guarantee of a minimum interest for the invested capital.[65]Among these, the concession of cash subsidies for kilometre of line was the only one used regularly during the 19th century, while the others were less relevant.

State aid was the principal fuel for the large investment in railways between 1855 and 1865, one of the most intense periods of spending on public works up until then.[66] It has been deemed impossible to quantify all of the subsidies and aid conceded by the State;[67] an idea of its size is offered by the estimate made by Gabriel Tortella, for whom public aid represented 49% of the capital laid out by the railway companies until 1867.[68] Public subsidies to the railway gave rise to all kinds of financial scandals and corruption, the most paradigmatic examples of which are those related to the Marquis of Salamanca – some of which have been already been mentioned. But such matters are not our primary concern. Our main focus is how subsidies from the national budget were used to support the centralized and radial design of the infrastructures, which couldn't have been supported by economic activity, by the market. And the need for subsidies for the development of a centralized and radial structure accented by the application of policies such as the connection of all of the provincial capitals with Madrid through the network of main lines.

Alfonso Herranz offers some very revealing figures on the progressive

Table 3.1 Internal Structure of the Spanish Railway System (1904–1905)

	Lines opened before 1873	Lines opened after 1873	The entire network
Length (km)	7,482	5,672	13,224
Density of passenger traffic (thousands of passengers–km per km of line)	166	89	132
Density of freight traffic (thousands of tons–km per km of line)	247	103	185
Gross income per km of line (pesetas)	29,125	13,422	22,313
Net income per km of line (pesetas)	15,720	4,667	10,926
Costs of exploitation/Gross income (%)	46	65	51
Net income/Capital costs (%)	5.63	2.2	4.36

Source: Alfonso Herranz Loncán, *Infraestructuras y crecimiento económico en España (1850–1935)* (Madrid: Fundación de los Ferrocarriles Españoles, 2008), p. 125.

increase in the need for subsidies. Table 3.1 presents figures of operation for different parts of the Spanish railway system in the years 1904–1905. It is necessary to keep in mind that the profitability of the Spanish system during these years was close to its historical maximum,[69] as a result of which the figures presented are singularly positive, far above what was normal. Even so, the net income for the lines opened before 1873 represented only 5.6% of the capital cost,[70] while the percentage was reduced to a meagre 2.2% in the lines opened after that year.

It is also necessary to remember that, while all of the railway lines enjoyed exemptions typical to all public works – such as franchise rights –, the direct or auxiliary State aid was especially concentrated on the lines declared to be of general interest, those that extended Madrid's connections in a radial fashion, while the transversal lines were developed in some cases without subsidies and in others with very limited ones.

In this sense, it is interesting to look at the information concerning direct and auxiliary subsidies conceded up until 1876, based on a report by the Ministerio de Fomento, sent to the congress in October/November of 1876, and which was reproduced during the course of a debate in the congress at the end of that year.[71] According to those figures, the lines in Catalonia, either finished or under construction, totalled 771 km, of which 387 km (50.2%) corresponded to subsidized lines, and 384 km (49.8%) to non-subsidized lines. Out of all the kilometres of subsidized lines, 284

(73.4%) corresponded to sections of the Madrid–Zaragoza–Barcelona–French border line on its route through Catalonia. The subsidies agreed to up to that moment for the lines of the railway in Catalonia amounted to 31.5 million pesetas, a figure that represented 6% of the total subsidies granted until then, 525 million pesetas according to the report by the Ministerio de Fomento. Nonetheless, the kilometres of lines in Catalonia represented 10.3% of those conceded up until then in Spain, 7,500 km.[72] Overall, the subsidies to railway lines in Catalonia were strongly concentrated on the radial line, while there was a predominant lack of subsidies for the transversal lines.

As has been stated above, the radial lines systematically benefited from the concession of subsidies and public aid. First of all, because they were given priority in the first expansion through the General Railway Law of 1855, the one of radialization (that is to say, the radial State). Secondly, as a result of the system of subsidies of a fixed quantity per kilometre of line, which was determined by auction. In this context, the lines with brighter economic prospects, such as the Catalan ones, were the object of greater competition between promoters, causing the subsidies to drop to zero in almost all of the cases (that is to say, a transversal market). This wasn't the case, however, for the lines given priority by law, whose prospects of profitability were poorer, but whose construction was a political priority.[73] And, in the final instance, there simply weren't enough public resources available for everyone when the network was already more developed. As Gómez Mendoza points out,[74] "despite the fact that the General Railway Law of 1877 promoted the laying of the transversal lines, the economic difficulties that the concessionary companies faced, a situation aggravated by the lack of public funds, impeded their construction." It goes without saying, when resources are not infinite, priorities must be established.

Thus, the promulgation of the Railway Law of 1855 with its generous outlay of subsidies was the key element behind the intense activity of railway line construction, which followed the priorities of the established radial lines. The large amount of public resources committed has led authors such as Gabriel Tortella[75] and Jordi Nadal[76] to consider that the railway policy seriously harmed Spain's industrial development in that period. That opinion isn't shared by Gómez Mendoza, who made a calculation of the social savings generated by the railway in Spain with a very favourable result for the railway,[77] an estimation more precisely examined by Herranz Loncán, with much more moderate results.[78]

These estimates of the railway's social savings, while valuable, have a great limitation: the absence of data did not allow making those analyses more precise in respect to what would have been obtained through possible alternative uses of the capital invested in the railway. In contrast, this was precisely the procedure used by Robert W. Fogel in his study of railways and economic growth in the United States,[79] an effort that was fundamental to his being awarded the Nobel Prize in 1993. Faced with the lack of such refinements of the analysis in the Spanish case, the thesis that the railway policy harmed Spain's industrial development and economic growth is widely accepted.[80]

Another question that has stirred great controversy is the one relating to the efficiency of the radial design of the railway network. Authors such as Nadal[81]argue that the design of the network responded to the interests of foreign companies in the export of mining products, and didn't adjust to the interests of national economic activity. Izquierdo's conclusion is very convincing when he states: "In terms of the possible regional impact, the effect of the railway was very weak. Only Madrid, due to the radial structure of the network, registered its effects, although at the price of great social cost [. . .] the radial character of the network blocked peripheral relations. Furthermore, the high transportation costs derived from its organization made the development of interior markets for the most part difficult."[82]

In contrast, other authors, such as Cordero and Menéndez, offer more benign assessments of the radial design, concluding that because "the capital of the monarchy's connections with neighbouring countries and the different regions of the country were unquestionable",[83] the most efficient and least costly way to achieve that goal was to build a radial-style network of at least 10,000 km, compared to a more balanced network of at least 15,000 km. In effect, there can be no doubt that to connect the capital with the rest of the country, it was less costly to limit work to connecting the capital with the rest of the country, and do away with transversal extensions that transcended that goal. As Mark Casson recently expressed,[84] if the same combination of services is demanded of the counterfactual system as that generated by the real system, it must, by necessity, be very similar to the one already existing. Even so, Cordero and Menéndez conclude that because the radial network was not completed with a more balanced expansion, "the initial insufficiency turned into a final defect." [85]

Many other authors have contributed to this controversy.[86] Nonetheless, it is appropriate to ask whether the question concerning the hypothetical efficiency of the radial and centralized design of the Spanish railway network is very pertinent. As has been shown by reviewing the debates in favour of the radial decisions, the concern for economic efficiency and for stimulating economic activity only emerged exceptionally in the debates and discussions, and didn't play a relevant role in the decisions. On the contrary, the principal motives for the radial network can be defined as: (1) to organize military logistics in the strategic centre of Madrid in case of foreign invasion; (2) to ensure the supply of foodstuffs and staples to the political capital; and (3) to connect the court, the monarchy and its state apparatus with all of the territories of Spain.

Fortunately, no military event has made it necessary to test the military performance of the network. In terms of its purpose of supplying the political capital, it would be difficult to express the obtained result better than Gómez Mendoza has: "Thanks to the railway, the court entered into contact, in the second half of the 19th century, with all of the productive areas of the country [. . .]. Madrid, at the end of the 19th century, maintained a balance deficit in its commercial exchanges [. . .] Furthermore, the volume of railway traffic ratifies the impression we have of Madrid as a large consumer centre, with hardly any production of its own to sell to other regions."[87] In this sense, the success of the enterprise was unquestionable, even if goods only travelled in one direction (toward the centre) of the radial lines,[88] and even if the image of a boxcar full of goods on the way to Madrid but empty on the way back was the living portrait of its economic inefficiency as a transportation system. Lastly, the expansion of the railway after the legislation of 1877 certainly completed the political capital's connections to all of the territorial terminals of political and administrative power . . . at the cost of a growing use of public subsidies and aid.

The radial design and the neglect of the transversal lines in the development of the networks was a general characteristic of the period. Parallel to the general railway legislation of 1855, and after the Madrid–Irún telegraph line entered into service that same year, a law was promulgated whose main objective was to built a radial network of telegraph lines to communicate Madrid with all of the provincial capitals, as well as with the French and Portuguese borders and with the overseas territories. The basic structure of the network was laid in only eight years, and according to Gómez Mendoza, "while the shortening of telegraphic distances was an unquestionable advantage for the residents of Madrid, it became a serious inconvenience for the rest of the population centres. In effect, the lack of a direct connection made it necessary for telegrams sent from cities such as Barcelona, La Coruña or Seville to pass through Madrid." [89] The mesh network would have to wait until the 20th century.

In Spain, just as had occurred with the roads in the 18th century, the case of the railways fulfilled in a systematic and massive way the premonitory assertion made by Adam Smith in 1776, in the sense that when no concern is paid to financing expenditures on public works through commerce, the result is that the work "happens to lead to the country villa of the intendant of the province, or to that of some great lord to whom the intendant finds it convenient to make his court."[90] And this was a definitive feature of the expansion of the Spanish railway, not shared by any of the European countries that spearheaded the development of the railway in the middle decades of the 19th century. It is also the case now in the current stage of railway development, marked by the expansion of the AVE. But before discussing the AVE, we must stop and examine another period that preceded it: the implantation and development of motorways in Spain.

4

Transversal Market, Radial State (II): The First Motorways

Motorways are roads with at least two lanes in either direction and free of intersections at the same level. The effective history of motorways in Spain began with the granting of two concessions at the start of 1967: The Jonquera-Barcelona and the Montgat (Barcelona)-Mataró. The connection established by the second concession coincided with that of the Barcelona-Mataró railway line, the first such line opened in Spain, in 1848.

This doesn't mean that prior to the 1960s there had been no debate concerning the implantation of motorways. Furthermore, on different occasions, improvement programs had been carried out on the traditional road system before the mid-20th century. A brief presentation of these antecedents is appropriate to our subject. Afterwards, a review is made of the beginnings of the motorway networks in the principal countries of the European Union. Placed within this context, the development of the Spanish motorway network in its different stages is looked at: from its beginnings with financing by direct tolls at the end of the 1960s, to the stage of financing by the public budget that begins in the mid-1980s. The first important milestone for the policy of financing by the public budget is the Plan General de Carreteras (PGC) (General Road Plan) 1984–1991, which culminates in practical terms in 1993. Although the concession of toll motorways by the central government resumed in the mid-1990s, financing by the public budget has maintained its hegemony as a financing model up to the present.

The most notable result of an analysis of the successive models of motorway financing is the following. In the first stage, characterized by the primacy of payment by users (tolls), the priority in the implantation of motorways translates into the creation of motorways in the Mediterranean corridor and the Ebro valley, the most dynamic corridors with the most vehicle traffic in Spain. Afterwards, the PGC 1984–1991 was entirely financed by the public budget, and primacy was given in the selection of priorities to the creation of toll-free motorways in the radial corridors that converge on Madrid. In sum, during the period in which financing by users predominates – the prospective demand – the incipient development of the network follows a transversal pattern. In contrast, when financing from the public budget– the State – assumes the central role the development of the network assumes a radial pattern. That is to say, transversal market, radial State.

Reforms in the Conventional System and Antecedents of Motorways in Spain

The second half of the 19th century was a period of intense road construction. While in 1840 approximately 4,000 km of roads existed, by 1856 this number had increased to almost 6,000.[1] The new roads filled out the radial network introduced in the 18th century, defined by the six fundamental radial routes ('six large royal roads') of the Road Plan included in the Public Works Plan of Ferdinand VI, whose precedent had been the six radial roads that formed the network of postal stage roads defined by Philip V in 1720.

In 1851, the law classifying roads was passed, which distinguished between four classes:[2] (1) main roads, which connected Madrid with the provincial capitals and maritime departments, financed wholly by the State; (2) transversal roads, which linked up to main roads passing through provincial capitals or important cities, and whose financing was shared by the State and the provinces; (3) provincial roads, financed by the provinces; and (4) local roads, financed by municipalities.

In the second half of the 19th century and the first quarter of the 20th, construction activity further increased, and by 1900 more than 36,000 km were built, which reached 57,000 km by 1924. This expansion of the road system was wholly financed by public resources, although through legislation on public works and roads passed in 1877 (the General Law of Public Works of 13 April and the General Law of Roads of 4 May) a legal framework had been established for the use of concessions, with the aim of raising private capital to finance their construction.[3] Nonetheless, no such concession was granted during the entire period of that legislation's validity.

After the strong quantitative expansion of the road system that took place between the mid-19th century and the first quarter of the 20th century, in 1926 a new relevant milestone appeared in the qualitative transformation of the system: the plan called the *Circuito Nacional de Firmes Especiales* (the National Circuit of Roads of Special Surfaces). The purpose of the plan was, maintaining the radial design of the system – established

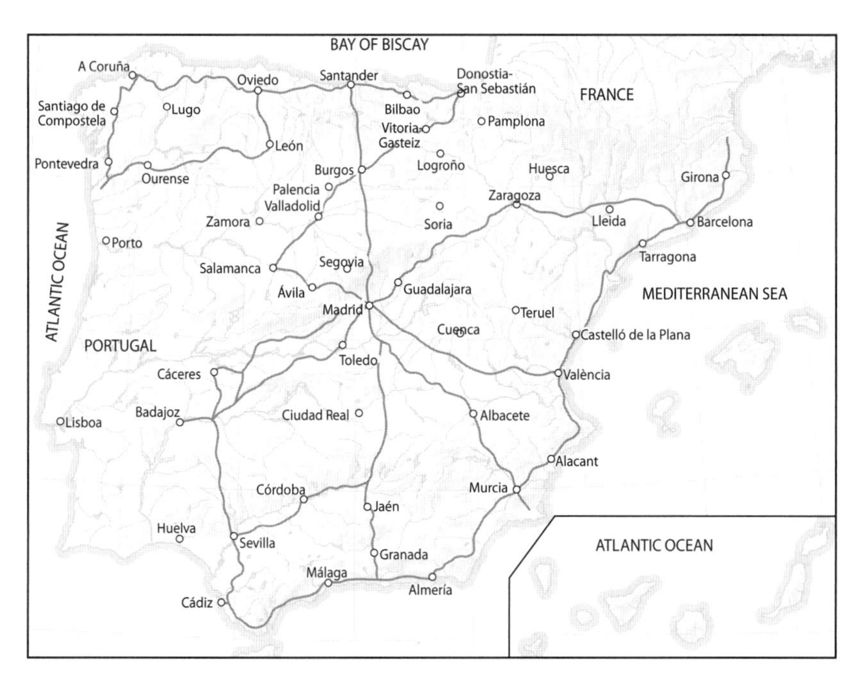

Map 4.1 National Circuit of Roads of Special Surfaces

in the 18th century and consolidated in the 19th – to reform the roads that joined the principal population centres. Map 4.1 shows the design of this circuit. The development of the plan modernized about 6,000 km of roads,[4] and was entirely financed by the national budget, to which specific taxes were added that were paid by the town councils of the municipalities through which the roads passed and by the concessionary companies of road transportation services.[5]

It was precisely during this period that the first attempt was made to implant motorways in Spain. At a time of great enthusiasm for the prospects of toll motorways, in July of 1928 the government authorized the Ministerio de Fomento to grant concessions for the construction and exploitation by way of tolls of the Madrid–València, Madrid–Irún and Oviedo–Gijón motorways (Royal Decree-Law of 28 July 1928), with the assignation of subsidies meant to complete the financing obtained by the tolls.[6] The Madrid–València aimed to make this Mediterranean city into the port of the capital, and a subsidy of two million pesetas was planned; the Madrid–Irún aimed to connect the capital with the French border for primarily tourist-related use, for which a subsidy of three million pesetas was planned. Lastly, the Oviedo-Gijón sought to alleviate the existing congestion between these two cities, and it was assigned a subsidy of 250,000 pesetas.[7]

But work on these motorways was not begun, and this was for reasons that were expressed even before the granting of the concessions: the unfeasibility of this type of special road in countries that hadn't yet completed ordinary networks,[8] and the existence of too little traffic – essentially urban – to support the costs[9] even with subsidies. That is to say, the market didn't support a radial design of toll motorways, for which there wasn't a demand, despite the concession of public subsidies to partially finance them. The beginning of the motorways network in the 1920s was thus frustrated. In the following decade, not a single study was made for motorways of private initiative,[10] and the implantation of motorways in Spain was postponed for another four decades, until the 1960s.

Keeping in mind the influence that Mussolini's fascist regime in Italy had on the dictatorship of Primo de Rivera, it is very probable that the idea of establishing private concessions for the construction of toll motorways in Spain followed the guidelines of the policy that had been applied in Italy since the end of 1922. This experience will be reviewed further on, along with those of other European countries.

During the Second Republic, an interesting change occurred: in 1934, plans were made to expand the Circuit of Roads of Special Surfaces by 1,161 new kilometres, of which 998 km corresponded to transversal roads (notably among which for their length were the València-Teruel-Zaragoza, Seville-Granada and the Salamanca-Cáceres roads).[11] This modification partially alleviated the initially highly radial design of the Circuit, but the coming of the Civil War impeded the practical realization of such plans.

A new program of repairs and improvements to the road system occurred in the mid-20th century. In 1951, the Road Modernization Plan was begun, which adapted routes for speeds of 100 km/h on most of the radial roads.[12]

Significant modernization of the road system began in the 1960s. With the opening of the economy to the outside world, established through the Stabilization Plan of 1959, the Spanish economy began to grow at an intense pace and transportation infrastructures became a bottleneck for economic activity, above all in the most dynamic zones of Spanish territory. In 1962, the report titled *Economic Development in Spain* by the World Bank[13] recommended efforts to repair and conserve the existing road system, and added that the only important road of new construction that would be necessary in the immediate future was the motorway on the Levante coast, along the coast of the Mediterranean, from the French border to Murcia.

The repair and conservation of the existing road network was made

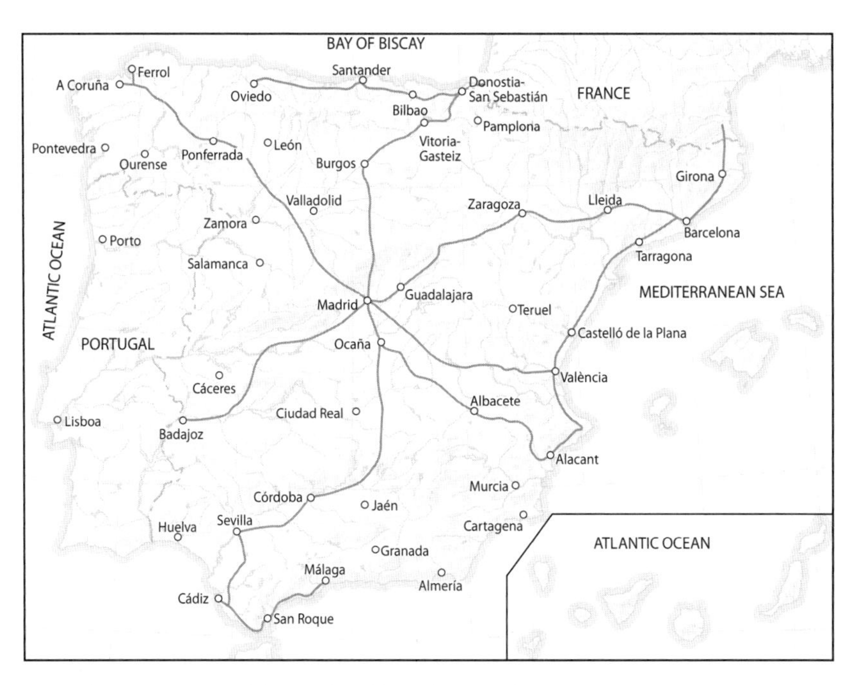

Map 4.2 *Redia* Plan (Network of Paved Routes)

through the *Redia* (Red de Itinerarios Asfálticos – Network of Paved Routes) plan, from 1967 to 1971. This plan promoted the modernization of a series of road network routes – although without their acquiring the characteristics of motorways – notably among which were the six traditional radial roads (the national ones, I to VI) and the Madrid–Alacant route. Other routes where repairs and modernization were planned were the N-340 on the La Jonquera–Alacant and Málaga–Cádiz trajectories, and the N-364 between San Sebastián and Oviedo.[14] Map 4.2 shows the design of the *Redia*. The plan was passed in 1967 and was financed wholly by budgetary resources, with a budget of 20,000 million pesetas.

In the view of Professor Cuadrado Roura[15] those plans "furthermore favoured, and in a unique way, the improvement of Madrid's links with the primary centres of the periphery [. . .] As can be seen, almost 75% of the affected network corresponds to roads connecting with Madrid (even with low daily traffic averages), marginalizing routes of a transversal or vertical character (the valley of the Ebro, the Via de la Plata – León-Extremadura – and the interior of Andalusia, for example), which could have played an important role in the development of some depressed areas of the country." Similarly, Professor Izquierdo de Bartolomé agrees that during that period "the territorial model consolidated its 'Centre-Periphery' configuration with the appearance of significant scale diseconomies that later gave rise to spreading effects, causing a modification in the spatial distribution of activities".[16]

Some long-term consequences of these changes in the territorial distribution of activities are clearly visible in Table 1.3 in Chapter 1, which registers the alterations in the weight of the GDP and in the population of each region, between the mid-1960s and the mid-2000s. It isn't necessary to repeat here commentaries on these results, which the reader can review in Chapter 1.

Surrounding References: The Development of the Motorway System in the Principal Countries of Europe

During the interwar period in Europe development began on motorway networks in the two large countries with dictatorships: Italy (with toll motorways) and Germany (with toll-free motorways). It wasn't, however, until the 1950s, following World War II, that the implantation of motorways became generalized in Europe's most important countries. The countries of central and northern Europe – of which Germany is a paradigmatic example – opted to finance their motorways through national budgets. In contrast, in southern Europe – especially in France and Italy – the toll option was chosen.

Germany

The first road with motorway characteristics in Europe was the Automobil-Verkehrs-und Übungs-Straße (AVUS), a small racing circuit in the southeast of Berlin which entered into service in 1921, although it was quite small in size. For this reason, in practical terms, one may consider the 20 km section between Cologne and Bonn as the first German motorway, which entered into service in 1932 on the north-south Hamburg-Frankfurt-Basel (Switzerland) route. Priority was given to this route as the first motorway corridor in Germany because it had the most commercial traffic. After these preliminary experiences, the network began to expand intensely in the mid-1930s under Hitler's government. In May of 1935, the Frankfurt–Darmstadt section of about 40 km entered into service, followed by 26 new sections in 1936.[17] The German case is interesting because, while it was financed by the national budget, it didn't give priority to routes affecting the political capital, Berlin, but rather to routes with greater traffic and commercial activity.

The expansion of the German motorways reached 2,128 km in 1942, which constituted a spectacular network at the time. The option of financing by the national budget may have been crucial in achieving such a large expansion of the system. The impression the German motorways made on General Eisenhower in the final years of World War II is considered to be one of the primary factors that led him – during his time as president of the United States – to encourage the construction of the interstate highway system, promoted through the National Interstate and Defense Highway Act of 1956.[18] The construction of the motorways in Germany recommenced in 1953, within the context of the country's reconstruction after the war, and by 1975 around 6,000 km had entered into service,[19] approximately half the current network. From the very beginning, German motorways were financed by the national budget.

France

The first motorway project in France began in 1937, with the construction of one toward the east from Paris, but World War II interrupted its development.[20] The effective implantation of motorways in France began in the 1950s. The initial pace of expansion of the network was quite slow. By 1960, only 160 km of motorways had been created, of which 10 were financed by toll and the rest through the national budget.[21] The network grew very quickly over the following two decades with the creation of almost 5,000 km of motorways, 75% of which were financed by tolls. Thus, by 1980, half of France's current extension of its motorway system, which is almost 11,000 km, had been built.

The toll concessions between 1956 and the end of the 1960s were assigned to companies under state control. The limited development of the network led the French government to open the concessions to private companies, and between 1970 and 1973 four such concessions were granted, totalling more than 1,000 km. But the majority of the new kilometres conceded in the 1970s continued to be made to state companies. Furthermore, because of the economic crisis of the early 1980s, private concessions faced serious financial problems, which led to the nationalization of three of the four private concessions.[22]

The hegemony of the public sector continued until the 2000s. In 2006, the government privatized the three principal concessions – Autoroute du Sud de la France (ASF), the Autoroute Paris–Rhin–Rhône –(APRR), and the Société Autoroute du Nord et l'Est de la France (SANEF) – which totalled around 7,000 km.[23] At present, almost three-fourths of the motorway network is toll-operated and managed by private companies. Their distribution around French territory is balanced, in contrast to the distribution of toll motorways in Spain.

Italy

The construction in Italy of motorways by way of concessions to private companies was encouraged from the start of the period of fascist government. In 1923, the Ministry of Public Works was reformed with the goal of stimulating cooperation between the State and private companies to promote public works. The reform made it possible to expand the system of concessions, provided broad legal flexibility,[24] and established the framework for applying a new policy of financing and managing motorways: the concession of construction and management to private companies, which received a toll paid by users as the primary source of income for financing the new motorways.

In October of 1922, Mussolini took control of the government and in December of that year he established an agreement with a private company created by Piero Puricelli, to whom he granted (even before the reform of the legislative framework made in 1923) the right to build and operate the motorway between Milan and the lakes of Como, Lugano and Maggiore.[25] The State provided a guarantee for the bonds issued by the concessionary and a subsidy from the government.[26] The first part of the Milan–lakes motorway was finished in September of 1924 and the second part in September of 1925;[27] it was Europe's first toll motorway.

From then on, and as a general rule, the State granted concessions to private companies for the construction and management of motorways for a period of 50 years. Because demand was low, the State provided an annual subsidy, in addition to the contributions made by the interested local governments. The private concessionary issued bonds guaranteed by the State and by the local governments.[28] As a consequence of this, the investment made by private companies represented a small fraction of the necessary capital,[29] and the obtaining of State's financial support was habitually a *sine qua non* condition.[30]

Beginning in 1923, six motorways were built in a brief period of time. The Milan–lakes was followed by the Milan–Bergamo, and then the Naples–Pompey, Brescia–Bergamo, Turin–Milan, Florence–sea, and Venice–Padua motorways. Traffic, however, wasn't sufficient to cover costs, and most of the concessions were nationalized in the 1930s to save the companies from financial collapse.[31] Only the Naples–Pompey, Turin–

Milan and Venice–Padua motorways remained in private hands, although the last of these only thanks to massive subsidies provided by local governments.[32] The State maintained the tolls on the nationalized motorways.

After World War II, the State recommenced the development of the motorway system, maintaining the toll as the financing method and granting concessions to a subsidiary agency of the *Istituto per la Ricostruzione Industriale* (IRI, created in 1933, and precursor to the *Instituto Nacional de Industria* in Spain), responsible for building and managing the motorways. Thus, in 1950, the construction of the Milan–Naples connection was commissioned, which received a state subsidy of 36% of the total cost. By 1970, after two decades, the Italian motorway system had reached 4,000 km. In 1975, it reached 5,900 km,[33] almost 90% of its present size, and of which 95% was managed by the public sector and only 5% by private companies.

As occurred in France, the private sector has taken the lead role in the management of motorways in the last decade. In 1999, the government privatized the concessions possessed by the public agency *Autostrade*, which included 60% of the system. At present, around 80% of the Italian motorway network is toll operated, and private companies manage more than 85% of these.[34] Their distribution around Italian territory is balanced.

Summary: Lessons from International Experience

As a general rule, the countries of central and northern Europe, as well as Anglo-Saxon ones, financed the development of their motorway systems through the use of public funds. The large Mediterranean countries, France and Italy, made use of direct tolls paid by users. While the private sector initially played a leading role in Italy during the years of the fascist regime, after the middle of the 20th century the motorway network expanded with motorways that were primarily publicly owned and managed. As much in France as in Italy, priority was given to expanding the network in the corridors with the most traffic, and the map of tolls presents a very balanced territorial distribution. The toll model was also adopted later by the small southern European countries, Portugal and Greece. In Portugal, the private sector was responsible for building and operating the network, while in Greece the expansion of toll motorways was carried out by a state company.

Why did the countries of southern Europe opt for the toll model? Financing infrastructures by way of the national budget presents two related requisites: (a) the political will to charge taxes, and (b) the presence of a modern and efficient fiscal system to ensure that tributary incomes are sufficient to finance these policies. In the period when work began on expanding the toll motorway networks, and still now so in the present, the countries of southern Europe have been less predisposed to general taxation than those of central and northern Europe. At the end of the 1960s in Germany, Holland, Belgium and Austria, the tax burden was around 25% of GDP, still lower than that of the Scandinavians and the United Kingdom. The tax burden in Spain was around 13%, much lower even than that of Greece.[35] Furthermore, the southern tax systems were the most archaic in Europe, with the possible exception of France. We thus find the fundamental reason behind the tolls: insufficient budgets and a lack of political will for increasing general taxation.

The Implantation and Development of Motorways in Spain

After the practical failure of the first motorway concessions (to be financed by tolls and subsidies) in the period of Primo de Rivera, which were never built, Spain reached the 1960s without having any interurban motorways.

The report by the World Bank in 1962,[36] mentioned above, had established that the only important road of new construction that would be necessary in the immediate future was the motorway running the length of the Mediterranean coast, from France to Murcia. This road would pass through zones of maximum traffic levels in Spain, levels that were furthermore growing with exceptional speed. It would pass through important industrial and agricultural zones and would serve some of the country's most important tourist zones. The report added that the increase in traffic could make the construction of fast lanes in other sections advisable in the near future.

Five years after the report by the World Bank, the *Programa de Autopistas Nacionales Españolas* (PANE) (Program of Spanish National Motorways) of 1967 was drawn up. This program planned for the construction of 3,160 km of toll motorways, arranged as shown in Map 4.3. The first sections were awarded up until 1973: La Jonquera–Barcelona–Tarragona, Montgat–Mataró and Bilbao–Behovia. They were followed by the concessions of Villalba–Villacastín-Adanero, Seville–Cádiz and Salou–València–Alacant. The possibility of having toll motorways raised great expectations throughout the country, as well as political and institutional pressures.[37] The bringing up to date of the PANE, the *Avance del Plan Nacional de Autopistas* (Advance of the National Motorways Plan) of 1972, planned 6,430 km of toll motorways, whose lay out is shown in Map 4.4.

By 1975, 2,042 km had been awarded through concessions, shown in Table 1.

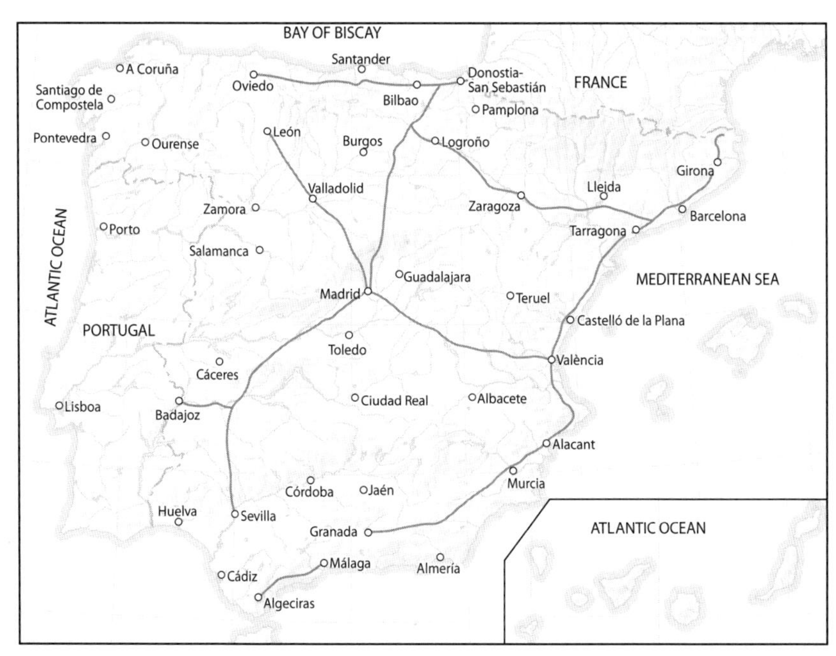

Map 4.3 Program of the Spanish National Motorways 1967

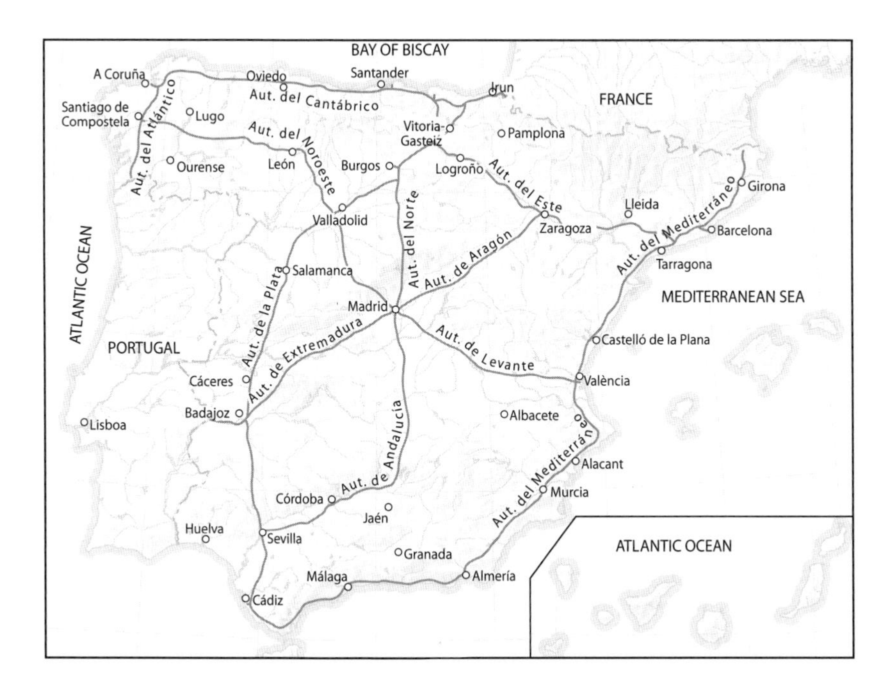

Map 4.4 Legend: Advance of the National Motorways Plan 1972

Table 4.1 Concessions of Toll Motorways up to 1975

Concessionaire	Section	Date	Length (years)
Acesa	La Jonquera–Barcelona	06.02.67	37
	Montgat–Mataró	06.02.67	37
	Barcelona–Tarragona	29.01.68	37
	Montmeló–Papiol	1974	–
Iberpistas	Villalba–Villacastín	29.01.68	50
	Villacastín–Adanero	30.09.72	50
Europistas	Bilbao–Behovia	23.03.68	35
Bética de Autopistas	Sevilla–Cádiz	30.07.69	24
Marenostrum	Salou–València	08.09.71	27
	València–Alacant	22.12.72	27
Audenasa	Tudela–Irurzun	08.06.73	41
Audasa	Ferrol-A Coruña–Santiago —Pontevedra–Vigo–Tuy	18.07.73	39
Acasa	Zaragoza–El Vendrell	25.07.73	25
Vasco-Aragonesa	Bilbao–Zaragoza	10.11.73	22
Eurovías	Burgos–Malzaga	26.06.74	20
Aucalsa	Campomanes–León	17.10.75	46

Note: Aumar took over the Sevilla-Cádiz section, and Acesa took over the Zaragoza-El Vendrell section.
Source: Germà Bel, "Financiación de infraestructuras viarias: la economía política de los peajes", *Papeles de Economía Española* (1999), 82, 123–139, p. 124.

In Spain, the toll model of financing was chosen in the 1960s even though the World Bank's report had made no suggestions in this respect. Nor was this initially the government's plan, but the insufficiencies of the Spanish tax system could have played an important role in that decision, as suggested by the view of Sansalvadó: "Although important documents like the General Road Plan of 1961 and the Planning of 1964 claimed the possibility of financing road infrastructures through the established tax figures, what is certain is that the insufficiency of our fiscal system was widely recognized".[38] At any rate, the option of toll financing was made explicit in the PANE of 1967.[39]

The deficiencies of the tax system and the lack of will to modernize it made it difficult to finance the motorways by way of the national budget, which was an option initially considered during the first half of the 1960s. Another factor that could have influenced the choice of tolls as a financing instrument was the anticipation of significant tourist traffic,[40] in large part arriving from outside of the country.

Lastly, a consistent explanation doesn't exist for the choice of a system of private concessions for the construction and exploitation of toll motorways, in a context in which France and Italy had opted for tolls under public management in the same period. The fact that the private Spanish concessionaries made use of state backing to get loans abroad clearly indicates that the State had at least as much access to foreign financing as the private concessions. It is probable that the influence of the options chosen by Italian motorway policy in the Mussolini years, present in the frustrated plans of Primo de Rivera, remained as a legacy during Franco's regime. This hypothesis deserves further investigation.

The system of direct tolls didn't prove to be too effective in expanding the network. The increase in the number of toll motorways under exploitation was very slow. Of the 6,430 km planned in 1972 and the 2,042 km awarded in 1975, only 1,807 km of toll motorways were in operation by 1985. The concessions of motorways were abruptly interrupted by the economic crisis of the 1970s. The 2,042 km awarded up to 1975 (not all under exploitation) didn't vary at all until 1987, when a new concession to a private company was granted: the Sant Cugat-Manresa Motorway (A-18), under the authority of the Generalitat of Catalonia.

Out of the total 1,807 km of toll motorways in service in the mid-1980s, somewhat more than two-thirds were in the Mediterranean corridor (La Jonquera-Alacant) and in the Ebro valley (Bilbao-El Vendrell). Map 4.5 shows the sections of toll motorways in service. By the way, it is curious and perhaps also relevant to note that these corridors also substantially coincide with the first Roman roads, from the first century AD, shown in Map 4.6.

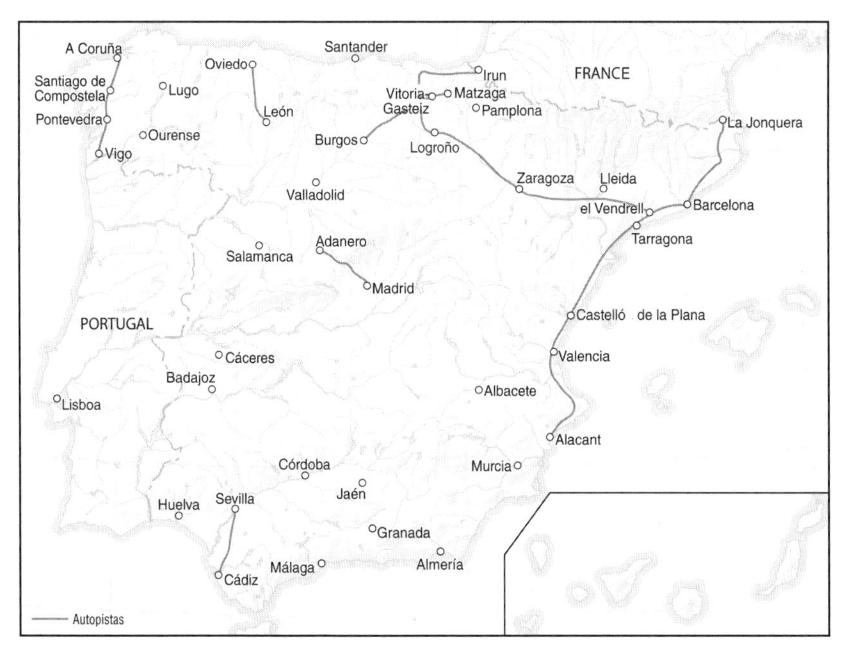

Map 4.5 Toll motorways entered into service between 1967 and 1985

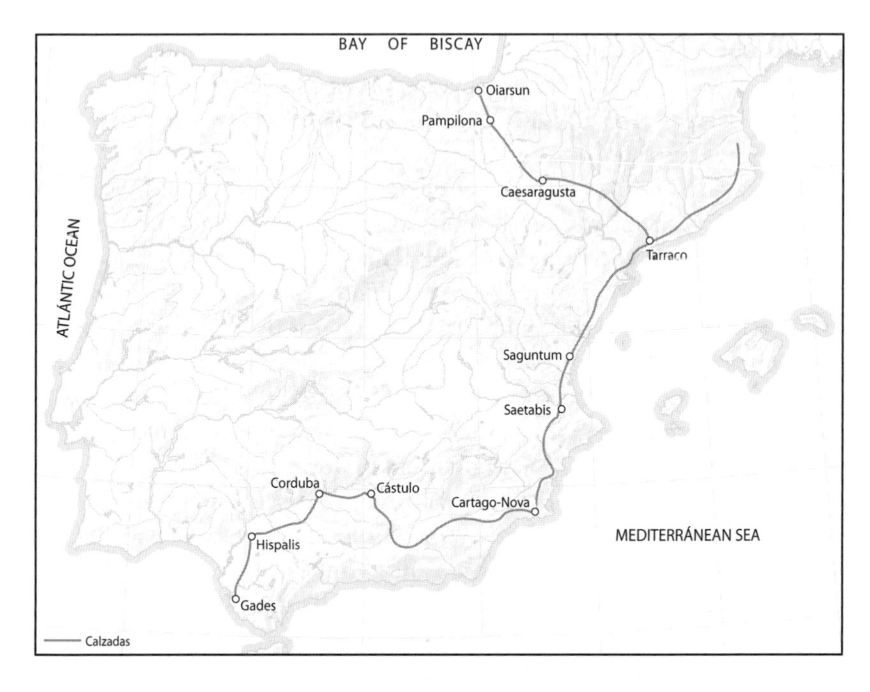

Map 4.6 Strabo's map of Roman roads. First century AD.

Already at that time the Romans dedicated special attention to roads on the main commercial routes!

It is essential to explain why toll motorways were built where they were. Financing by users offers incentives to prioritize routes that have the most commercial activity and the best growth prospects, which redound on recovering costs. For this reason, as is only logical, the first important concessions (1967–68) were made on the corridor with the most economic growth and, therefore, with the greatest increase in traffic – particularly in terms of freight – and the best prospects for profitability: the sections between La Jonquera and Tarragona, and between Montgat and Mataró.[41] That is to say, on the corridor that the World Bank had recommended in its 1962 report. At the end of 1973, the only trajectories that had been awarded in quite a complete way were La Jonquera–Alacant and El Vendrell–Bilbao. Indeed, the Mediterranean and the valley of the Ebro were the corridors where economic activity and heavy traffic grew the most. Because they were the most dynamic corridors in terms of passenger and freight traffic, they offered greater potential for obtaining toll incomes.

Beginning in the mid-1970s, debates appeared concerning a series of problems posed by the toll model in Spain. In 1974, the *Informe sobre las*

Autopistas Nacionales de Peaje (Report on National Toll Motorways)[42] highlighted the reduction in the rate of traffic growth, the rise in costs of external resources and the high cost of construction of the Spanish toll motorways. The economic crisis of the 1970s cast many doubts on the outlook for investments in new motorway sections, given that these didn't present as rosy a picture for traffic expectations as those that had been originally awarded. Indeed, with the economic crisis, concessions entirely ceased. Nobody was interested in losing money investing in corridors with lower expectations of profitability.

In addition to the very limited expansion of the established network, another element of dissatisfaction with the policy of toll motorway concessions was the damage inflicted on the public treasury in the mid and long-term. Since their beginnings, motorway concessions included mercantile, tax and financial clauses favourable to the concessionaries, clauses that were systematized in a stable way by the Law 8/1972, of construction, conservation and exploitation of motorways under concession. These clauses imposed very onerous burdens on the Treasury, especially in the case of the exchange rate insurance covered by the State for capital raised abroad with the goal of financing motorway construction. Through this mechanism, the State undertook to provide the concessionary the foreign currencies for the payment of debt service at the same exchange rate prevailing on the day of acquiring the loan. In fact, the exchange rate insurance was later repealed for new concessions, in the Road Law of 1988. By 1996, the cost of the exchange rate insurance for the State was 2,884.17 million euros, which meant an expense of more than four euros for each euro effectively spent by private investors.[43]

In the final period of the government of the Unión de Centro Democratico (UCD) in the summer of 1982, the minister of Public Works announced the need to complete the motorway system with up to 4,000 km by the year 2000, and proposed forming a public company that would finance the construction of 1,500 km of toll motorways and assume responsibility for their management. The indicated sections were: Alacant–Murcia, Madrid–Zaragoza, Madrid–Toledo, Bilbao–Santander, and Santiago–Pontevedra.[44] The significance of these new sections was to complete the route suggested by the World Bank for the Mediterranean, culminate the connection between Barcelona and Madrid, modernize the Cantabrian corridor, connect the main urban zones of Galicia and link Madrid with Toledo.

Nonetheless, these pre-electoral announcements – which seemed to be inspired by the practices followed in France and Italy in the preceding decades – never reached fruition given that the parliamentary election of 28 October 1982 resulted in the defeat of the governing party.

From Toll Financing to Budgetary Financing: The Toll-Free Motorways

The Partido Socialista Obrero Español – PSOE – won an absolute majority in the elections of 1982, and took possession of the government in December. In 1984, the new government created the Empresa Nacional de Autopistas (ENAUSA) (National Motorways Company), which absorbed various bankrupt concessions incapable of realizing awarded sections: Ferrol–A Coruña–Santiago–Pontevedra–Vigo–Tuy (Autopistas del Atlántico, AUDASA), Tudela–Irurzun (Autopistas de Navarra, AUDENASA) and Campomanes–León (Astur–Leonesa, AUCALSA). And, in more general terms, established a budgetary financing model for the new motorways – termed *autovías* as opposed to *autopistas* – in the General Road Plan (PGC) 1984–1991.

With this decision, the model of road infrastructures distanced itself from the model of the large Mediterranean countries and moved closer to the models of central and northern European and Anglo-Saxon countries. Various motives existed for this change in policy. First of all, there were tax reasons. Budgetary financing demanded overcoming the difficulties posed by the tax system of the late Franco period. With the introduction of the *Impuesto sobre la Renta de las Personas Físicas* (Income Tax for Individuals [IRPF]) in 1977, a big step had been made in that direction. The Socialist government adopted a guideline for bringing taxation closer to the norm of the countries of the European Community. This decision, in addition to the use of public debt, made possible the budgetary financing of roads, among other programs. Furthermore, entry into the EEC and access to regional policy funds made it possible to collect additional budgetary resources for the construction of motorways.

Secondly, the type of design established for most of the toll-free motorways in the General Road Plan, based on the possibility of widening already existing routes, made possible a significant reduction in spending costs. These types of roads were termed *autovías*, a term that is all but exclusive to Spain, and which in this text is only used in the terminological context of the PGC 1984–1991 (with a meaning equivalent to 'toll-free motorways').

In addition to lower spending costs derived from making use of the already existing roads, it was possible to do away with additional spending (on greater access-limitation of the roadway and installations for charging tolls). The combination of more available tax resources and lower spending costs facilitated the process of equipping motorways. In fact, while the plans made at the end of the UCD's term of government pursued the goal of 4,000 km of motorways by the year 2000, the motorway system under state management already reached that expansion by the end of 1990, thanks primarily to the entering into service of 1,707 km of toll-free motorways between 1986 and 1990.

At this point it is appropriate to take a more detailed look at the content of the General Road Plan 1984–1991 and its practical development. The primary actions related to toll-free motorways, in terms of kilometres, programmed by the PGC can be found in table 2 of the PGC.[45] The *autovía* program totalled 3,250 km, with an initial budget of 330,000 million pesetas (1,980 million euros).[46]

The development of the PGC, in respect to the creation of toll-free motorways, was all but complete by 1993. The amount of resources used to realize the plan was much greater than initially estimated, above all due to

Table 4.2 Program of *autovías* of the General Road Plan. Sections in service by 31 December 1993

Toll-free motorway	Km in operation		
North (Madrid–Burgos)	222.5		
Northeast (Madrid–Zaragoza)	280.8		
Northeast (Lleida–Cervera)	46.1		
Northeast (Igualada–Martorell)	40.0		
Levante (Madrid–Valencia y Alicante)	436.8		
Andalusia (Madrid–Sevilla)	519.8		
Andalusia (Jerez de la Frontera–Pto. Sta. María)	6.2		
Extremadura (Madrid–Badajoz)	290.4		
Northwest (Adanerov–Benavente)	157.5		
Sevilla–Huelva	64.0		
Asturias (Campomanes–Oviedo)	34.8		
East (Utiel–Valencia)	57.2		
Murcia–Cartagena	55.3		
Las Pedrizas–Málaga	41.7		
Madrid–Toledo	59.4		
SUBTOTAL RADIAL MOTORWAYS		2,312.5	75.9%
Mediterráneo (by pass València, Alacant–Murcia, Puerto Lumbreras–Baza and Almería–Adra)	362.1		
Costa del Sol (Málaga–Algeciras)	117.2		
Atlantic (Vigo–Frontera portuguesa)	30.9		
Santander–Torrelavega	17.7		
Alcoy–Cocentaina	3.4		
Castilla (Burgos–Tordesillas)	175.2		
Oviedo–Pola de Siero	26.4		
SUBTOTAL TRANSVERSAL MOTORWAYS		732.9	24.1%
TOTAL		3,045.4	100.0%

Source: Built on information from the Instituto de Estudios del Transporte – Ministerio de Obras Públicas, Transporte y Medio Ambiente.

the large increase in spending on *autovías* (7,500 million euros), which consumed almost half of the total resources of the plan. This was due, on the one hand, to the diversion of costs planned for the initially included actions, and on the other, to the ex-post inclusion of new actions.

The immediate consequence was the spectacular expansion of the motorway system in Spain. By 31 December 1993, 3,045.4 km of toll-free motorways had entered into service, built under the aegis of the PGC, while another 385.6 km were under construction. In total, there were 3,431 km, around 200 km more than initially planned. During the same period, the number of kilometres of toll motorways awarded by the State that entered into service was well below a hundred. Table 4.2 shows the kilometres of toll-free motorways in service up to the end of 1993, detailed by route.[47]

From Table 4.2 one can see that the basic roads of the radial network (N-I to N-VI) concentrated most of the actions. Additionally, the transformation into motorways of the N-301 and the N-330 had been centred on sections that served the Madrid–Levante Sur connection. Lastly, the A-69 is the natural extension of the N-IV toward Huelva. The only actions that had a measure of effect on transversal corridors occurred on the N-340,

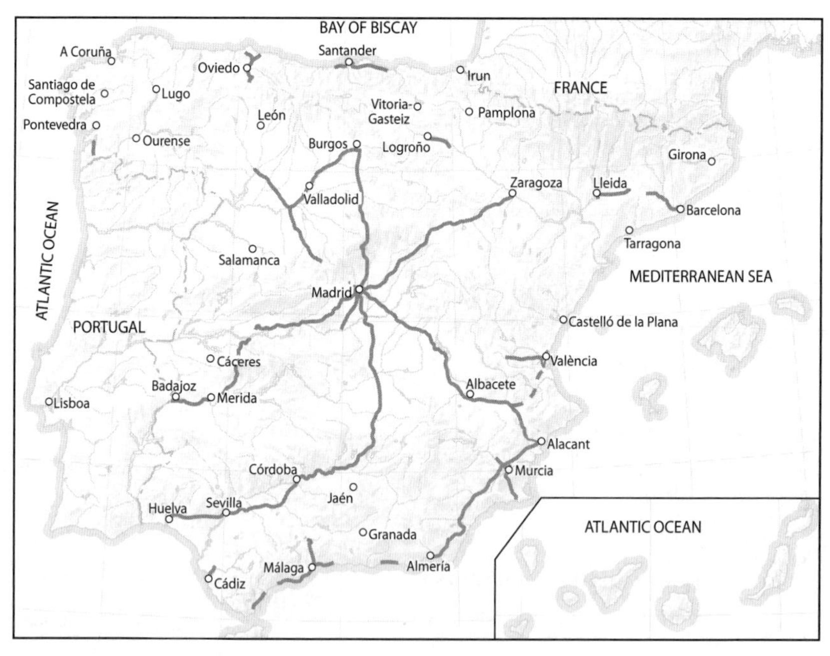

Map 4.7 Toll-free motorways (*autovías*) entering into service between 1985 and 1993

between Alacant and the province of Cádiz, and on the transversal N-620, which served to communicate the French border and the Portuguese border. Map 4.7 shows the position of two sections of toll-free motorway in service in Spanish territory.

In 1994, the general secretary for Surface Transportation Infrastructures, Emilio Pérez Touriño, gave a clear description of what realising the *autovías* of the PGC 1984–1991 meant: "It is a network whose characteristic is to have provided our country's radial quality with high-capacity roadways [. . .] in terms of high-capacity infrastructure, the network has concentrated on culminating the radial connections of our country, in addition to some other relevant actions".[48]

Another different question is whether the priorities established in the General Road Plan 1984–91 were correct. Clearly, some of the radial motorways were located on interurban routes that didn't have motorways and which had high daily traffic averages. The most relevant exceptions to these factors are found in some routes of the second stage, such as the Madrid–Badajoz and Burgos–Tordesillas motorways, which had relatively lower daily traffic averages. But greater weight was given to the fact that they were routes connecting Portugal with the centre of the peninsula (the first of the above) and with European routes (the second), in addition to political criteria defended by the idea of 'territorial rebalance'.

Elsewhere, an additional factor of great relevance was apparent in a model of budgetary financing. The four autonomous communities where the most motorways were built between 1985 and 1993 are Castilla-La

Table 4.3 Daily traffic averages (DTA) in 1983 and situation in PGC, 1984–1991

Road	DTA 1983 minimum	Section with lowest DTA	*Autovía* in PGC 1984–1991?	DTA 2008
N-340 Málaga–Algeciras	6,960	San Roque	Delayed	33,399
N-340 Algeciras–Cádiz	5,658	Algeciras–Tarifa	Not planned	11,888
N-630 Sevilla–Mérida/Badajoz	3,108	El Ronquillo	Not planned	8,154
N-V Madrid–Trujillo	5,125	Navalmoral Mata–Trujillo	Yes	10,665
N-V Trujillo–Badajoz	3,088	Trujillo-Mérida	Yes	7,387
N-I Madrid–Aranda de Duero	5,919	Sur de Aranda	Yes	17,424
N-I Aranda de Duero–Burgos	5,609	Norte de Aranda	Yes	20,039

Source: Maps of Traffics 1983 and 2008. Ministerio de Obras Públicas y Urbanismo y Ministerio de Fomento.

Mancha, Andalusia, Castilla y León, and the Valèncian Community, all Objective 1 regions of the European Community. This made it possible to obtain very high levels of co-financing with the Regional Policy of the EEC, through ERDF.

Nonetheless, it also seems debatable – taking jointly into consideration criteria of traffic levels and territorial rebalance – whether some of the priorities selected were more consistent than other alternatives that weren't selected, or whose execution suffered long delays in time. Table 4.3 presents the daily traffic averages in 1983 (figures available at the moment of drawing up the PGC 1984–1991) at the gauging stations of low traffic on some roads of Andalusia, Extremadura, and Castilla y León. All of these regions were Objective 1 of the EEC.

The routes of the upper section of the table correspond to transversal corridors: the Mediterranean corridor extended to Cádiz and the Ruta de la Plata, respectively. The lower routes correspond to radial roads connecting with Madrid. It is not possible to apply a rationale of demand, nor of inter-territorial solidarity in prioritizing the *autovía* between Navalmoral de la Mata and Trujillo above that of the route between Cádiz and Algeciras. The comparison between this and the Trujillo–Badajoz section is even more telling. Something similar is suggested by comparing the Cádiz–Algeciras and Aranda de Duero–Burgos routes. On the other hand, in strict terms of pure territorial rebalancing, it is possible to state that the Algeciras–Cádiz and Seville–Badajoz routes should have been prioritized, given the socio-economic characteristics of the areas they communicate, among the less developed in Spain.

The most plausible reason for having prioritized the sections of the lower part of the table is their connections with Madrid, which – although rhetorically defended in such worthy terms as 'territorial rebalancing' – obeys criteria of centralization much more than solidarity. Of course, almost 20 years after the PGC 1984–1991 was culminated, many conventional roads have been transformed into motorways. For example, the N-630 (today the A-66) between Seville and Mérida/Badajoz is now a motorway. But the time sequence in the modernization of infrastructures is not neutral in the spatial effects that these have on economic activities.

Furthermore, among the specific examples that concern us, most of the trajectory between Algeciras and Cádiz (126 km) continues to have the characteristics of a conventional road. The 57-kilometre trajectory Cádiz–Vejer de la Frontera has motorway characteristics (now the A48). Nevertheless, the 67 km section of the N-340 between Vejer de la Frontera and Los Pastores (Algeciras) continues to be a conventional road, which means more than half of the route between Cádiz–Algeciras remains without being modernized. It is true that the regional A-381 motorway is now in service between Jerez de la Frontera and Los Barrios (in the vicinity of Algeciras), which provides a good connection between Cádiz and Algeciras . . . although the distance it covers is almost 50% longer. It is also true that the direct route between both of the large cities of the province of Cádiz – part of the Mediterranean corridor – continues to have the characteristics of conventional road, while sections with much less average daily traffic (but which connect radially with Madrid) have had motorway characteristics for almost two decades.

Having reached this point, the fundamental idea of this chapter has been established: the structural modernization of the roads was begun in the 1960s with the implantation of motorways, almost always on the corridors with the best prospects for traffic and the generation of paid incomes. During a second stage, the State assumed a leading role through budgetary financing, which was used to radialize the motorway network – prioritizing the radial roads that converge on Madrid. The parallels with the financial pattern followed by the expansion of the railway are quite striking. Furthermore, it illustrates very clearly the existence of an underlying pattern, maintained over time, which orients infrastructure policy according to reasons unrelated to transportation policy in the strict sense. Transversal market, radial State.

The Return to Pro-Toll Policies?

Although the principal thesis of this chapter has been established, it is still interesting to review, if only briefly, the basic outlines of motorway policy since the mid-1990s. In particular, in respect to the occasionally expressed intention of implanting tolls in the zones of Spain that lack them, in order to thereby alleviate the existing territorial asymmetry.

In 1993, the year in which the realization of the PGC 1984–1991 was culminated, the state-controlled motorway network was 5,494 km, of which 3,730 were toll-free (68%) and 1,794 were toll (32%). These figures don't include the 220 km of dual-carriageway roads, given that in many cases their technical characteristics were very inferior to those of a motorway (for example, due to the existence of same level intersections, and the progressive implantation of roundabouts that transform the roadways into urban type use, etc.). The percentage of toll-free motorways in the state network continued to grow, until reaching 4,123 km (70% of the total) in 1996, while the weight of the toll motorways remained at 30%. In that year, there was a change of political leadership in the central government with the arrival of the Partido Popular.

With the change, the new government's policy was less adverse to toll motorways. The basic aspects of the new, more favourable policies towards tolls were: (1) agreements to extend concessions, and (2) the *Programa de Autopistas de Peaje* (Toll Motorway Program), of 1997.[49]

Agreements to extend concessions came into increasing use during the 1990s, following the antecedent established by the agreement between the Ministry of Public Works and the ACESA concessionary in 1990, by which the concession was extended in order to finance the soft-toll of the new Mataró-Palafolls motorway (a motorway originally planned to be toll-free in the PGC 1984–1991). A milestone in this policy was the extension of the concessions to a maximum period of 75 years, introduced in December of 1996 in the Ley de Acompañamiento de los Presupuestos of 1997 (Legislation Accompanying the Budget), by the new government of the Partido Popular. This modification left the path definitively clear for the practice of renegotiations, and in its day implied a break with the rules of the game that contravened the administration's obligations to the citizenry, given that before this legal modification the motorway concessions had a maximum lifespan of fifty years. Nonetheless, the new government also announced that it was going to extend the concession of toll motorways throughout Spain, to rebalance their presence in Spanish territory.

Unquestionably, the toll policy was more ambitious than it had been under the governments of the PSOE, which had only awarded two relatively short sections, Mataró–Palafolls, in 1990, and Málaga–Estepona, in 1996. In the context of the new pro-toll policies, the *Programa de Autopistas de Peaje* of the central government was of special relevance, whose first stage – shown in Table 4.4 – was presented in February of 1997. The results of the preliminary studies by the ministry suggested that five sections (the three access ones to Madrid, the Alacant–Cartagena, and the Madrid–Guadalajara) presented financial profitability. However, in keeping with the view of Rafael Izquierdo, "the rest (León–Astorga, Ávila–NVI, Segovia–San Rafael, Estepona–Guadiaro, and Santiago–Alto de Santo Domingo) required state contributions that oscillated, according to the calculations realized, between 40% and 65% of the total spending".[50]

These actions totalled 441.5 km, which along with the 83 toll km between Málaga and Estepona awarded in 1996, meant almost 70% of the new toll motorways in the national system.[51] The network of toll motorways controlled by the State, which was 1,764 km in 1993, reached a total extension of 2,493 km at the end of 2008.[52] A significant percentage of these new sections are found in the four new radial toll accesses to Madrid,

Table 4.4 Program of Toll Motorways Stage I

Toll motorway	Km	Budget Million euros
Access to Madrid M-40–Arganda (R3)	38.8	125.0
Access to Madrid M-40– Ocaña (R4)	60.7	130.4
Access to Madrid M-40–Navalcarnero (R5)	23.5	88.3
Alacant–Cartagena	96.0	220.6
Madrid–Guadalajara (R2)	45.2	250.7
Ávila–N-VI	22.9	70.5
Estepona–Guadiaro	22.1	133.4
León–Astorga	47.3	137.0
Santiago–Alto Santo Domingo	56.0	330.6
Segovia–San Rafael	29.0	70.5

Source: Ministerio de Fomento.

parallel to the toll-free motorways A-2, A-3, A-4 and A-5, thanks to which the capital now has duplicated, high-capacity accesses (toll-free and toll).

Most of the new toll actions have been supported by subsidies from the national budget, conceded both at the moment of the concession as well as afterwards. The most recent example is the concession of aid to the radial toll accesses to Madrid in the General National Budget of 2010, defended on the grounds of the extra costs of the expropriations. No doubt, the fact that traffic levels on the radial toll accesses are much lower than initially anticipated has been a key factor for the concession of that aid.

Nonetheless, the central question here is: have the new toll-related actions corrected the asymmetry in terms of the model and inter-territorial aspects of the financing of motorways in Spain? With the practical completion of the PGC 1984–1991, the percentage of toll motorways operated by the State had been reduced to almost 30%. At the end of 2008, the state-run motorway system had an extension of 10,126 km. Of these, 7,633 km were toll-free (75%) and 2,493 km were toll (25%). The policy of reducing the asymmetry . . . had increased it! This shouldn't come as a surprise. In the last 15 years, new sections of toll-free motorways have continually entered into service. And although the pace of the creation of new sections has fallen in respect to the PGC 1984–1991, as is logical, the toll-free motorway's hegemony in respect to the toll motorway has increased, as clearly demonstrated in Figure 4.1. Insincere policy or incompetent execution?

Spain has a mixed system for financing motorways that is quite peculiar in the context of the European Union. In addition to its mixed character, another differential feature is even more exceptional: the large inter-territorial variability of the weight of the tolls, reflected in Graph 4.2, which includes the weight of the toll in the State network of motorways of

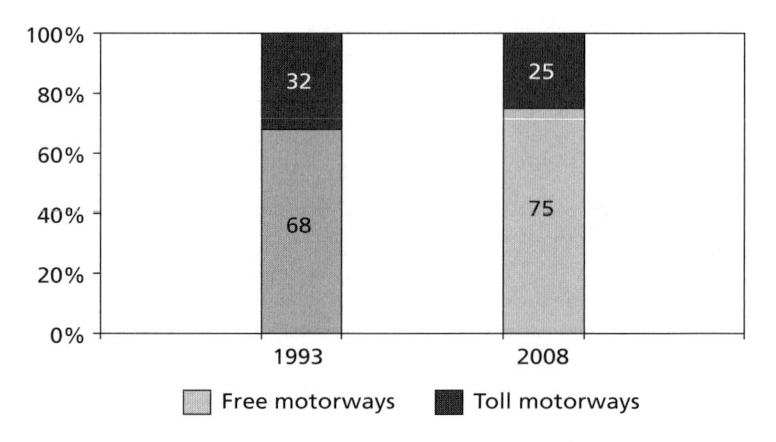

Graph 4.1 Composition of the national motorway system (toll-free and toll)

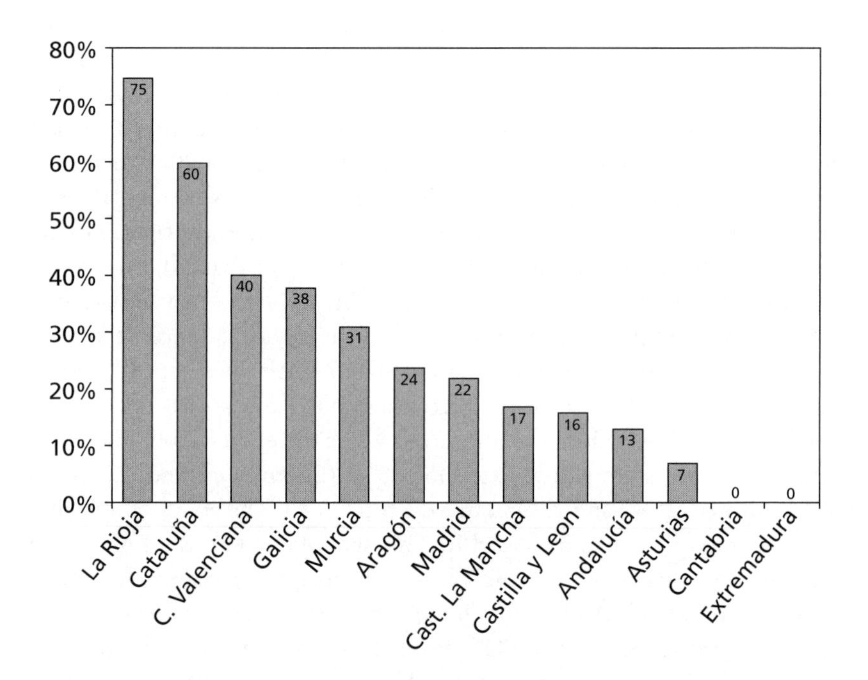

Note: In the Canary and Balearic Islands the island governments have exclusive authority over roads. In Navarra and the Basque Country, exclusive authority pertains to the *foral* (provincial) governments, although in this case some exceptional toll sections exist on the Vasco–Aragonesa motorway, under state control. All tollways under state control are privately managed.
Source: *Anuario Estadístico 2008* (Ministerio del Fomento, 2009), p. 158

Graph 4.2 Percentage of tolls on state network motorways (toll-free and toll) in each region each region. The weight of the tolls is greatest in regions such as La Rioja (75%) and Catalonia (60%), and significantly above Spain as a whole in regions such as the Valèncian Community (40%), Galicia (38%) and Murcia (31%). Nonetheless, in Cantabria and Extremadura the weight of tolls on state motorways is zero, and in others it is a good deal lower than in Spain as a whole: Asturias (7%), Andalusia (13%), Castilla y León (16%) and Castilla-La Mancha (17%).

Forty years after the first motorways entered into service, the superposition of financing models in the process of the motorway system's development in Spain has led to the existence of a mixed model in spending and maintenance – budget and toll. This model is characterized, furthermore, by significant territorial asymmetry. This asymmetry causes inequalities between Spanish citizens and companies in respect to the payment of services of similar quality. This sharply contrasts with the pronounced equalitarianism of Spaniards in respect to the financing of the rest of the public services overseen by the State. Even so, it has become one of the most constant elements of our motorway model, which is quite unique among the countries of our vicinity.

Conclusion: Transversal Market, Radial State

The development of the motorway system in Spain began in the 1960s. In a first stage, financing was fundamentally made by users through the concession of toll motorways. For this reason, the first toll motorways were implanted above all in the primary routes of road traffic, on the Mediterranean corridor and in the valley of the Ebro. The development of motorways supported by the market, basically financed by users, followed a transversal pattern.

In a second stage, spending and services were financed fundamentally by the national budget. The big milestone of this second stage was the General Road Program 1984–1991, whose principal result was the creation of a large number of toll-free motorways. Most of those motorways converge on Madrid, causing the radialization of the network. It is appropriate to recall, in this context, that toll-free motorways were implanted on some radial roads although their traffic levels were (and are) less than those of transversal roads that haven't been transformed into motorways. Madrid, which in the 18th century had already become kilometre zero for the traditional road system in Spain, now assumes the condition of kilometre zero for the motorway system. The development of the motorways supported by the State, by the national budget, followed a radial pattern.

In 1720, Philip V transformed the design of surface communications in Spain by introducing through law the radial map of postal stage roads, articulated in six radial routes. These six routes were defined as the fundamental radial routes ("six large royal roads") of the Road Plan included in the Public Works Plan of Ferdinand VI. This king, through the Royal Decree of 1747, decreed the possibility of building roads paid for out of the Royal Treasury, an option exclusively applied to the six 'royal roads', which eventually turned into the six radial roads beginning in the reign of Charles III. But the financing of 'lesser' roads continued to depend on municipalities . . . And this was so up until the 20th century, when the PGC 1984–1991 established the financing of new motorways through the national budget, and centred their expansion on the six radial roads. The historical regularity is clear and overwhelming: radial State.

5

The New Spain (I): Railway Modernization Starting from Kilometre Zero

The concept of the high-speed train is generally used to designate a railway capable of reaching speeds of around 250 km/h or more, which involves the construction of its own specific track.[1] This type of railway in Spain has been termed *Alta Velocidad Española* ('Spanish High-Speed' or AVE, its acronym in Spanish), an identifying term that has no equivalent in other developed countries where this type of railway lacks national connotations. The first AVE was implanted on the Madrid–Seville route and began its service in 1992. The new route was used to apply a parallel decision to install the new tracks at international track width. This decision, whether correct or not (a debate outside the scope of our objectives), was independent of the necessary requisites for implanting the high-speed train. The entering into service of the Madrid–Seville AVE, with intermediary stations at Ciudad Real, Puertollano and Cordoba, occurred shortly before the inauguration of the Universal Exposition of Seville in 1992.

The choice of the Madrid–Seville line as the first for the implantation of the AVE in Spain was surprising, paradoxical and novel. The element of surprise was the fact that the first line chosen for the AVE wasn't the one with the highest density of traffic – then or now – which was the Madrid–Barcelona line. The paradoxical element was that, given that the international track width was chosen with the goal of integrating the Spanish network into the European one, a peninsular high-speed island was formed instead of beginning with the modernization of some of the connections with France (still unresolved as of the present). The novel element was that, for the first time since the royal roads of the 18th century, a structural modernization of ground infrastructures began at kilometre 0, something that with the implantation of the railway in the 19th century had only occurred after the General Law of 1855.

While novel, the fact that the modernization of the AVE began at kilometre 0 is consistent with the logic of infrastructure policy in Spain in recent centuries, as has been analyzed in preceding chapters. The implantation of the railway in the 19th century began on lines that, in most cases, were not publicly subsidized; after 1855, radialization was legislated and a policy of substantial budgetary subsidies was carried out, effective above all for the radial lines. The implantation of motorways began in the 1960s with a financing model by users through direct tolls, in which the corridors of the Mediterranean and the valley of the Ebro were given priority. In the 1980s, the model was changed for one of budgetary financing of motorways, with a plan (PGC 1984–1991) whose primary goal was to transform the radial roads that converged on Madrid into toll-free motorways.

In the case of the AVE, from the very first moment, its creation has been financed by the national budget, given that investment on the infrastructure is barely recouped, and even the costs of its operation are subsidized. Given this form of financing, no other form of development – in light of historical precedents – could have been expected: the creation from the start of a radial AVE network with its origin at kilometre 0. Given the absence of the market (which would never have made this kind of an investment in Spain), radial State.

Surrounding References: The Development of High-Speed Rail in the Principal Countries of Europe and in Japan

In recent decades, above all since the end of the 20th century, many countries have built high-speed railway lines, at speeds of 250 km/h or higher. Table 5.1 shows the expansion of this infrastructure by early 2010.

Japan was the pioneering country in the implantation of high-speed rail. In Europe, France and Germany followed Japan's example in the 1980s, as did Spain beginning in 1992. As can be seen in the table 5.1, and despite being the fourth country to implant high-speed rail, Spain is the European Union country with the largest prospective expansion of its network, if we consider the lines in operation and those under construction (and if we also take into account the ones being planned). Actually, after the Madrid–València line entered into service in December 2010, the Spanish network became the longest one in Europe. And it will be – according to present planning – the world's leading country with the most extensive high-speed network, with the exception of China, that is undergoing a fast expansion of its network. The experiences of the countries that implanted high-speed

Table 5.1 High-speed railway lines in service in early 2010. Speed ≥250 km/h

Continent	Country	First year of service	Km in service (1)	Km under construction (2)	Projected (3)	Total (1)+(2)+(3)
Europe – UE	Germany	1988	1032	316	599	1947
	Belgium	1997	209	–	–	209
	Spain	1992	1515	2219	1702	5440
	France	1981	1872	299	2616	4787
	Holland	2009	120	–	–	120
	Italy	1992	760	55	395	1210
	Poland	–	–	–	712	712
	Portugal	–	–	–	1006	1006
	United Kingdom	2003	113	–	–	113
	Sweden	–	–	–	750	750
Europe-No UE	Russia	–	–	–	650	650
	Switzerland	2007	35	72	–	107
Asia	Saudi Arabia	–	–	–	550	550
	China	2008	3182	7313	2901	13396
	South Korea	2004	330	82	–	412
	India	–	–	–	495	495
	Iran	–	–	–	475	475
	Japan	1964	2145	590	583	3318
	Taiwan	2007	345	–	–	345
	Turkey	2009	235	510	1679	2424
America	Argentina	–	–	–	315	315
	Brazil	–	–	–	500	500
	United States	–	–	–	900	900
Africa	Morocco	–	–	–	680	680

Notes: [a] Between 1978 and 1991 the *direttissima* line between Florence and Rome began service, with speed up to 250 km/h. Its technical characteristics are not those of high speed.

[b] In all countries lines with speed below 250 km/h are excluded. The unique exception to this is China, because of the difficulty in decomposing the tranches with speed between 200 and 250 km/h.

[c] 362 km at speed of 240 km/h exist in the Northeast corridor of the USA (Boston–New York–Washington DC).

Source: Author's, based on data from the department of high speed rail in the International Union of Railways (UIC), updated with the companies' web pages.

rail before Spain are interesting and provide valuable lessons that should be revised before analyzing Spain's own experience.[2]

Japan

The world's first high-speed railway (*Shinkansen*) entered into service in 1964, with the Tokaydo Shinkansen line that connected the cities of Tokyo and Osaka with an extension of 515 km. This event made Japan the pioneering country in the implantation of high-speed rail services. The second line – Sanyo Shinkansen – entered into service in 1972 and was finished in 1975. It connects the cities of Kobe and Moji, with an extension of 537 km. The connection between these lines was completed by the section between

Osaka and Kobe, of about 40 km. In this way, at the end of the 1970s, before high-speed rail entered into service in Europe, Japan already had more than 1,000 km of high-speed rail. In the early 1980s, work was begun on the Joetsu Shinkansen (Tokyo–Niigata) and Tohoku Shinkansen (Tokyo–Morioka) lines. In 1982, service began on sections of the Joetsu line, whose total extension is 270 km (along with some shared sections with the Tohoku). In 1982, service also began on sections of the Tohoku line. The line is 593 km long and its last section, Morioka–Hachinoche, was completed in 2002. By early 2010, the Shinkansen (≥250 km/h) network in Japan had somewhat less than 2,000 km in service.

The primary motivation for the development of high-speed rail in Japan was to improve mobility in corridors where traffic had reached high levels of congestion caused by the rapid economic growth following World War II. The urban structure of the country, with densely populated metropolitan areas separated by a few hundred kilometres and a large demand for ground transportation, has favoured the development of high-speed rail.[3] At present, the Shinkansen network crosses the island of Honshu, the largest archipelago, and transports more than 300 million passengers every year. While at first a mixed service of passengers and freight was pursued, the strong passenger demand and the needs imposed by the traffic of freight on track maintenance determined the network's orientation in favour of passenger service.

Studies on the economic impact of high-speed rail reveal that the services sector has benefited the most in Japan, and that services to industry experienced a high concentration in the cities of Tokyo and Osaka, the primary hubs of the network and the country's largest metropolitan areas.[4] Tourist activity experienced significant growth, as did business travel, above all intra-business, but overnight stays in hotels by business travellers declined in Tokyo and Osaka. In terms of the impact on commercial activity, Tokyo was the primary beneficiary of trips for this motive. Nonetheless, the (unfounded) a priori expectations of economic benefits derived from the high-speed train led to political pressure and demands for stations in smaller cities, which affected the viability of the system, causing a rise in debt and annual losses. As a result, the debt of Japan Railways in 1987 was more than 25 billion yen (equivalent to 200,000 million euros); this caused a financial crisis that led to the privatization of most of the railway network that year, including high-speed rail.[5]

France

Construction on the first line of the *Train à Grande Vitesse* (TGV) began in 1975, between Paris and Lyon, with a length of 419 km. Commercial TGV service on the line, called the Paris-Southeast, started in 1981. The primary motive for the construction of the TGV as a specific network in France was the high levels of traffic congestion between the two cities. Between 1980 and 1992, the number of people travelling by train between the cities almost doubled, with the users of the TGV between Paris and Lyon in this latter year totalling almost 19 million.[6] The success of the TGV led to the application of a spending plan to build connections from Paris to Le Mans (1989), Tours (1990) and Calais (1993). The expansion continued on the Rhône-Alpes (1994) and Mediterranean (2001) corridors. At the start of 2010, the TGV network had 1,872 km in service. The TGV lines transport more than 100 million passengers a year.

In practice, the TGV in France has been developed according to state policy guidelines based on containing costs and commercial viability.[7] The expansion of the network has followed criteria of investing only in lines where spending was socially profitable; the lines have been financed according to their expected profitability, with a required minimum rate of financial and social return of 12% (which has been flexibly applied).[8] For this reason, those in charge of railways in France – who haven't mixed politics with spending – have always been reluctant to satisfy demands of a territorial type that go against the principle of social profitability. Priority has been given to service on corridors with sufficient traffic, connecting cities of a significant size. For this reason, it has almost always been necessary to connect cities with Paris to justify the investment. The first three lines built connected the French capital with the country's other four main cities: Lyon, Marseille, Bordeaux and Lille. This has generated a star-shaped network, centred on Paris. It is interesting to note that the use of conventional services for connections with lower traffic density, as well as for the access of the TGV to the large cities, has been maintained given that the costs of expropriation and construction would have been exorbitant.

In terms of the TGV's economic impact, the city of Paris has received the largest share of the benefits, attracting activity from smaller cities. The absorption effect of the principal hub is visible in the fact that after the TGV entered into service on the Paris–Rhône/Alpes corridor, the (roundtrip) trips originating in Paris grew 52%, while the (roundtrip) journeys whose destination was the capital rose 144%.[9] Although on a much smaller scale than Paris, other large cities, such as Lyon and Lille, have received benefits through the increase of economic cooperation and exchange with the capital.

Just as in Japan, the TGV has led to the centralization of service activities in the large hubs of the network and has favoured intra-organizational trips. Journeys with this end originating in Paris increased 21%, while those that have Paris as their destination grew 156%.[10] On the contrary, the effects on industrial activities have been insignificant and the TGV's impact on decisions to locate companies within the services sector appears negligible.[11] Lastly, the additional information available on business trips made during the first half of the 1980s indicates that after the TGV entered into service the number of travellers who stayed at least one night at their destination fell from 74% to 46%.[12]

Germany

The beginnings of the commercial operation of high-speed rail – *neubaustrecken* – in Germany (the InterCity Express [ICE]) occurred almost a decade later than it did in France, following a process of construction that was plagued by long delays caused by orographic problems as well as legal and political ones.[13] Furthermore, the ICE was used to transform the characteristics of the German railway system. This system was characterized by the preponderance of the east–west lines built prior to World War II, even though industrial traffic had since come to follow a primarily north-south direction. For this reason, the modernization of the railway was taken advantage of to facilitate the transportation of freight from northern ports to industrial areas in the south. This is why the first two lines – *neubaustrecken* – were the ones joining Hannover with Fulda and Würzburg (opened in 1988 and completed in 1994) and Mannheim with Stuttgart (completed in 1991); their primary goal was to resolve problems of congestion and, as has been mentioned, improve freight transportation from the north to the south. The high-speed lines (ICE ≥250 km/h) in service in 2010 had an extension of somewhat more than 1,000 km. The network provides service to more than 70 million passengers a year.

It is important to highlight that on many occasions the option chosen has been to improve the conventional lines for speeds between 200 and 230 km/h (similar to the optimum level of service of the Euromed train between Barcelona and Alacant in Spain). For example, between Hamburg and (1) Berlin, (2) Bremen–Münster, and (3) Hannover–Dortmund. Also in the connections between Hannover and Wolfsburg, Berlin and Leipzig, Frankfurt and Mannheim, and the southern part of the Nurembur–Munich line. Therefore, the German strategy has been very different from the one pursued by Japan and France: instead of building only new lines exclusively for high-speed rail, many conventional lines have been modernized for high speeds (200–230 km/h). Furthermore, the high-speed lines (≥250 km/h) in Germany are compatible with freight traffic (with the exception of the Cologne–Frankfurt line). As a result, the network is shared by high-speed trains, high-speed passenger services (and other more conventional ones) and freight traffic.

Railway modernization in Germany has had mixed results in terms of costs. Making passenger and freight traffic compatible (which implies limiting the maximum speed to between 250 and 300 km/h) on the new high-speed lines has led to higher costs, but also to greater benefits for the connected industrial centres.[14] On the other hand, the fact that a large part of the conventional network has been modernized to high-speed rail has led to lower costs on these lines in respect to costs registered on the new lines of the ICE.

Nevertheless, the high cost of construction of the new lines of the ICE has led to a questioning of the usefulness of continuing to spend on this type of infrastructure, which generates very limited environmental benefits in comparison with other, alternative focuses of railway modernization, and more restrictive policies in respect to road transportation.[15] This is why the number of kilometres of high-speed rail under construction and being planned in Germany (Table 5.1, above) is much lower than in European countries with a similar surface area but less economic power and population, such as France and Spain.

In terms of the economic effects of the ICE in Germany, the system was designed to spread out benefits rather than to concentrate them in the largest hubs of the network. Freight transportation was given special priority because it contributed more to generating income and economic productivity than did passenger transportation. The urban structure of Germany lacks mono-centric characteristics, such as that of Paris in France. Thus, the ICE system has been based on a complex interconnection of services, with exchanges that offer connections of between one and two hours between most of the principal German cities, and more frequent services on the principal lines.[16]

Italy

High-speed rail in Italy has the 240-km Rome–Florence line as a precedent, known as the *direttissima*, which entered into partial service in 1978 and was completed in 1992. This line allows speeds of up to 250 km/h, but its technical characteristics are not comparable to those of high-speed rail, the *Rete Alta Velocità/Alta Capacità* (AV/AC). Work on the AV/AC network was begun in 1991, with the concession to the *Società TAV* for the construction and operation of the Milan–Naples and Turin–Venice lines. The concession was expanded in 1992 to include the Milan–Genoa line. The Società TAV was a mixed company, with 60% of its capital privately held and 40% in the hands of the state company Ferrovie dello Stato.[17] But the private partners were reticent to contribute the required capital, and in 1998 the Ferrovie dello Stato acquired the 60% in private hands. The first sections in service were the Rome–Naples in 2005 and the Turin–Novara in 2006. At present, the AV/AC network offers complete service on the Turin–Milan–Bologna–Florence and Rome–Naples–Salerno lines. The AV/AC network has an expansion of 760 km (1,000 km if you include the Rome–Florence *direttissima*).

The initial plan called for the construction of a high-speed network that was supposed to function independently of the conventional network, as in Japan, France and Spain. But in 1996, this was changed for a more integrated concept of the network, for which reason the plans for high-speed rail were replaced by the Alta Velocità/Alta Capacità (High-Speed/High-Capacity). The definitive focus pursued a greater integration between the high-speed network and the conventional one; this would enlarge the railway's transportation capacity, expand the effects of high-speed rail in the territory and avoid the degradation of the conventional lines in the areas between cities served by high-speed rail (the so-called 'tunnel effect'). Such a decision implied significantly increasing planned costs; real costs, meanwhile, have grown far beyond the initial estimates as work has been carried out.

In the case of Italy, in general, it is necessary to keep in mind that high-speed rail fundamentally competes with road transportation, given that air service between the cities connected up until now by the AV/AC network is of little importance due to the short distances between these cities. Nonetheless, the recent introduction of AV/AC service in Italy means that systematic information regarding its economic impact and mobility is not yet available.

Summary: Lessons from International Experience

A review of the international experiences of high-speed rail provides some lessons that are of great use for understanding its economic, territorial and environmental effects and impacts.

High-speed rail projects are most effective when they resolve problems of insufficient capacity in congested corridors, and when they make it possible to optimize industrial connections, improving accessibility to freight transportation. Connecting with other corridors in order to promote regional development usually leads to the economic failure of the project.

The construction of exclusive tracks for passenger trains only makes sense on lines with very high levels of traffic. When this is not the case, greater success is had by building tracks of compatible use for both passengers and freight, although this translates into less ambitious speeds and somewhat higher costs, given that they promote industrial connections. This is important because passenger transportation by high-speed rail has a very limited aggregate economic impact, in contrast to what happens with freight transportation. The problem of spending costs can be alleviated if high-speed lines are combined with the improvement of conventional lines on corridors with low traffic levels. In the case of France, the connection with commuter trains has also been used for access to large metropolitan areas, which avoids the costs of expropriation and construction, particularly high in these areas. Nevertheless, the location of high-speed stations outside the urban centre usually results in failure when there is a lack of adequate multi-modal connections.

In sum, the very high spending costs demanded by the high-speed railway, along with the elevated operating costs of its services, demand a very high level of traffic. According to estimates made by professors Ginés de Rus and Gustavo Nombela, spending on high-speed rail is difficult to justify when the estimated demand for the first year is below the interval of 8 to 10 million passengers for a line of 500 km, a distance in which high-speed rail is clearly competitive with airplane and road travel.[18] Thus, the construction of high-speed lines should only be carried out in relations that connect very populated metropolitan areas with important problems of road traffic congestion and deficient air connections. This is the case with the lines built in France and Japan, as well as with the main German lines.

In terms of the impact on mobility, high-speed rail saves significant time in comparison to conventional services, and its competitive advantage lies in the interval between (approximately) 150 and 650 km. For distances less than these, road travel is very competitive. At the upper limit, air transportation provides a similar total travel time. Beyond this, the advantage of air transportation grows as the distance increases. It is important to take into consideration, furthermore, the great comfort and reliability (lack of delays) of high-speed rail travel, compared to competing modes of travel. In keeping with these guidelines, the studies realized for the Paris–Lyon and Madrid–Seville lines[19] have shown that air travel is the primary victim of high-speed rail service, much more so than road transportation. In the case of Spain, the most recent information from the railway operator indicates that the AVE boasts 85% of the market share on the Madrid–Seville line, with almost total hegemony on the corridor.

Another important subject is the environmental impact of high-speed rail. A systematic, aggregated and complete study of the effects of high-speed rail on the reduction of CO_2 has yet to be produced. Even so, some information is available, above all in respect to energy consumption. One of the most complete and sophisticated studies[20] so far on the environmental evaluation of high-speed rail suggests that the energy consumed per seat and kilometre by the airplane is 240% greater than that of high-speed rail. Nonetheless, the energy consumed by high-speed rail is greater than that of road vehicles, both in terms of gas and petroleum, and much greater than that of conventional intercity trains. Another excellent technical study[21] confirms that the conventional intercity train is more efficient than high-speed rail, but the results for road transportation are similar to those of high-speed rail. In all, while it is more efficient than the plane, high-speed rail is not an especially useful instrument for combating CO_2 emissions, given that it is less efficient than modernized conventional trains. Furthermore, the construction of new and separate high-speed rail lines generates very significant CO_2 emissions (in addition to using up space and generating noise and visual pollution) that environmental analysis of high-speed rail doesn't take into consideration.

Lastly, let us focus our attention on economic and regional effects. The international experience clearly indicates that high-speed rail helps to consolidate productive processes already underway and facilitates intra-organizational trips. But it doesn't generate new activities nor does it attract companies or investments.[22] In fact, for cities with worse economic conditions than their neighbours, high-speed rail connections can cause a dislocation of economic activities and a negative aggregate impact.[23] High-speed rail encourages the centralization of activities in the large hubs, especially in the services sector. The primary hubs of the network – more dynamic – can benefit at the expense of intermediary cities, which are usually the big losers of high-speed rail.[24] For this reason, the efforts by many smaller-sized cities to get high-speed rail stations can be unfruitful and even counterproductive.[25]

In addition to business trips, tourism is the other sector that receives a large boost when high-speed rail enters into service. The number of tourists increases in the cities connected to the network. But for both tourism and business trips, the number of overnight stays at the destination decreases, given the greater facility of making the return trip on the same day.[26] The overall effects are ambiguous: the impact on restaurants can be positive, but hotel services may be negatively impacted by the reduction in the average number of overnight stays. Lastly, the impact on population and housing growth, if it exists, is marginal.

The Alta Velocidad Española (AVE)

The star of infrastructure policy in Spain in recent years has been and is the Alta Velocidad Española (Spanish High-Speed, or AVE), incompatible with freight traffic. Expenditure on AVE lines clearly demonstrates the primacy this infrastructure modality has enjoyed; enormous amounts of material resources and technical and human effort have been dedicated to it. Furthermore, everything indicates that this will continue to be the case up until the year 2020, in keeping with the *Plan Estratégico de Infraestructuras de Transporte* (PEIT, Strategic Plan of Transportation Infrastructures) by the Ministerio de Fomento (Ministry of Public Works). Given that everything in life has its limits, neither resources nor efforts have been left over to promote freight railway, whose large loss of market share in Spain in the present decade, even more than ridiculous, has been pathetic. Let us now look at the primary questions related to the AVE.

Implantation and Development of the AVE

The first AVE railway line entered into service in 1992 between Madrid and Seville and made possible a (direct) trip between both cities in two hours and twenty minutes. Spain decided to build a segregated high-speed network, as had been done in Japan and France (although in those countries, conventional lines are compatible because they share the same track width), and in contrast to Germany and Italy. Furthermore, Spain opted to purchase the railway technology abroad rather than to develop its own technology,[27] a fact that also distinguishes the Spanish case from the other experiences reviewed above. In 1995, work began on the Madrid–Zaragoza– Lleida–Barcelona–French border AVE line, which began operating between Madrid and Lleida in 2003, and reached Tarragona at the end of 2006. The AVE began its commercial operations in December of 2007 from Madrid to Segovia-Valladolid, and to Málaga, in this last case from the Madrid–Seville line. Also from this line (in the Sagra) a branch had been opened earlier to Toledo. The AVE reached Barcelona in February of 2008, and almost the entire section up to the French border is under construction.

In December of 2010, the Madrid–Cuenca–València line entered into service, with a branch to Albacete. The planned pace of realizing new sections is intense, and Spain has now become the country in the world with the most operating kilometres of high-speed rail (> 250 km/h), after China. The goal expressed in February of 2007 by the president of the government Rodríguez Zapatero[28] has thus been fulfilled (with permission from the Asian giant). The fulfilment of President Aznar's wish, expressed in April

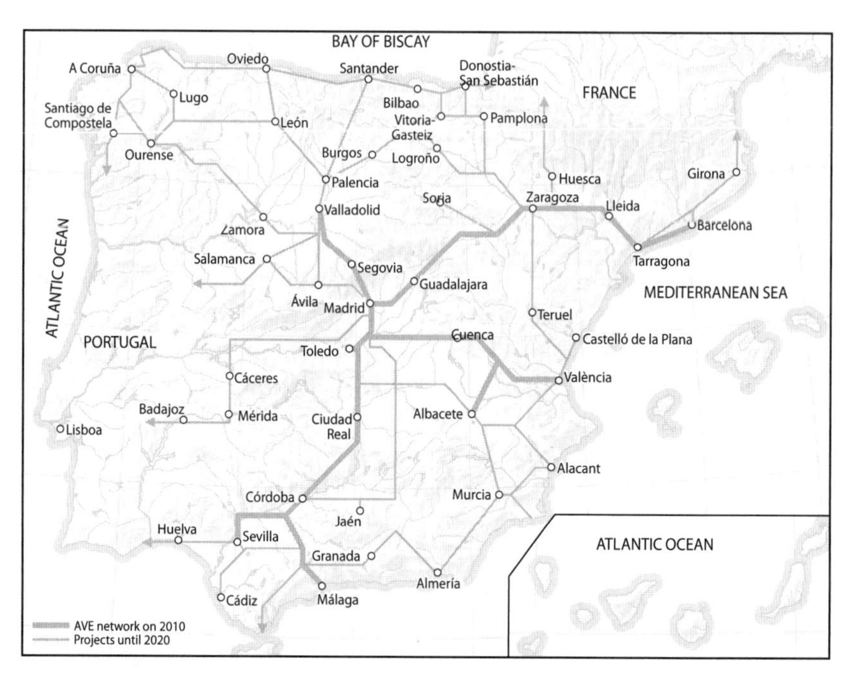

Map 5.1 AVE network in Spain in service in 2010 (bold lines) and planned actions up until 2020 (thin lines)

of 2000 to connect Madrid with all of the provincial capitals by 2010 will have to wait until 2020 (if budget cutbacks permit it). Map 5.1 shows the approximately 2,000 km in service at present (in bold lines), as well as the ones planned up to 2020 (the map includes high-speed routes at speed greater than 250 km).

It is important to highlight the fact that exclusive use for passenger travel will not be extended to all of the planned lines, given that in some cases high-performance lines, combining passengers and freight will be implanted, whose mixed character will moderately lower speeds. Nonetheless, it is difficult to predict at present what the final composition of the network will be between lines exclusively for passenger travel and mixed ones, given that this is the only significant aspect of transportation infrastructure policy over which no consensus exists between Spain's principal political parties, the PSOE and the PP. The government of the PSOE has planned for most of the routes to be built in the future to offer mixed passenger/freight services, just as the minister of Fomento, Magdalena Álvarez, had correctly argued in her appearances before the Congress to report on the PEIT.[29] But in keeping with their pronouncements in congress, the PP is in favour of the maximum speed (only possible on tracks exclusively for passenger travel) to join Madrid with each and every one of the peninsular provincial capitals. It is evident that Spaniards not living in provincial capitals are children of a lesser god. As for everything else, only the future can tell how the network will continue to evolve.

Impacts on Mobility

It is unquestionable that the AVE provides high levels of comfort and satisfaction to its users, who also avoid paying a large part of the costs thanks to subsidies that cover practically the entire cost of the infrastructure (something much harder to find in medium/long distance journeys in other modes of travel). Having noted the AVE's contribution to the comfort of its users, we shall now examine its overall impact. In this sense, the balance cannot be favourable.

In terms of its effectiveness as a transportation infrastructure, the first thing to say is that it has been very effective in dominating, when not establishing a hegemony over, the quota of passengers on the principal connections served by the AVE at competitive distances. Thus, according to the operating company, in 2009, the AVE achieved 85% of the Madrid–Seville market share, more than 70% of the Madrid–Málaga, and very near 50% of the Madrid–Barcelona, in detriment, above all, to air travel. Note how the share descends as the distances increase, from the 471 km of Madrid–Seville to the 621 km of the Madrid–Barcelona.

For distances above 600–700 km, the AVE's results are much more modest. In the case of Spain, routes exist between Barcelona and Seville and Málaga, which can be made non-stop after the bypass service in Madrid began functioning in 2009 (the radial character of the Spanish network makes it necessary to pass through the capital to travel between the north and the south of the peninsula, even though this means travelling greater distances). The bypass reduced the journey between Barcelona and the Andalusian capitals by some 50 minutes; Table 5.2 provides a picture of the offer in these relations almost a year after this improvement.

In effect, the AVE's market share in these distances is much more discreet. The reason for this is because the onboard time when travelling by the AVE is five hours and 30 minutes, while by plane it is one hour and 35 minutes. The total travel time (door to door) by the AVE is almost double the time by plane. Furthermore, the fact that the frequency of the AVE is only one unit (except at exceptional points) means it offers much less convenience than travelling by air, which offers a frequency of eight and nine trips to Málaga and Seville, respectively. What is more, and despite the subsidy

Table 5.2 Offer by the AVE and air service between Barcelona and Seville/Málaga. Daily seats (total in both directions) for 17 May 2010 and prices (for only one direction)

Trip	Seats AVE	Seats plain	Price AVE (minimum)	Price plain (minimum/ maximum)	Operating units
Barcelona–Málaga	632	2,640 to 2,880	83.30	29.00 // 69.44	AVE: 2 (1 round trip) Plain: 16 (8 round trips)
Barcelona–Seville	632	3,060 to 3,240	99.00	39.44 // 70.00	AVE: 2 (1 round trip) Plain: 18 (9 round trips)

Source: Author, based on information obtained from the web page of RENFE and several airlines, on 17 April 2010.

of the infrastructure, the price of an AVE ticket is substantially greater than that of an airplane ticket.

When analyzing the impact of the AVE on mobility, one must never forget that the convenience of a mode of travel depends crucially on not only the distance/time of the journey, but also the frequency of non-stop service. This last is generally a more important limitation for the passenger AVE than it is for air travel. This is why the most experienced European operator of high-speed rail, the French *Société National des Chemins de Fer* (SNCF), is much more sceptical than is usually the case in Spain about the possibilities of high-speed travel between Spain and France. Upon being asked in February of 2010, how many hours a trip between Madrid and Paris would take in 2012, Guillaume Pépy, president of the SNCF replied: "Madrid–Paris will be possible, but I don't think it will be a particularly interesting destination. It's a lot of kilometres against the plane, which doesn't make any stops! The big success will be Madrid–Montpellier, Barcelona–Perpignan, Barcelona–Marseille, Barcelona–Lyon . . . You can't think solely about the people travelling the entire trajectory."[30] The idea of connecting Spain with Europe by way of the AVE has always been, in Spain, a more romantic rather than practical approach to the effective service provided by each mode of transportation. The cost in time and the cost of the ticket impose important limitations.

Even so, we again point out that the traffic quotas of the AVE in connections such as the Madrid–Barcelona and those joining Madrid with the main capitals of Andalusia are impressive. However, when we transform quotas into volumes of traffic, the image that forms is dismal. In 2010, on all of the sections providing service, 16 million passengers were transported (some 20 million passengers are expected for 2011). Thus, with a high-speed rail network already more extensive than Japan's and France's, the AVE transported barely 6% of the number of passengers transported in

Japan, and less than 20% of those in France (and much less than a quarter of those transported in Germany by the ICE Express, whose network is much smaller). It so happens that those countries have greater population densities and an urban structure much more appropriate to passenger rail travel. And, even so, they have been more selective in prioritizing their lines and in the expansion of their networks. Spain, in contrast, has an urban structure much less fitting to railway transportation, but we have nonetheless become leaders in the offer of high-speed rail (with permission from China). Every bit a symbol of modernity, no doubt.

Economic Impact

In Spain, the public debate on the AVE has been mainly political and attention has not been paid to the social return on such an investment. This has happened because, apart from its political motivations, the AVE is considered a symbol of modernity and enjoys the support of its users, who, after all, pay low prices (relative to its real cost) thanks to large public subsidies.[31] But the cost-benefit analysis conducted on expected results for the Madrid–Seville line showed that this relationship could not be economically justified given its negative net benefits, and its relatively low traffic, despite its large market share on the corridor.[32] More recent cost-benefit analysis on the profitability of the Madrid–Barcelona line showed that even on this route the potential demand would not offset the large investment, and that time savings would be small in aggregate terms, even if a high share of traffic were captured.[33]

In effect, the policy of expanding high-speed rail has led to extraordinarily high spending costs. Table 5.3 presents some cost figures for the AVE

Table 5.3 Costs of construction of AVE lines most recently entered into service

Line	Full service	Km (1)	Construction cost (million nominal €) (2)	Construction cost (million 2010) (3)	Cost/km (million nominal) (2)/(1)	Cost/km (million 2010) (3)/(1)
Madrid–Seville	1992	471	2,704	4,626	5,7	9,8
Córdoba–Málaga	2007	155	2,672	2,825	17,3	18,2
Madrid–Valladolid	2007	184	4,429	4,621	24,1	25,4
Madrid–Barcelona	2008	621	9,018	9,934	14,5	16,0
Madrid–Valencia	2010	365	6,629	6,629	18,2	18,2

Note: Information not available for the section La Sagra-Toledo. The section Zaragoza-Huesca is not included because it lacks HSR technical characteristics.
Source: Based on table 2, in Daniel Albalate, and Germà Bel, "Cuando la economía no importa: Auge y esplendor de la alta velocidad en España", *Revista de Economía Aplicada* (2011), XIX (55), 171–190, p. 184.

lines that have entered into service in recent years, obtained from the website of the Ministerio de Fomento.

The almost 1,800 kilometres of lines in Table 3 have meant an investment of almost 30,00 million (current) euros. This investment almost double the spending made on airports over the entire decade of the 2000s (the following chapter will analyze airport policy in detail). Note that we don't include in these calculations the spending made in recent years on lines that have not yet entered into service. Nonetheless, all of the high-speed lines in service combined (including here also the La Sagra–Toledo and the high-speed Zaragoza–Huesca) transported 16 million passengers in 2009, while Spanish airports managed 193 million passengers and more than half a million tons of cargo in the same year. If we consider passenger-km figures, the difference becomes even clearer, because the average distance travelled by plane is much greater than that by AVE. These comparisons offer a clear idea of the limited total effectiveness of the AVE in Spain, much inferior to what has been obtained in countries like Japan, France and Germany due to the high traffic densities in their respective high-speed rail systems.

The social return of the AVE in Spain is negative, if we take into consideration its costs and benefits. Estimates by De Rus and Nombela, given earlier, indicate that a high-speed rail line of 500 km requires between eight and ten million passengers beginning in the first year to provide public benefits. But the Madrid–Barcelona line, running 621 km, transports around six million passengers. In all, the kilometres in service in Spain transported many fewer passengers than those necessary to generate public benefits. The fact that an important part of the spending on AVE lines has been co-financed with funds from the European Union doesn't constitute a real alleviation; such aid could have been spent on infrastructures with great social and economic benefits, such as freight railway networks or infrastructures for communications technology. The cost of not having sufficiently invested – not even close – in these types of infrastructures is a liability stemming from having conceded priority to passenger-only high-speed rail.

It is also very worrying that the AVE generates operating losses, as the European Commission has made clear by declaring illegal aid to cover the operating losses of its long distance services, which include high-speed rail. Such aid reached the figure of 248 million euros in 2007, and may have risen to 400 million euros in subsequent years.[34] The prospects for the future are even bleaker, given that lines will progressively come into service with ever lower traffic densities, inferior to the levels of lines already in service at the moment. Indeed, in February 2011 the Spanish government claimed that Renfe have obtained 2.5 million euro profits from AVE in 2010. However, this calculation implies neither infrastructure cost recovery nor full rolling stock cost recovery!

The facts have turned out to support the views of renowned analysts of the history of the railway system in Spain. Such as those by Uriol Salcedo, who already back in 1992 questioned, " What will the demand for high-speed lines be in Spain? We're afraid the subject hasn't been studied in depth and that the results won't be good, in terms of traffic and in terms of incomes and costs".[35] Or Gómez Mendoza, who more recently concluded in an article with a very expressive title ("*Del ferrocarril al AVE. ¿Los mismos errores históricos?*" "From the Railway to the AVE. The Same Historical Errors?"), that "in contrast to what occurred with the train in the second half of the 19th century, the benefits of high-speed rail are quite limited [. . .] the decision to assign enormous public resources to furnish high-quality resources to a minority of the Spanish society is one of dubious fairness".[36]

Territorial Impacts

Finally, an analysis should be made of the AVE's territorial impact. It has often been stated that cities serviced by the AVE have experimented significant population and housing growth. Ciudad Real is perhaps the most frequently cited example. Certainly, Ciudad Real has grown significantly since 1992, but is the AVE the factor behind such growth? To formulate a reply to this question, we can compare population growth and housing increase in Ciudad Real and the other city of Castilla-La Mancha with AVE service since 1992, Puertollano, with the rest of the capitals of Castilla-La Mancha. We shall also include the cases of Murcia and Cartagena for their relative similarities to Ciudad Real and Puertollano.

A very useful piece of information is obtained from an analysis of the evolution of the population and housing stock between 1991 (the year before the AVE entered into service) and 2001, the last year for which we have an official census. Furthermore, this interval of time is very appropriate because no significant improvement of infrastructures occurs in the cities we examine of Castilla-La Mancha distinct from Ciudad Real and Puertollano. As Table 5.4 shows, Ciudad Real experiences a relatively moderate population increase in respect to the group of cities that we are using as a control group (none of which had AVE service in 2001). The case of Puertollano is even more spectacular, given that it is the only city that lost population in the period analyzed. The city of Cordoba, which also received the AVE in 1992, is not included in the comparison because it is less comparable. At any rate, its

Table 5.4 Population growth and increase of housing stocks in Ciudad Real, Puertollano and comparable cities

	Population 1991	Population 2001	1991–2001	Housing 1991	Housing 2001	1991–2001
Ciudad Real	57,030	63,251	10.9%	21,664	28,799	32.9%
Puertollano	50,910	48,086	– 0.6%	19,118	22,669	18.6%
Albacete	130,023	148,934	14.5%	51,892	67,448	30.0%
Guadalajara	63,649	68,248	7.2%	23,958	29,825	24.5%
Cuenca	42,817	46,341	8.2%	18,647	23,902	28.2%
Toledo	59,802	68,382	14.3%	22,164	30,167	36.1%
Murcia	328,100	370,745	13.0%	119,437	148,850	24.6%
Cartagena	168,023	184,686	9.9%	84,916	102,045	10.2%

Source: Source: Census of 1991 and 2001. Nationals Statistics Institute (INE).

population growth between 1991 and 2001 was less than 2%. In the case of Seville, its population growth was even less: 0.2%.

In terms of housing stocks (Table 5.4), we find a very similar result. Despite being one of the cities to grow the most, Ciudad Real is surpassed by Toledo and equalled by Albacete. The case of Puertollano is even clearer: its housing stock only grows more than that of Cartagena. With respect to Ciudad Real, good reasons exist for thinking that an important part of the increase in its housing stock is due to the creation of a new university campus, much more than to the service offered by the AVE, in keeping with what the analysis of the population shows.

It seems more likely that the AVE can have a significant impact (still difficult to measure, given the brevity of time it has been operating) on the cases of Toledo and Segovia. The AVE in these two cities is functional for the daily trip to Madrid; the travel time and its monetary cost permit this. In this way, the AVE functions as a "luxury commuter train". Of course, it remains to be seen whether the effect will be to invigorate the smaller hubs of the network, or rather to suck activity into the largest hub, Madrid. Comparable experiences indicate that the second of these options occurs more frequently.

So, Why Will We Be the European Country with the Most Kilometres of High-Speed Rail?

The countries that have preceded us in the development of high-speed rail networks have given priority to questions such as the potential traffic demand of the lines to be modernized (related to the density of traffic on the corridor), the needs of freight traffic as a function of the railway system

. . . that is to say, to questions characteristic of transportation policy. The case of Spain, European leader in the number of high-speed rail kilometres, is different. The implantation and development of the AVE doesn't follow an approach based on its transportation function, which infrastructure policy decisions should take into account.

In an article published in *El País* on 6 October 2003 jointly with Carme Miralles-Guasch,[37] we stated that the development of the AVE seems to have been the result of a series of romantic fantasies by governments of every political stripe. The first line built, Madrid–Seville, responded to the desires of some leaders from a neglected region to equip their territory with an ultra-modern infrastructure as a symbol that the south, occasionally, "also exists". The first line petitioned, toward the French border, responded to the desire of some regional leaders eager for a faster connection to the heart of Europe. Nothing better for this purpose than to acquire some high-speed tracks with international track widths to perforate the borders. Now, the multitude of projects for AVE lines to every imaginable destination responds to the explicit desire by leaders, reaffirmed in their Spanish nationalism, to bring all of the provincial capitals within three hours reach by train to the national capital and, in this way, "bring about cohesion".

And we added, "At any rate, however, it isn't time yet, nor is it our aim to strike up a debate on the expansion of the AVE in Spain. The mirror effect has some unavoidable consequences in politics, and it is thus a fait accompli. Nonetheless, a fait accompli allows for reflection and learning. And another fait accompli is that we have sacrificed a great deal of resources and many priorities to the AVE, which the rest of the infrastructures have paid for, above all conventional ones and those that improve urban mobility [. . .] some day [the AVE] will be finished and the quantitative insignificance of spending on other surface transportation infrastructures will be obvious."

Unfortunately, this has turned out to be the case. Eight years later, the priority of the AVE continues to be a central element of Spanish politics. This has meant neglecting and leaving in the background other infrastructures that are much more important for the economy. Particularly, the freight railway, as much in terms of available lines as in the flagrant lack of railway connectivity between ports and logistical centres – to ensure the mobility and connection of goods entering by sea or air with the national and international markets. This is why during the "marvellous decade" of railway spending in Spain – that of the 2000s – the freight railway's market share declined from more than 7% to less than 4%. Bad news for social well-being, because such a decline has done nothing to reduce road traffic congestion and CO_2 emissions, and has moreover kept road traffic accidents from being further reduced.

Our diagnosis, however, was based on a mistaken premise. It is not a question of reflection and learning, as we thought. It is rather, in reality, a matter of the function granted to transportation infrastructures in Spain. The goal of the AVE's expansion, as was declared with crystal clarity in April of 2000 by José María Aznar, is to improve Madrid's connections with all of the peninsula's provincial capitals, regardless of the cost and independently of the real transportation function such a connection fulfils. And this continues to be the case. If we had known then that such a goal had already been established as a legal imperative by the General Railway Law of 1870 – to complete the course begun by the General Law of 1855 – we would have better understood the logic of this policy. A logic that is unique among the countries of our milieu. This is why we are the country with the most kilometres of high-speed rail in Europe. Even if their degree of use (measured, for example, by passengers per km of network) is precarious in respect to the pioneers – Japan and France – and to those that followed them. And regardless of the cost.

The AVE's development and its radial expansion will continue; they respond to a political logic cast in iron and an inevitable political dynamic.

The political logic consists in using the law and budget subsidies to make real that which the economic dynamic would in no way support on its own: the radialization of communications networks in Spain. This is why on 21 April 2010, the minister of Fomento officially announced the construction of a high-speed line between Ávila and Segovia (to connect it with that of Madrid), while there continues to be left behind the transformation of the section between Castellón and Tarragona into high-speed rail (which, by the way, I also don't think is a socially desirable investment). The goal of the AVE's expansion is to connect Madrid with all of the provincial capitals; and Tarragona is already connected with Madrid while plans are being made to connect Castellón in such a way as well. Goal achieved. What about the fact that the section between Castellón and Tarragona is intermediary between Barcelona and València, the second and third Spanish metropolitan areas, and that on some sections of this route only one track exists? If this causes surprise it is only because one has chosen not to listen to the already mentioned reason for the expansion of the AVE's network offered by the ex-president Aznar on 25 April 2000: "A high-speed railway network that, in ten years, will locate all of the provincial capitals at a distance of less than four hours from the centre of the peninsula". And this continues to be the case.

On the other hand, the political dynamic has satisfied what in Spain has been adopted as an indicator of inter-territorial equality in the realm of transportation infrastructures: to equally communicate all of the provincial capitals with the political capital. In fact, the two main justifications given by the minister of Fomento for the new Ávila–Segovia line is that it will reduce the travel time from Ávila to Madrid to less than 40 minutes, which "will contribute to the territorial cohesion of Castilla y León". Such a conception has nothing to envy of the Railway Law of 1870. Obviously this time it occurs in relation to the AVE, and this provides us with one of the most poignant images of contemporary Spanish politics: that of so many mayors and regional presidents requesting an infrastructure that will suck economic activity out of their cities/regions to the benefit of the network's largest hub, just as repeated analyses of the experiences of pioneering countries show.

In sum, the guideline for the development of high-speed rail in Spain has followed what has been the norm (generally) since the first half of the 18th century. And it is fully consistent with the pattern that has presided the establishing of priorities in the development of infrastructures ever since 23 April 1720, the date of the promulgation of the *Reglamento General para la Dirección y Gobierno de los Oficios de Correo Mayor y Postas de España en los viajes que se hicieren* ('General Regulation for the Management and Governing of the Postal and Stage Services of Spain, in Journeys Made'), mentioned in Chapter 2. That is to say, in the constituent act of the radial State.

6

The New Spain (II): Airport Management from Kilometre Zero

Aeropuertos Españoles y Navegación Aérea (AENA), attached to the Ministerio de Fomento, manages in a global way practically all of the airports that channel commercial air traffic within Spanish territory.[1] AENA is the owner of all of the facilities associated with the airports and jointly with the ministry plays a decisive role in key aspects such as decisions on fees spending, the assignation or coordination – as the case may be – of rights to land and take off (slots), and negotiations with airline companies.

Here too, Spain constitutes an exceptional case, because it is the only Western country with various cities and airports of a large size exclusively managed by a sole entity dependent on the central government. Only the case of Romania is similar, but the size of that country's air market is much smaller. This chapter will analyze this unique situation.

Airports play a fundamental role in the economic development of the territory they service, generating an important part of the wealth and providing connectivity with the rest of the world to their territorial area.[2] In recent decades, changes of great importance have occurred that have altered the traditional ways in which airports function. Among these changes, two are particularly notable: (1) the liberalization of air transportation within large economic regions, first in the United States, and somewhat later in Europe, and more recently the transcontinental agreements termed "open skies" between the USA and the EU, which have intensified the possibilities of competition between airlines and between airports; and (2) the introduction of new business models in the air transportation sector, particularly that of "low-cost" airline companies, which have radically altered the map of the offer and have forced important changes in the conventional companies which operate within networks. These transformations have encouraged a generalized process of reform in airport management throughout the world. Airports have ceased to be considered solely and exclusively as providers of a public service, with great importance now placed on their condition as economic entities that must interact in an agile way in such a changing environment.

This competitive environment throughout the chain of value of air transportation explains why in Europe, and in almost all developed countries, management is carried out on an individual level for each airport, with frequent pre-eminence given to territorial administrations as the responsible bodies for providing the service, and with different degrees of cooperation between the public and private sectors. Individualized management stimulates competition between airports to attract, according to the case, low-cost airlines, network airlines or both types. Furthermore, it facilitates transparency in the mechanisms of financing for loss-making airports. All of this leads to a greater efficiency in airport management.

Given the present model of airport management in Spain, no possibility exists for a differentiated commercial policy. Furthermore, a mechanism of a single fund is used for the assignation of the economic resources they generate. The single fund implies a system of cross-subsidies between airports, which is neither transparent nor efficient.

The persistence of the centralized and joint management model of airports in Spain, within an international context that has made this model obsolete, is explained by the possibilities its conservation offers to the political and civil servant authorities on a central level to define a specific role for each airport and in this way give a hierarchical order to Spanish urban areas and the relations between them. Instead of following criteria characteristic of transportation policy, airport management from kilometre zero makes it possible to use airports as an instrument of political power and territorial policy. In the 21st century, at a time when the management of infrastructures has acquired ever-greater importance, the centralized control of airports makes it possible to stimulate the radial character of air networks in Spain, and through this, their global connectivity.

The Emergence of Airports in Spain and the Development of the Management Model

The first Spanish aerodrome was installed in 1911 at Cuatro Vientos (Madrid). According to Gómez Mendoza,[3] "the close ties of the aeronautic industry with military demand and the preference of the military for Madrid as the base for their operations in this area explain why Madrid became an important hub in the Spanish air network". Later, this aerodrome was followed by the Barcelona-El Prat in 1918, and the Ingenio-Telde in Gran Canaria and Málaga, both in 1919. The aerodromes were licensed concessions in parallel with the concession for the operation of airlines.

During the dictatorship of Primo de Rivera the first specific regulation appeared for the organization of the functioning of the aerodromes, the *Reglas para la elección de terrenos destinados a aeródromos o aeropuertos y para su funcionamiento* ("Regulations for the choice of lands to be used as aerodromes or airports and for their functioning"), on 19 June 1926. A year later, on 19 July 1927, the Royal Decree Law of National Airports was passed which distinguished between aerodromes and airports. The latter were classified into three types: (1) airports in the service of the State, (2), in public service or of general interest, and (3) private ones.[4]

The construction and operation of airports of general interest were assumed by local councils or boards. The Juntas de Aeropuertos (Airport Councils) were supported by provincial and local administrations, which was "a good example of administrative and managerial decentralization".[5] A later regulation established that the Airport Council would make use of incomes generated to finance maintenance and work on the airport, with the goal of being self-financing. In sum, it was a model very near to what today is understood by individual management.

In 1930, the Junta Central de Aeropuertos (Central Council of Airports) was formed as a body that assumed all responsibility for the design and construction of airports as well as their operation. In a drift characterized by "a centralizing interest of the authorities over airports",[6] in early 1931 the government of Admiral Aznar suppressed the local councils of the airports of Madrid and Barcelona and moved their functions to the Junta Central de Aeropuertos.

During the Second Republic, the transfer of civil aviation services to the Generalitat of Catalonia was passed in 1933. Within the general context of instability of that period, authority for those services was recovered by the central government in October of 1934, and then once again returned to the Generalitat after the victory of the Frente Popular in the elections of 1936.

After the Civil War of 1936–1939, authority over airports passed to the Ministerio del Aire (Air Ministry) and in November of 1940, the *Ley de Régimen y Características de Aeródromos y Aeropuertos* ("Law of Organization and Characteristics of Aerodromes and Airports") was passed.[7] The law classified the airports into military, commercial and private ones, and all of these were under military jurisdiction. The Junta Central as well as the local councils of airports were suppressed, and the management of commercial airports was assumed by the Dirección General de la Aviación Civil (General

Management of Civil Aviation). In 1957, a reorganization was made of some aspects of airport organization. On the one hand, for the purpose of collecting fees, three categories of airports were established, which is still in effect today (although with changes in their composition). On the other hand, the Organismo Autónomo Aeropuertos Nacionales (Autonomous Body of National Airports) was created. This autonomous body is the distant predecessor of the present-day AENA, created in 1991 with the aim of offering greater flexibility and agility to public management.

The centralized and global model of airport management was adopted after World War II by the countries with communist dictatorships, where airports were under the control of military authorities. This was also the case with the two sole countries of continental Western Europe (Spain and Portugal) with centralized and global management, also subject to military control. Military control coincided also in the other continental case of a non-communist origin, that of Greece.[8] In essence, therefore, the management model we now have is the – modernized – heir of that organizational structure of Spanish airports.

Surrounding References: The Model of Airport Management in Surrounding Countries

In Europe, airports have traditionally been considered to be providers of a public service. This is why public ownership, with varying degrees of involvement by the respective territorial governments, has predominated until very recently. Nonetheless, the privatization processes applied in recent decades have also affected the airport policy of many countries. For this reason, different ownership structures are now apparent in airports around Europe and there has been a growth in the creation of the companies – public, private or mixed – that assume responsibility for airport management.[9]

In some countries, the central government still maintains ownership and control over the management of airports. In these cases, airports are often managed in a global, joint way, "as if" dealing with a "national network" (which doesn't in fact exist). Among the countries of the European Union, centralized and global management exists in Spain, Estonia, Finland, Lithuania, Portugal and Romania. All of these countries – with the sole exception of Spain – are characterized by having only one large airport and quite a small air market. For example, the total traffic of Finland is similar to that of the airport of Málaga and a good deal less than that of Palma de Mallorca, and Helsinki moves more than 90% of its traffic

Chart 6.1 Models of management (individual vs. centralized) in the European Union

Form of Management	Type of Market	Countries of the EU
Centralized and joint	Large	Spain
	Small	Estonia, Finland, Lithuania, Portugal, Romania.
Hybrid	Large	Ø
	Small	Sweden, Greece
In transition from joint to individualized management	Large	Ø
	Small	Poland
Individualized management	Large	Germany, France, Great Britain, Italy.
	Small	Austria, Belgium, Bulgaria, Cyprus, Denmark, Slovakia, Slovenia, Holland, Hungry, Ireland, Latvia, Luxemburg, Malta, Czech Republic.

Note 1: The "large" type market indicates around 100 million passengers or more per year. The country with the most passengers among countries with a "small market" is Holland, with less than 50 million per year.
Note 2: Outside the EU, in the case of Norway, management is centralized and joint. The rest of the Anglo-Saxon countries (USA, Canada, Australia and New Zealand) have individualized management, as does Switzerland.
Source: For European Union countries and others of the OECD, Germá Bel & Xavier Fageda, *Aeroports i Poder* (Barcelona: Edicions 62, 2007). Websites for the airports of countries of Central and Eastern Europe.

outside of the country. Thus, Spain is the only case in which airports with a significant volume of traffic are managed in a joint, global way, as shown in Chart 6.1.

Sweden has a mixed model with some of its airports subject to centralized and joint management, while another part (with less traffic) is managed individually. Curiously, among the latter is the Stockholm-Skavsta airport, the capital's second and the country's third in terms of traffic, managed by the TBI company, of which AENA is a partner. In Greece, Athens is managed in an individual way while the rest of the airports are managed in a centralized and joint fashion.

The rest of the European countries have individualized management models. This is the predominant trend in the larger-sized European countries: Great Britain, Germany, Italy and France. Individualized management is also predominant in many smaller countries: Austria, Belgium, Bulgaria, Cyprus, Denmark, Slovakia, Slovenia, Holland, Hungary, Ireland, Latvia, Malta and the Czech Republic. Each airport is managed by a public, private or mixed company. With the significant exception of the United Kingdom, the government usually remains the owner of the airports, meaning that privatization processes essentially involve the sale of the company that manages the facilities.

In sum, developed countries comparable to Spain in surface area, population and size of air market, have a management model of airports based on individual management, airport by airport, or of groups of airports in the same metropolitan area. The main characteristics of airport models in Germany, Great Britain, France and Italy are reviewed below.

Germany

Generally, the owners of the management companies of German airports have been local or regional governments, along with the federal government, in variable proportions. The federal government held a minority share and this depended on the type of airport and the state (*land*) where the facility was located. The primary motor driving the change in the structure of ownership of airport operators practiced since the early 1990s has been the divestments made by the federal government and on a much smaller scale, by regional and local governments. Such divestments have been made in a context of progressive deterioration of public finances. As a result of this process, the federal government now maintains only a very reduced share (and doesn't participate in management) of the airport operators of Berlin, Cologne/Bonn and Munich.

Furthermore, various airports have been privatized, generally in a partial way. The Fraport consortium, of which the state of Hesse and the city of Frankfurt are majority stakeholders, manages the airports of Frankfurt (the country's largest), Hannover and Saarbrücken. For its part, the Airport Partners GmbH consortium is a stakeholder in the airports of Hamburg, Monchengladbach and Düsseldorf. This last case – although not as well-known as Frankfurt and Munich – is interesting, given that it is Germany's third airport and 50% of the managing company belongs to the city of Düsseldorf.

Furthermore, the second terminal of the Munich airport (the second German airport, in which the regional government holds a majority stake and which is entirely public) has been built and managed by a mixed company made up by the airport management company itself (60%) and Lufthansa airlines (40%).[10] In sum, private investors have been capable of acquiring partial ownership and management of the three largest airports in Germany, and at the same time they have acquired relevant positions in other small airports nearby. Nonetheless, the corresponding local and regional governments are still the main – when not the sole – shareholders of the 19 commercial German airports (and also generally of the airports with less traffic).

The United Kingdom

Before the reforms made in the 1980s, territorial authorities formed the institutional foundation of the management system of British airports. The exception to this rule was the British Airports Authority, which depended on the central government and which had been created in 1965 to centralize the management of London's main international airports. After 1965, the Authority assumed responsibility for the management of the capital's three main airports (Heathrow, Gatwick and Stansted). In 1971, it acquired the three main Scottish airports (Aberdeen, Edinburgh and Glasgow).[11]

The White Paper of 1985 determined the need to expand the commercialization and privatization of airports in the United Kingdom, with the goal of increasing management efficiency and alleviating the burden that loss-making airports represented for the public sector. This position was consistent with general policy in the United Kingdom during the 1980s, which was strongly slanted in favour of privatization. In 1986, the British Airports Authority was dismantled and the BAA company was created, which was privatized in 1987. Furthermore, the corporatization (the transformation from bureaucratic management to public company) of the rest of the airports with significant volumes of traffic was undertaken.

With the exception of BAA, the owners of the new management companies of airports were local governments. Private investors were given the opportunity of becoming shareholders in airport authorities. In fact, since 1990, many airport authorities have been partially or totally sold to private investors. As a result, most of the operators are now private, although some exceptions endure, such as Manchester, East Midlands and some smaller airports.

One of the most important recent events in airport policy in the United Kingdom (and in Europe as a whole) has been the process of review and investigation (and the subsequent establishing of a packet of remedies) concerning conditions of competition between the airports of BAA – acquired by Ferrovial in 2006 – in the United Kingdom. At that moment, BAA owned and managed Heathrow, Gatwick, Stansted in London; Glasgow, Edinburgh and Aberdeen in Scotland; and Southampton, purchased in 1990. Furthermore, the state of competition between the airports of BAA was investigated. The review and investigation was carried out by the British authority on competition (the United Kingdom Competition Commission [UKCC]), which decided it was necessary to break up the BAA group because of the damages to users and airlines caused by a lack of competition. For this reason, it made BAA sell Gatwick and Stansted airports, and one of the two larger airports in Scotland (Edinburgh or Glasgow). Ferrovial sold Gatwick in 2009. After several unsuccessful appeals by BAA against that request, the Competition Commission has decided in July 2011 to speed up the sale by BAA of Stansted, and either Edinburgh or Glasgow.

Finally, it is opportune to point out that the problem of the survival of airports with little traffic is centred in airports located in remote zones of Scotland. In such cases, the central government offers a wide array of aid, ranging from current subsidies and capital, to obligations of public service on routes that guarantee direct air connections with the main English and Scottish cities. Furthermore, those small airports that continue to be owned by the local government receive subsidies from this level of government, if necessary.

France

The State played a fundamental role in establishing the airport sector in France. It was the owner of the grounds and also the creator of the facilities. Nonetheless, since the 1950s, a system of concessions was set up through which local chambers of commerce came to manage all of the commercial French airports except for those of Paris.[12] In the present day, the three commercial airports of Paris (Charles de Gaulle, Orly and Le Bourget) are managed by the company Aéroports de Paris (ADP). The principal owner of ADP is the French state, with 68.4% of the capital. The rest of the ownership is in the hands of minority private investors. The stock of ADP is traded on the Paris exchange.

In the 2000s, a new de-centralizing drive occurred in France. In addition to maintaining the system of local management, during a first stage of this reform the State transferred ownership of the most modest provincial airports (such as Corsica, Perpignan, Béziers, Carcassonne and Tarbes) to territorial organizations. In the last two years, the largest airports outside of Paris (such as Lyon, Toulouse or Bordeaux) have come to be managed as public limited companies, and different private investors have taken stakes in their management, partially replacing the chambers of commerce. The State maintains ownership of the facilities of medium-sized airports, and has granted concessions for 40 years to the operating companies.

The State has maintained an initial presence in the operating companies (without interfering in management) and has reduced its stake, similar to what the German federal government has done since the early 1990s. The end goal of airport policy is to eliminate the presence of the State in all of the regional and provincial airports.[13] A greater privatization of Aéroports de Paris is not out of the picture in the near future.

Italy

The property and ownership of airport facilities in Italy belong to the central government. However, management is provided by limited liability companies. These companies manage the different airports individually and through long-term concessions. Traditionally, the sole shareholders of the managing companies of airports were local and provincial governments. But since the mid-1990s, there has been a growing participation by the private sector in airport management. The financial difficulties that limit the activity of the regional and local governments are a plausible explanation for this trend.

In 1997, 70% of the operating company of the Naples airport was acquired by BAA. That same year, the privatization process of Aeroporti di Roma S.p.A (operator of Fiumicino and Ciampino) began, and was completed in 2000. The private group Gemina S.p.A. holds 95.8% of the company, while 3% belongs to different territorial bodies. There is also minority private participation in the airports of Turin, Venice and Florence. In general, local and regional governments, at times with some participation from private operators, are the owners of most of the airport management companies in Italy. This is the case, for example, with the system of Milan airports (Malpensa and Linate), whose managing body is essentially owned by municipal (84.6%) and provincial (14.5%) governments.

Finally, it is good to keep in mind that as much the central government as local and regional ones have played a very significant role in financing spending on enlarging the capacity of all types of airports, from the large international airports to ones with less traffic. The use of current subsidies for airports on behalf of the different levels of government has been more modest. Financial incentives to airlines encouraging them to operate on routes with low densities of traffic have also been limited.

Summary: Lessons from International Experience

The model of individual management of airports is the norm in all developed countries with large surface areas and populations and large air markets. It has been the traditional model in most cases, and in the early 1990s has been adopted by some countries, such as Australia and Canada, that had a centralized model similar to that of AENA.

In terms of the form of ownership of airport management, the cases of the United Kingdom, Germany, Italy and, incipiently, France, demonstrate that the same country can experiment with very different forms of ownership of airport operators. In essence, what really matters in respect to efficiency is competition, much more so than ownership *per se*.

Reforms toward individualization in the management of the airports are more closely associated with improving efficiency in the development of operations. In effect, airline companies push for greater efficiency in the provision of airport infrastructure. This pressure forces political authorities to offer an institutional framework that permits competition between airports. This is a key aspect behind enabling an airport to offer its customer, the airline, the best product, in terms of both prices and quality of service.

The discipline that individual management imposes on all airports can limit the size of the subsidies necessary to keep afloat the loss-making ones.[14] Furthermore, in an individual management model, the financing of loss-making airports can be dealt with in different ways. On the one hand, it can be done through specific subsidies to the airports. Such subsidies, whether capital or current, can come from the central government (Ireland), the regional government (Germany), local governments (Australia, the United Kingdom), or all levels of government (Italy). On the other hand, the financing of loss-making airports can also be carried out by way of a fund created using a part of the surplus generated by large airports, as the case of Canada illustrates. The subsidies can also be applied to the airline companies, as alternative ways of sustaining loss-making airports by guaranteeing a minimum level of traffic.[15] The cases of Ireland and the United Kingdom reveal the importance such support mechanisms can have to the companies.

At any rate, what is very clear is that it isn't necessary to have a centralized model such as the Spanish one to articulate mechanisms of financial support for airports with deficits and self-financing difficulties but which are deemed necessary to maintain in operation.

The Rhetoric of the Centralized Management Model in Spain: Solidarity and Efficiency

The traditional argument brandished to preserve the model of centralized management, with a sole fund, of airports in Spain has been the alleged solidarity it offers to the smallest airports, which makes it possible – it is said – to financially support airports that don't generate the necessary traffic to be self-sufficient, and thus ensure equality for all Spaniards. More recently, the supposed efficiency of this model has also been alleged.

In fact, the debate over the reform of the management of airports in Spain intensified in the early 2000s, as demonstrated by my articles "Aeropuertos: El diagnóstico" and "Aeropuertos: La alternativa" published in *El País* on 20 February and 1 March of 2002, respectively. In that context, on 4 June 2002, the minister of Fomento, Álvarez Cascos, declared that if the 12 most important airports were separated, the other 33 would cause losses to the State, "and somebody has to explain how they would be financed". Thus, he inferred, solidarity with the non-principal airports made it necessary to maintain the centralized system.

This line of reasoning in terms of solidarity with the smallest and equality among Spaniards is voiced repeatedly by those members of the Partido Popular responsible for infrastructures, who are in the opposition by Autumn 2011. For example, in December of 2008, Andrés Ayala, spokesman for the PP in the Comisión de Fomento (Public Works Commission) of the national congress, emphasized that one of the fundamental principles of his party's policy was "the principle of equality and solidarity with all Spaniards and territories of Spain. Madame minister: AENA and the functioning of our airport model must have a global view of the public interest and not a territorial one. Thus, it is essential to maintain that principle of equality and solidarity as an element of the model of AENA . . . We don't want, Madame Minister, and we would like to emphasize this – the principles of solidarity and equality for all Spaniards in the treatment of this public service which is air transportation to be broken."[16]

The response by the minister of Fomento, Magdalena Álvarez, to the PP spokesman's request was unconditional: "And here, we have achieved and made a virtue out of the territorial solidarity of the airports and– indeed, Mister Ayala, I am in complete agreement with you in that the good functioning of AENA is attributable to both the socialist governments and to the governments of the Partido Popular";[17] this response satisfied the PP spokesman: "Madame minister, the PP parliamentary group is going to maintain its position. Your position is also similar, very similar to the program of the Partido Popular, which is neither a good nor bad thing, we simply have coincided".[18]

In a more recent parliamentary debate, on 12 January 2010, Rafael Simancas, spokesman for the socialist group in the Comisión de Fomento, alluded to the need of "ensuring that any decentralizing dynamic is fully compatible with the fulfilment of our obligations to guarantee the survival and viability of economically dependent airports and of carrying out the constitutional resolve of maintaining the solidarity, cohesion and equality of all Spaniards in terms of mobility and connectivity in all territories of Spain."[19]

Simancas furthermore requested the minister of Fomento, José Blanco, "to not hesitate in the least in maintaining, exactly as the minister has planned, the network model of our airports, because it ensures an efficient system, guarantees full connectivity for all citizens, wherever they may live, and fulfils the principles of solidarity, cohesion and equality among all Spaniards".[20]

As occurred with the previous minister in late 2008, the positions expressed by the minister also merited the adhesion of the PP's spokesman, Andrés Ayala: "Mister Blanco: competition, sustainability, efficiency, maintaining state ownership, sensitivity toward the reinforced public service necessary with the islands and with Ceuta and Melilla, solidarity and equality and network functioning [. . .] These are the principles deduced from your intervention and which have been clearly stated by this spokesman and thus, the Partido Popular, which has already maintained these principles, Minister, is going to support this model".[21]

There is no question that solidarity – traditionally – and efficiency more recently are the reoccurring arguments that uphold the persistence of the centralized management model. Are these arguments supported by reality?

The Reality of the Centralized Management Model in Spain: Lack of Solidarity and Inefficiency

For a long time, from the end of the 1990s until January of 2010, the central government didn't make public the operating financial information on an airport-by-airport basis, with the excuse that this information didn't exist (?), despite the fact that it had been regularly supplied up until 1998.

During that period, the only disaggregated economic information available on an airport level was the spending made on a regional level, given the legal obligation that exists to make such information public once it has been passed by the Cortes Generales. The latest published figures correspond to 2008, and Table 6.1 shows the volume of spending on airports in each region for the period 1985–2008, in constant value (euros of 2008), in column (1). It must be noted that this period is substantially longer than a complete spending cycle, and thus the results are not distorted by specific spending. The percentage that each airport region absorbs from the total is also included, in column (2), as well as the percentage of the total number of passengers administered by each airport region during the period, in column (3).

The figures of the table show that:

Table 6.1 Regional distribution of spending on airports by the central government, and percentages of spending and of the total number of passengers. 1985–2008

Region	(1) Total investment 85–08 Millions euro 2008	(2) % Investment 85-08	(3) % Passengers 85-08
Madrid	10,109.2	44.5%	22.2%
Catalonia	4,579.8	20.2%	15.3%
Andalusia	2,135.1	9.4%	10.0%
Canary Islands	2,082.3	9.2%	20.7%
Balearic Islands	1,467.8	6.5%	18.3%
Valencia C.	768.4	3.4%	6.3%
País Vasco	411.4	1.8%	2.1%
Galicia	408.0	1.8%	1.9%
Castilla y León	209.1	0.9%	0.2%
Aragón	173.0	0.8%	0.2%
Asturias	95.4	0.4%	0.6%
Murcia	82.6	0.4%	0.4%
Melilla	82.5	0.4%	0.2%
Cantabria	56.9	0.3%	0.2%
Navarra	55.1	0.2%	0.2%
Extremadura	5.6	0.0%	0.0%
Total	22,722.2		

Note: The regions of Castilla-La Mancha and La Rioja are not included because the airports of Albacete and Logroño were not in service during most of the period. Their share of both the spending and passenger traffic is quite small.
Source: Devised by the author from spending figures from the Ministerio de Fomento; traffic figures from the Ministerio de Fomento and AENA.

- The spending on airports reflects a very strong concentration in the region of Madrid (almost exclusively in Madrid-Barajas); the region's portion of the total spending (44.5%) is double the percentage of passengers it administers (22.2%). It is opportune to point out that these calculations probably underestimate the concentration of the spending in Madrid. In keeping with the economic figures on an airport level supplied by the government on 12 January 2010,[22] the debt attributable to the airports of Madrid was 6,212 million euros at the end of 2009, a figure that represented 54.4% of the total debt of the airports of AENA.
- The next region with the most spending is Catalonia (above all, Barcelona-El Prat); its share of the spending is 20%, somewhat

greater than its share of passenger traffic. The debt attributable to the Catalan airports of AENA is 2,035.2 million euros, a sum that represents 17.8% of the total debt, just slightly above its share of passengers.

- In Andalusia, the share of spending and the share of passengers are in balance. In the island regions, the share of spending is much lower than the share of passengers.
- Among the regions with medium traffic, the Valèncian Community and the Basque Country present spending below their share of passengers, while the situation is more balanced in Galicia.
- Lastly, among the regions with low traffic, the results are varied: Castilla y León, Aragon and Murcia appear as relatively favoured in terms of spending, while Asturias has a spending deficit. The situation is relatively balanced in the rest of the regions with low traffic.

Is it reasonable that Madrid – the richest region in Spain – concentrates a share of spending that is double its share of traffic? The subject can be viewed from different angles. But, however one looks at it, it is impossible to sustain that a criteria of inter-territorial solidarity has presided over the spending on airports in Spain. In fact, upon analyzing the regional distribution of spending on airports with robust empirical techniques, one finds that this distribution has a positive systematic association with the per capita GDP and the traffic at the airport, which is exactly the opposite what a principle of inter-territorial solidarity would demand.[23] Furthermore, one also finds a positive systematic relation between spending and shared political identity between central and regional governments. Not at all surprising.

The economic figures on an airport level provided by the government on 12 January 2010 make it possible to delve deeper into the subject of

Chart 6.2 Glossary of terms related to the economic accounts of airports

Term	Meaning
Unit Load (WLU)	Basic unit of traffic volume. A passenger is equivalent to 100 kg of load. Thus, the total number of unit loads is derived from adding the "number of passengers" + kg of freight/100
Gross Operating Profit	The operating results of each airport. The gross profit indicates the economic efficiency of airport management, given that it takes into account the management of the facilities as well as investment decisions.
EBITDA	Earnings before interest, taxes, depreciation and amortization. This is the operating result, without taking into account investment, its financing and amortization. The EBITDA indicates the technical efficiency of airport management, given that it doesn't take into account investment decisions and their consequences.
Attributable Debt	Debt that corresponds to each airport out of the total debt.

solidarity, by way of the information supplied in Table 6.2. Before discussing these figures, Chart 6.2 summarizes the meaning of the main terms and indicators, in order to thus provide a more agile analysis.

Table 6.2 Economic figures for airports managed by AENA

AIRPORT	(1) Passengers 2009	(2) Unit loads WLU	(3) Gross operational profit (GOP) (Million Euro)	(4) Ratio GOP/WLU (Euro)	(5) EBITDA (Million Euro)	(6) Ratio EBITDA/WLU (Euro)	(7) Attributable debt (Million Euro)	(8) % Total debt
Madrid Barajas	48,270,581	51,298,577	–300.9	–5.9	138.9	2.7	6,097.0	53.4%
Barcelona	27,311,765	28,209,893	–42.0	–1.5	96.6	3.4	1,813.8	15.9%
Palma Mallorca	21,203,028	21,373,889	37.8	1.8	62.5	2.9	0.0	0.0%
Málaga	11,622,443	11,656,453	12.8	1.1	51.0	4.4	572.8	5.0%
Gran Canaria	9,155,670	9,415,598	6.5	0.7	14.7	1.6	0.0	0.0%
Alacant	9,139,607	9,171,604	43.5	4.7	46.7	5.1	0.0	0.0%
Tenerife Sur	7,108,073	7,161,785	13.9	1.9	20.1	2.8	0.0	0.0%
Girona	5,286,975	5,287,688	18.0	3.4	24.5	4.6	51.0	0.4%
València	4,748,981	4,846,993	–1.2	–0.2	14.0	2.9	127.2	1.1%
Lanzarote	4,701,480	4,742,948	–0.9	–0.2	9.1	1.9	0.0	0.0%
Eivissa	4,572,814	4,604,191	4.0	0.9	11.2	2.4	0.0	0.0%
Tenerife Norte	4,054,147	4,237,197	–5.6	–1.3	5.1	1.2	94.5	0.8%
Sevilla	4,051,268	4,101,079	–2.3	–0.6	5.5	1.3	0.0	0.0%
Fuerteventura	3,738,492	3,757,625	–2.3	–0.6	10.1	2.7	128.5	1.1%
Bilbao	3,654,951	3,681,866	0.1	0.0	15.1	4.1	174.3	1.5%
Menorca	2,433,672	2,459,886	–14.2	–5.8	–1.4	–0.6	135.6	1.2%
Santiago	1,943,900	1,963,786	–10.2	–5.2	–1.3	–0.7	96.5	0.8%
Reus	1,706,609	1,706,705	–7.1	–4.1	–0.5	–0.3	97.3	0.9%
S. Javier-Murcia	1,630,521	1,630,607	1.5	0.9	7.1	4.3	73.6	0.6%
Asturias	1,316,088	1,317,219	–4.2	–3.2	0.8	0.6	68.2	0.6%
Granada-Jaén	1,187,736	1,188,148	–6.6	–5.6	–1.3	–1.1	75.4	0.7%
Vigo	1,103,291	1,111,258	–6.9	–6.2	–1.6	–1.5	65.7	0.6%
Jerez	1,079,787	1,080,763	–12.2	–11.3	–6.7	–6.2	81.0	0.7%
A Coruña	1,068,823	1,071,220	–4.4	–4.1	0.5	0.4	72.9	0.6%
La Palma	1,042,969	1,053,807	–12.9	–12.3	–4.9	–4.7	187.1	1.6%
Santander	958,157	958,268	–4.7	–4.9	0.1	0.1	83.9	0.7%
Zaragoza	528,313	897,676	–8.7	–9.6	–1.5	–1.6	139.5	1.2%
Almería	791,830	791,992	–7.5	–9.4	–1.6	–2.1	80.0	0.7%
Valladolid	365,683	366,435	–4.9	–13.3	–1.4	–3.7	55.8	0.5%
Pamplona	335,590	336,036	–6.4	–19.2	–3.2	–9.4	78.0	0.7%
San Sebastián	314,262	314,573	–6.8	–21.5	–4.3	–13.5	52.7	0.5%
Vitoria	39,933	313,813	–16.5	–52.6	–10.5	–33.6	92.3	0.8%
Melilla	293,692	297,198	–10.9	–36.6	–5.5	–18.4	105.3	0.9%
El Hierro	183,470	185,010	–5.9	–31.6	–3.6	–19.5	51.3	0.4%
León	94,282	94,319	–6.9	–73.5	–1.6	–17.1	86.7	0.8%
Badajoz	75,353	75,353	–1.1	–14.6	–0.3	–4.1	19.6	0.2%
Salamanca	53,088	53,088	–2.8	–53.5	–1.3	–24.7	31.1	0.3%
La Rioja	35,664	35,664	–6.2	–173.8	–3.6	–102.1	49.0	0.4%
La Gomera	34,609	34,715	–5.1	–147.8	–2.9	–83.8	33.5	0.3%
Burgos	27,710	27,710	–5.3	–191.3	–1.9	–68.6	59.9	0.5%
Torrejón	26,650	26,652	–3.0	–113.7	–2.0	–73.2	36.5	0.3%
Ceuta	20,566	20,576	–2.1	–103.5	–1.4	–67.6	16.9	0.1%
Córdoba	15,459	15,459	–3.9	–252.3	–1.9	–121.0	68.8	0.6%
Albacete	15,262	15,262	–2.9	–191.3	–1.6	–105.5	24.1	0.2%
Huesca-Pirineos	6,341	6,341	–6.2	–977.8	–2.1	–326.4	67.7	0.6%
Cuatro Vientos	229	229	–9.3	–40.480.3	–6.4	–27.947.6	78.5	0.7%
Sabadell	0	0	–7.9	∞	–4.9	∞	73.1	0.6%
Son Bonet	0	0	–2.4	∞	–1.7	∞	16.1	0.1%
Total	187,349,814	192,997,155	–433.0	–2.2	450.8	2.4	11,412.6	100.0%

Source: Information provided by the Ministerio de Fomento to parliamentary groups and the press at the Comisión de Fomento (Public Works Commission) of the national congress, 12 January 2010. For passengers and WLU, the AENA website.

We can now address questions related to solidarity and the efficiency of the model.

1 Is the spending (reflected in the attributable debt) distributed in a balanced way?

This question has been addressed above with spending and passenger figures for the period 1985–2008. In looking now at the attributable debt, one notes that the concentration in the airports of Madrid (Barajas, Torrejón and Cuatro Vientos) is 54.4%, even greater than what was found in the historical analysis of spending (column 8 of Table 2). The forecast for 31 December 2010, also provided, indicates that Madrid will concentrate by that date 51.9% of the debt. Nonetheless, its share of passenger traffic in 2009 was 25.8%.

In the case of the airports of Catalonia (Barcelona, Girona, Reus and Sabadell), the situation is much more balanced. The debt was 17.8% of the total in 2009 (column 8 of Table 6.2), and it was forecast to be 18.1% in 2010, while its share of traffic in 2009 was somewhat greater, 18.3%.

Basically, this is practically the entire history of the debt of AENA, given that only the airport of Málaga (5% of the total debt) in Andalusia (7.7%) adds anything worth mentioning.

In sum, the total investment of AENA reflects an exorbitant concentration in the airport of the political capital, whose share of the spending is more than double its share of traffic. At the other extreme, the large, highly tourist-oriented airports and the medium ones have received investment far below their volume of traffic, although all of them are in zones relatively poorer than the capital. Solidarity and equality?

2 Do the large and profitable airports subsidize the deficits of smaller and loss-making airports?

The premise contains an error noted previously by other studies, even if without detailed figures:[24] the largest Spanish airports don't run a surplus, but rather a deficit.

The figures from column 3 show the deficit for each airport, and adding up the figures for all of the airports with deficits (37, plus the heliport of Ceuta), one gets a total sum of 570 million euros. In turn, the nine airports with surpluses have a total profit of 137 million euros. Overall, AENA has an operating deficit of 433 million euros.[25]

The Madrid-Barajas airport, the largest in Spain, ran a 301 million euro deficit in 2009, a figure that represents 53% of the gross operating losses of all the loss-making airports! At a great distance from Madrid-Barajas, the airport with the second-largest deficit is Barcelona-El Prat, with a loss of 42 million (7% of the total deficits).

But, how much in the red were airports with commercial traffic[26] managing less than a million unit loads (WLU) per year? This figure is important, given that in keeping with studies by the European Commission, airports with more than a million unit loads tend to be self-sufficient (depreciation included) and "those that are not, are either offering large discounts in their aeronautic fees, or else have fundamental problems of efficiency in their management".[27] Well then, the airports of AENA with commercial service and traffic lower than a million WLU had a total deficit of 118 million euros, that is, 20% of the total deficit, and 39% of that of Madrid-Barajas.

In Spain, the largest airports are not profitable and do not finance the smaller ones. The airports that finance the others are the large tourist ones and some medium ones. And the ones that enjoy solidarity are, above all, the airport of Madrid-Barajas and, to a much smaller extent, that of Barcelona-El Prat.

The Spanish airport model lacks solidarity and, furthermore, is very inefficient from the economic point of view. This is why AENA loses the most money at its business among all of the world's airport operators.[28] To justify this situation, blame is placed on the large amount of investment realized; if one ignores the spending, they say, then the organization is profitable. Well, since the 1960s, the proposition has been established in economic analysis that in areas of public service, public companies have incentives to over-invest (while the contrary is true for private ones). And the over-investment realized by AENA has been very exaggerated. It is difficult to find anywhere in the world examples of airport expansion with a relative (and absolute) cost as high as that recently realized in Madrid-Barajas and Barcelona-El Prat. Perhaps, those realized in Dubai and Beijing.

Now, having shown that AENA suffers from economic inefficiency, we shall move beyond investment and evaluate its technical efficiency. Columns 5 & 6 of Table 6.1 will help us in this endeavour.

3 Do airports earn what they should with operating profits?

As an exercise, we can overlook for a moment the investment on each airport, as well as the corresponding costs of amortization and financial costs involved. Although this doesn't make much sense in strict economic terms, it permits debating the argument that investment explains the anomaly of the deficit in the larger airports. Column 5 shows us the earnings before interests, taxes, depreciation and amortization (EBITDA), and its figures indicate that 19 airports achieved operating profits. Another two had almost balanced results. The information shows that Madrid-Barajas had the largest operating profit, with 139 million euros, followed by Barcelona-El Prat, with 97 million euros.

Nonetheless, column 6 offers us a much more precise indicator of technical efficiency: the EBITDA per unit load, or unit operation earnings. A priori, the earnings of airports must grow as their traffic increases, given the existence of economies of scale in their operation. For this reason, with appropriate technical management, airports with a large volume of traffic should have larger unit earnings. But this isn't the case in Spain. At least nine airports have an EBITDA unit larger than Madrid-Barajas, and five have an EBITDA unit larger than Barelona-El Prat.

The situation becomes even clearer if we eliminate the comparison with the island airports, given that in all of these there is a discount on the fees paid for domestic (within Spain) and inter-island flights, which artificially lowers their incomes from fees. If we look only at the non-island airports with operating profits, only the airports of Seville, Santander, A Coruña and Asturias present an EBITDA unit lower than that of Madrid-Barajas. In the case of the last three of these, it is necessary to keep in mind an important fact: due to their relatively low volume of traffic, less than 1.5 million unit loads, they operate well below the optimum scale level. For this reason, it is normal for their unit earnings to be low.

Technical efficiency in the management of AENA airports is manifestly improvable. This has been analyzed using other figures relative to the overall efficiency of AENA,[29] and by other studies, such as one by Martín, Román and Voltes-Dorta,[30] who examine in detail the efficiency of Spanish airports for earlier years – until the end of the 1990s – and find that Spanish airports function with an inefficiency of between 15% and 26%.

Some of the reasons for this inefficiency in the management of airports are closely tied to the management model in Spain. For example, the three airports with the most traffic apply the same fees, although the cost of operation is different for each of them. Because of their type of facilities and traffic, airports such as Madrid-Barajas and Barcelona-El Prat have higher unit costs than others such as Málaga, Alacant, Palma de Mallorca, Bilbao and València. This generates inefficiencies in the system as a whole, and cross-subsidies from these latter airports to those of Barcelona and, above all, Madrid. Although some upward differentiation of fees in Madrid and Barcelona has been introduced in 2011, there is still a long way to go on that direction. Of course, the practice of applying unit fees without direct relation to costs is not something that occurs in other comparable countries, where fees reflect the costs of the airports, except when these airports are so small as to not be self-sufficient.

As has been mentioned, in all countries subsidies are applied to the smallest airports when they play a role of guaranteeing mobility. That said, it is also appropriate to ask if it makes sense to have made large investment in recent years to realize commercial operations in airports in zones with little local demand and which are serviced by motorways and occasionally also by high-speed rail. This is the case of airports such as those of Córdoba, Huesca-Pirineos, Albacete and Burgos (also those of Ciudad Real, Lleida-Alguaire, or Castelló, promoted by territorial governments). Commercial traffic at these airports is tiny and, in contrast to airports located on smaller islands, doesn't constitute an obligatory mode of mobility. Nonetheless, these airports subject the system to important deficits and have generated important volumes of debt. Unquestionably, the policy of expanding commercial airports in Spain would have benefited from the existence of an individual management model, in which questions relating to the obligation of public service at smaller airports would be scrutinized with a greater sense of reality (in terms of transportation).

Why Do They Call It Solidarity, Equality and Efficiency, When It Is Merely Political Control?

As has occurred with other types of transportation infrastructure in Spain, concepts such as solidarity, equality and (much more recently) efficiency are the key words used to justify the persistence of a management model of airports that is unique among the countries of our vicinity, a model whose roots lie in the periods of military control over airport facilities, which guaranteed centralized control over air traffic.

Airports play an important role in the modern connectivity of metropolitan areas and urban areas of a certain demographic and economic size. As with other activities, cities compete for economic activity. This competition occurs between cities in the same country, between cities in the same economic region (such as the European Union) and also in the global space. And the management of airports is one of the instruments for applying individual strategies and developing the potential of the territory served by the airport. What is important, therefore, is not which government can manage the airports, but whether or not these function in a monopoly system.

The centralized management model in Spain permits the central government to control management of the airports and particularly decisions related to spending, fees and commercial policy. Especially notable in terms of this last area is the assigning of time slots for the operation of airplanes and commercial relations with the different airlines. And this situation will not be substantially modified for the purposes of the Government to privatize 49 percent of AENA, and to concession to private management commercial and terminal services in Madrid-Barajas and Barcelona-El Prat. Retaining centralized control over those elements makes it possible to define the mission for each one of the airports within the system, and establish a hierarchy between them. This has nothing to do with solidarity or equality. It is furthermore inefficient, because it suffers from all of the defects of a monopoly in sectors where this is not economically justified.

But airport policy in Spain, like other infrastructure policies, doesn't correspond to criteria related to transportation policy, but rather to political criteria of territorial organization. This is why reforming management models to adapt them to what is normal is an impossible mission. Not because it cannot be done, but because it isn't desired.

Epilogue: And Now, A Spain Like France?

Our journey has arrived at port. It began on the postal stage routes of Philip V, who on 23 April 1720 changed (literally) the map of Spain by designating six routes as "royal roads"; the six radial routes that have since that time structured Spain. Ferdinand VI attempted to modernize them as roads and upon encountering reluctance from the municipalities to finance the king's roads, arranged through the Royal Decree of 1747 for the possibility of financing them by way of the royal treasury. His successor, Charles III, decisively applied this policy and through the Decree of 1761 collected general budgets to finance the six royal and preferential roads, and "delegated" the financing of the rest of the roads to those who had interest in them.

The demand caused by commercial traffic played a more important role in the development of railways in Spain in the mid-19th century, which began with a series of trajectories financed by interested parties. Of course, there were notable exceptions, such as the projects promoted by the Marquis of Salamanca, who was able to apply a special financial magic to attract, like a magnet, financial aid from the State. Worries over the railway isolation that threatened Madrid was one of the main factors leading to the promulgation of a general legislation, contained in the General Law of 1855. In essence, this law established the preferential character of six radial lines designed to connect Madrid with various ports and international borders of the peninsula. These lines absorbed the lion's share of the enormous amount of public resources assigned as subsidies for the construction of the railway. Shortly afterwards, in 1870, new legislation extended Madrid's connections to all of the provincial capitals, at public expense if necessary.

The policies of transportation infrastructures and services set in motion in the 18th and 19th centuries show how legal regulations and funds from the national budget were used to organize political power and satisfy the needs of the Crown and its capital. This was done independently of the priorities of the economic system and the needs of connection between centres of economic production. The latter were systematically left out of the established priorities, and neglected in the assignation of national budgetary resources, if they received them at all. Transversal market, radial State.

Administrative and political goals were always given higher priority, while transportation efficiency and its contribution to economic productivity were relegated. This was the standard pattern in the development of transportation infrastructures in Spain over the course of recent centuries. And this pattern has continued to function in the infrastructure policies applied in the last fifty years, as demonstrated by the analysis of the construction and expansion of motorways, the development of high-speed rail, and airport policy. All of this has provided a hard to surpass contribution to the practical realization of the political project that has been in effect since the early 18th century: to make a Spain like France, with a Madrid like Paris.

Indeed, this succession of policies has closely accompanied the transformation of Madrid's status. Political capital status, achieved in the early 18th century, has been completed by the status of economic capital gained in the last two decades. The result is the conversion – at last – of Madrid into the Paris of Spain. A transformation that satisfies the vast majority of the political and economic elites, and the population of Spain. At the end of the day, the desire to emulate France has enjoyed very wide acceptation from the very moment in which it was formulated.

Furthermore, the role of Madrid as capital has reinforced its legitimatization in recent decades among a broad cross-section of the Spanish population. The process of regional autonomy begun after the democratic transition has increased the perception of inter-territorial differentiation and the perception of the existence of inequalities. Although, in reality, never before in contemporary Spain has a greater real inter-territorial equality existed in the provision of basic public services. For example, concerning a service as basic and essential to social and community welfare as the Public Health System, intra-autonomous region inequalities are at present more worrying than inter-territorial inequalities, which are moderate in comparison to those found in surrounding countries.[1] Nonetheless, perhaps because in Spain inequality between territories is of much greater concern than inequality between people, the process of regional autonomy has sparked great anxiety, and for many Spaniards the national capital has become instituted as the anchor of homogeneity and equality between territories.

Also for this reason, Madrid's status as absolute (political and economic) capital is an irreversible phenomenon. And with this, its function as the Paris of Spain. As José Luis García Delgado has said, "Madrid can fulfil an authentic *structuring* function of Spanish territory, economically and geographically, institutionally and culturally".[2] However, it's not as if Paris and Madrid are exactly the same. For example, the airports of Lyon, Toulouse or Bordeaux are NOT controlled from Paris, the goal of the French government is NOT to connect Paris with all of the departmental capitals by way of the TGV (which is why France doesn't need as many kilometres of high-speed rail as Spain), and tolls on motorways are as present in the radial communications of Paris as they are in the rest of the country. Although, of course, it is necessary to understand that Paris has "always" been Paris.

Madrid's access to the status of absolute capital has eliminated one of the age-old tensions of Spanish territorial policy: the contradiction between political power and economic power. But Spain is not yet like France. In this sense, in recent years there has been a perceptible recuperation of the project to build a country like France. In the moments following drastic changes in political life in Spain, as was the case with the Second Republic, the "French" project was put on hold, placed on stand-by. The same occurred during the Transition and the first years of democracy, after the end of the Franco regime. Now the waters have returned to their course: the project has recovered its original direction.

Some of the emerging problems on Spain's political agenda clearly illustrate this. Notable among these are market unity and the recovery of State authority over education.

I dealt with the issue of market unity in my articles "Spain, Capital Paris" and "Market Unity or National Unity?", published in *La Vanguardia* on 24 April and 4 June of 2009, respectively. In particular, in the second of these, I explained how in the United States – which is probably the world's most unified large market – many tax and regulatory specificities exist between the different states and nobody feels that this threatens market unity. And what risk is there to market unity within a region of the European Union? Although, I added, "of course it would be quite ingenuous to think that the problem is merely one of lack of information. The obsession with market unity is a symptom (only one among many) of something deeper: the growing perception in Spain that decentralization has reached a 'limit' it should never have reached, because it threatens National Unity. Rectification is in the air and that is where we're heading. Would it be too much to ask to not use the term market unity when in reality what is meant is National Unity? At least this way we would understand each other better."

The fact that an intelligent person would say something stupid such as that market unity is threatened in Spain doesn't belie their intelligence (unless they end up believing the stupidity after repeating it too often). Rather, it indicates that they want to say something else. In this case, that Spain's drifting has ended, and that the time has once again come to reach cruising speed toward the goal of unity.

Something similar is present in the growing debate over recovering State authority of education. The proposals in this direction, far from being concerned with the quality of the educational system and the welfare and cohesion of the Spaniards of the future, are morbidly obsessed with "re-directing" the linguistic and cultural particularities that are expressed in the educational systems. After all, language and culture constitute mirrors in which difference is reflected, and difference unsettles, distorts homogeneity. How difficult it is to live in a complex world!

Matters such as these are going to mark the agenda of territorial policy in the Spain of the future, and it seems plausible to me that they will lead to changes in direction that the majority (or, at any rate, a sufficiently decided part) of Spanish society desires. The result could end up being a country like France, which will probably no longer resemble the Spain we have known. Would this be what was anticipated by the reflection of a Spanish thinker – so often quoted and so little read – known as José Ortega y Gasset?:

> "For me there's no doubt about this: when a society falls victim to particularism, it can always be claimed that the first to be a particularist was precisely the central power. And this is what has happened in Spain [. . .]. Castile has made Spain, and Castile has unmade it." (*España Invertebrada*, 1921, p. 61)

Notes

Preface

1 Germà Bel, "Financiación de infraestructuras viarias: la economía política de los peajes", *Papeles de Economía Española* (1999), 82, 123–139.
2 The content of the PhD Dissertation was published in Alfonso Herranz Loncán, *Infraestructuras y crecimiento económico en España (1850–1935)* (Madrid: Fundación de los Ferrocarriles Españoles, 2008).
3 Santos Juliá, "Madrid, capital del Estado (1833–1993)", in Santos Juliá, David Ringrose & Cristina Segura, *Madrid. Historia de una capital* (Madrid: Alianza Editorial, 1994 [ed. 2000]), pp. 315–576 (p. 406).
4 José Luis García Delgado, "Madrid, capital económica", *Arbor* (2001), 169 (666), 359–369, pp. 361–363.
5 *Ibid.*, p. 363.
6 See, for instance, Germà Bel, "Política de transporte: ¿Más recursos o mejor gestión?", *Economistas* (2007), 111, 279–284; Germà Bel, "Las infraestructuras y los servicios de transporte en la LES", in Jesús Fernández-Villaverde, Luis Garicano & Manuel Bagüés, eds., *La Ley de Economía Sostenible* (Madrid: FEDEA, 2010), pp. 102–105.
7 As it can be seen in Josep Vicent Boira, "El eje mediterráneo y las redes transeuropeas de transporte (RTE-T): Historia de un desencuentro. De la cumbre de Essen (1994) a la dimensión exterior (2006)", *Papers* (2007), 44, 44–63.
8 Enric Juliana, *La deriva de España. Geografía de un país vigoroso y desorientado* (Barcelona: RBA, 2009).

1 A Madrid Like Paris?

1 John H. Elliot, *Imperial Spain 1469–1716* (London: Edward Arnold Publishers, 1963).
2 More information on investment in different transportation modes can be found in Germà Bel, "Las infraestructuras y los servicios de transporte en la LES», in Jesús Fernández-Villaverde, Luis Garicano & Manuel Bagüés, *La Ley de Economía Sostenible* (Madrid: FEDEA, 2010), pp. 102–105 (p. 103).
3 *Ibid.*, p. 103.
4 Josep Oliver Alonso, dir., *La apertura exterior de las regiones en España* (València: Tirant lo Blanch, 2003), p. 259.

5 More details on the Mediterranean corridor can be found in Mateu Turró, "L'EURAM, porta d'Europa. Reflexions a partir del llibre blanc de les infraestructures de l'EURAM», in EURAM, *Llibre blanc de les infraestructures. Euroregió del arc mediterrani* (València: EURAM, 2010), pp. 389–434.
6 Basic data on toll motorways obtained from *Anuario Estadístico de 2008* of the Ministerio de Fomento, 2009.
7 Detailed information on toll motorways in Europe is available in Daniel Albalate, Germà Bel & Xavier Fageda, "Privatization and regulatory reform of toll motorways in Europe", *Governance* (2009), 22 (2), 295–318.
8 For an explanation of the management models in Europe, see Germà Bel & Xavier Fageda, *Aeroports i Poder* (Barcelona: Edicions 62, 2007); or Germà Bel & Xavier Fageda, "Privatization, regulation and airport pricing: An empirical analysis for Europe", *Journal of Regulatory Economics* (2010), 37 (2), 142–161.
9 As stated by Pasqual Maragall one decade ago, "Before, Madrid was the political capital, and Barcelona and Bilbao, and València later, the industrial and economic capitals. Now is the almost the reverse. Now Madrid is, first of all, the economic capital" (Pasqual Maragall, "Madrid se va", *El País*, 27 February 2001).
10 Pablo Alcaide Guindo, "Avance de las magnitudes económicas españolas en 2009 y serie provisional del Balance Económico Regional. Años 2000 a 2009", *Cuadernos de Información Económica* (2010), 214, 1–64 (p. 22).
11 Information prepared by the company Iberinform, within the Grupo Crédito y Caución. Downloaded (11 February 2010) from http://www.iberinform.es/Noticias_Iberinform/noticia/mitad-empresas-espana-ranking-5000-madrid-2009.html.
12 Those firms that have their headquarters in a different country have been excluded from the ranking of largest firms.
13 Santos Juliá, "Madrid, capital del Estado (1833–1993)", in Santos Juliá, David Ringrose & Cristina Segura, *Madrid. Historia de una capital* (Madrid: Alianza Editorial, 1994, ed. 2000), pp. 315–576 (p. 497).
14 See, for instance, Jordi Pujol, "El desgarro", in Jordi Pujol, *Un modelo malogrado* (Barcelona: Centres d'Estudis Jordi Pujol, 2009), pp. 21–25.
15 Alfred North Whitehead, *Process and Reality* (Cambridge: Cambridge University Press, 1929).
16 Willard van Orman Quine, "On what there is", *Review of Metaphysics* (1948), 2 (5), 21–38
17 Adam Smith, *The Wealth of Nations*, 1776 (3rd ed., London: W. Strahan & T. Cadell, 1784, vol. III.V.I, pp. 94–96).
18 See a fine account in Santos Juliá, "Madrid, . . . ", *op. cit.*
19 Adam Smith, *The Wealth of Nations*, *op. cit.*, vol. I, pp. 22–23.
20 José Ortega y Gasset, *España invertebrada* (1921; 2nd ed., Madrid: Espasa Calpe, 1967), pp. 36–37.
21 Denomination given since 1996 to the former Ministry of Public Works, Transportation, and Environment.

22 Diego Mateo del Peral, "Los orígenes de la política ferroviaria en España (1844–1877)", in Miguel Artola (dir.), Ramón Cordero, Diego Mateo & Fernando Menéndez, *Los ferrocarriles en España 1844/1943. Tomo I. El Estado y los ferrocarriles* (Madrid: Servicio de Estudios del Banco de España, 1978), pp. 31–159 (pp. 75–76).
23 José María Aznar, *Debate sobre la investidura del candidato a la Presidencia del Gobierno*. Diario de Sesiones del Congreso de los Diputados. Pleno y Diputación Permanente. Year 2000, nº. 2 (25 April), p. 29.
24 Comisión de ingenieros, "Ante-proyectos del Plan General de Ferro-carriles. Memoria", *Revista de Obras Públicas* (1864), 12 (17 & 18), 198–204 & 208–215 (p. 200).
25 José Luís Rodríguez Zapatero, *Una idea actual de España*. 1 February 2007 (emphasis mine). This speech was partially printed in the newspaper *El Mundo*, 2 February 2007, pp. 6–7. It can be downloaded from http://www. pedrojhernando.com/aelpa2007/informacion/zapatero-ideaactualespa%C3%B1a.pdf.
26 Diego Mateo del Peral, "Los orígenes . . . ", *op. cit.*, pp. 123 y 125.
27 See, for instance, Norihiko Yamano & Toru Ohkawara, "The regional allocation of public investment: efficiency or equity?", *Journal of Regional Science* (2000), 40 (2), 205–229; and Ángel de la Fuente, "Second-best redistribution through public investment: a characterization, an empirical test and an application to the case of Spain", *Regional Science and Urban Economics* (2004), 34 (5), 489–503.
28 See, for instance, Achim Kemmerling & Andreas Stephan, "The contribution of local public infrastructure to private productivity and its political economy: evidence from a panel of large German cities", *Public Choice* (2002), 113 (3/4), 403–424; and Antoni Castells & Albert Solé-Ollé, "The regional allocation of infrastructure investment: the role of equity, efficiency and political factors", *European Economic Review* (2005), 49 (5), 1165–1205.
29 An extended discussion of this idea can be found in Germà Bel, "Comment VIII", in Núria Bosch, Marta Espasa & Albert Solé Ollé, eds., *The political economy of inter-regional fiscal flows. Measurement, determinants and effects on country stability* (Cheltenham: Edward Elgar, 2010), pp. 320–325.
30 Germà Bel & Xavier Fageda, "Preventing competition because of "solidarity": Rhetoric and reality of airport investments in Spain", *Applied Economics* (2009), 41(22), 2853–2865.
31 *El País*, 5 June 2002.
32 Salvador de la Encina, *Comparecencia de la señora ministra de Fomento (Álvarez Arza) para informar sobre las líneas básicas del nuevo modelo de gestión aeroportuaria*. Diario de Sesiones del Congreso de los Diputados. Comisión de Fomento. Year 2008, nº. 177 (16 December 2008), pp. 19–20.
33 This ended a long period, since 2000, in which that information was not made publicly available.
34 Ministerio de Fomento, *Previsión de resultados económicos de los aeropuertos españoles.*

Ejercicio 2009. Ejercicio 2010. Information released by the Minister of Fomento to the Spanish Congress, 12 January 2010, p. 3.

2 From Administrative Capital to Political Capital

1 David R. Ringrose, *Madrid y la economía española, 1560–1850. Ciudad, Corte y País en el Antiguo Régimen* (Madrid: Alianza Universidad, 1985) ([1st ed. in English, Berkeley: University of California Press, 1983], p. 209. Population estimates provided by Ringrose allow comparing Madrid with other Castilian cities, and observing their evolution over time.
2 John H. Elliot, *La España Imperial 1469–1716* (Barcelona: CL & Vicens Vives, 1996).
3 Alfredo Alvar Ezquerra, *Felipe II, la Corte y Madrid en 1561* (Madrid: CSIC, 1985), p. 29.
4 Manuel Fernández Álvarez, *Felipe II y su tiempo* (Madrid: Espasa Calpe, 1998, 6th ed.), p. 149; John H. Elliot, *Imperial Spain, op. cit.*
5 Alfredo Alvar Ezquerra, *El nacimiento de una capital europea. Madrid entre 1561 y 1606* (Madrid: Turner Libros, 1989), pp. 275–284.
6 Manuel Fernández Álvarez, *Felipe II, op. cit.*, p. 149.
7 Cristina Segura, "Madrid, capital imperial (1561–1833)", in Santos Juliá, David Ringrose & Cristina Segura, *Madrid. Historia de una capital* (Madrid: Alianza Editorial, 1994, ed. 2000), pp. 11–151 (p. 15).
8 David R. Ringrose, *Madrid y la economía . . . , op. cit.*, p. 112.
9 *Ibid.*, p. 209.
10 David Ringrose, "Madrid, capital imperial (1561–1833)", in Santos Juliá, David Ringrose & Cristina Segura, *Madrid . . . op. cit.*, pp. 153–314 (p. 159).
11 David Ringrose, "Madrid, capital . . . ", *op. cit.*, p. 197.
12 David R. Ringrose, *Madrid y la economía . . . , op. cit.*, p. 175.
13 Alberto Gil Novales, "Política y sociedad", in Manuel Tuñón de Lara, dir., *Historia de España. Historia de España. Tomo VII, Centralismo, Ilustración y agonía del Antiguo Régimen (1715–1833)* (Barcelona: Editorial Labor, 1980), pp. 175–320 (pp. 212–213).
14 David Ringrose, "Madrid, capital . . . ", *op. cit.*, p. 162.
15 Carlos Álvarez-Nogal & Leandro Prados de la Escosura, "The decline of Spain (1500–1850): conjectural estimates", *European Review of Economic History* (2007), 11 (3), 319–366, p. 354.
16 David Ringrose, "Madrid, capital . . . ", *op. cit.*, p. 295.
17 John H. Elliot, *La España Imperial 1469–1716* (Barcelona: CL & Vicens Vives, 1996), p. 455.
18 David Ringrose, *España, 1700–1900: el mito del fracaso* (Madrid: Alianza Editorial, 1996), p. 139.
19 Emiliano Fernández de Pinedo, "Coyuntura y políticas económicas", in Manuel Tuñón de Lara, dir., *Historia de España, . . . op. cit.*, pp. 9–173 (pp. 73–74).
20 David Ringrose, "Madrid, capital . . . ", *op. cit.*, p. 296.

21 John H. Elliot, *La España Imperial 1469–1716* (Barcelona: CL & Vicens Vives, 1996), p. 457.
22 José Álvarez Junco, *Mater Dolorosa. La idea de España en el siglo XIX* (Madrid: Taurus, 2001), pp. 102–103.
23 Although positions in favour of a different 'Enlightenment' did indeed exist, as shown by Ernest Lluch, *La Catalunya vençuda del segle XVIII. Foscors i clarors de la Il·lustració* (Barcelona: Edicions 62, 1996).
24 *Ibid.*, p. 122.
25 Borja de Riquer, "Aproximación al nacionalismo español contemporáneo", *Studia Historica. Historia Contemporánea* (1994), 12, 11–29.
26 Jaume Vicens Vives. *Aproximación a la Historia de España* (Barcelona: Vicens Vives, 1952, 4th. ed., 1966), p. 197.
27 Ignacio de Luzán, *Memorias literarias de París* (Madrid: Imprenta de don Gabriel Ramírez, 1751), p. 2. (Taken from Mario Onaindía, *La construcción de la nación española* [Barcelona: Ediciones B, 2002], p. 53).
28 Mario Onaindía. *La construcción, . . . , op. cit.* p. 327.
29 *Ibid.*, p. 328.
30 Miguel Artola. *Los afrancesados* (Madrid: Alianza Universidad, 1989).
31 José Álvarez Junco, *Mater Dolorosa . . . , op. cit.*, p. 535.
32 *Ibid.*, p. 535.
33 Jesús Astigarraga, "Necker en España, 1780–1800", *Revista de Economía Aplicada* (2000), 8(23), 119–141, pp. 130–133.
34 Royal Decree of 30 November 1833 on the civil division of the Spanish territory in the Peninsula and the adjacent islands in 49 provinces. *Gaceta de Madrid* nº 154, 3 December 1833.
35 Jaume Vicens Vives. *Aproximación . . . , op. cit.*, p. 164.
36 David R. Ringrose, *Madrid y la economía . . . , op. cit.*, p. 389.
37 Raymond Carr, *España 1808–1939* (Barcelona: Ariel, 1970), p. 203 (1st ed. in English, Oxford: Oxford University Press, 1996).
38 José Álvarez Junco, *Mater Dolorosa . . . , op. cit.*, p. 537.
39 Santos Madrazo, *El Sistema de Transportes en España, 1750–1850* (Madrid: Ediciones Turner, 1984), pp. 27 and 151–152.
40 José I. Uriol, "Las calzadas romanas y los caminos del siglo XVI", *Revista de Obras Públicas* (1985), 132 (3237), 553–563, p. 557.
41 José I. Uriol, "Los viajes por la posta en el siglo XVIII y en los primeros años del siglo XIX", *Revista de Obras Públicas* (1977), 124 (3151), 837–856, p. 837.
42 *Ibid.*, p. 841.
43 José I. Uriol, "Las carreteras y los canales de navegación en los reinados de Fernando VI y Carlos III", *Revista de Obras Públicas* (1978), 125 (3159), 533–546, p. 535.
44 Gonzalo Menéndez Pidal, *Los caminos en la Historia de España* (Madrid: Ediciones Cultura Hispánica, 1951), p. 122.
45 José I. Uriol Salcedo, *Historia de los caminos de España. Vol. I Hasta el siglo XIX* (Madrid: Editorial AC, 1990), p. 242.

46 Francisco Wais San Martín, "Recuerdo a Bernardo Ward y sus caminos", *Revista de Obras Públicas* (1963), 111 (2981), 563–566, p. 563.
47 José I. Uriol, "Las carreteras y los canales de navegación en los reinados de Fernando VI y Carlos III. Auge de la construcción de carreteras y canales. Carlos III", *Revista de Obras Públicas* (1978), 125 (3160), 625–636, p. 626.
48 Gonzalo Menéndez Pidal, *Los caminos . . .* , *op. cit.*, p. 123.
49 José I. Uriol, "Las carreteras y los canales . . . ", *op. cit.*, pp. 626–627.
50 Antonio Gómez Mendoza, "Madrid, centro de la red de comunicaciones", *Arbor* (2001), 169 (666), 343–358, p. 349.
51 Santos Madrazo, *El Sistema de Transportes . . .* , *op. cit.*, pp. 62–63, 159.
52 José I. Uriol, "Las carreteras y los canales . . . ", *op. cit.*, p. 630.
53 Carlos Álvarez-Nogal y Leandro Prados de la Escosura, "The decline of Spain, . . . ", *op. cit.*, p. 354.
54 Gonzalo Menéndez Pidal, *Los caminos*, . . . *op. cit.*, p. 124.
55 Alfredo Alvar Ezquerra, *El nacimiento . . .* , *op. cit.*, pp. 107–188.
56 David Ringrose, "Madrid, capital . . . ", *op. cit.*, p. 179.
57 David Ringrose, *España . . .* , *op. cit.*, p. 138.
58 David Ringrose, *Madrid y la economía . . .* , *op. cit.*, p. 129.
59 David Ringrose, *Los transportes y el estancamiento económico de España (1750–1850)* (Madrid: Editorial Tecnos, 1972) (1st ed., in English, Durham (NC): Duke University Press, 1970), p. 49.
60 David Ringrose, "Madrid, capital . . . ", *op. cit.*, p. 277.
61 Antonio Gómez Mendoza, "Madrid, . . . ", *op. cit.*, p. 348.
62 David Ringrose, *Madrid y la economía . . .* , *op. cit.*, p. 106.
63 David Ringrose, *Los transportes . . .* , *op. cit.*, p. 143–147.
64 Antonio Gómez Mendoza, "Madrid, . . . ", *op. cit.*, p. 356.

3 Transversal Market, Radial State (I): The First Railways

1 Mark Casson, *The World's First Railway System* (Oxford: Oxford University Press, 2009), p. 126.
2 Francisco Wais, *Historia de los ferrocarriles españoles I* (Madrid: Fundación de los Ferrocarriles Españoles, 1987, 3rd ed., ed. 1968), p. 26.
3 *Ibid.*, pp. 27–28.
4 *Ibid.*, pp. 29–30.
5 Emilio de Diego García, "El ferrocarril: La Habana-Güines", *Cuadernos de Historia Moderna y Contemporánea* (1983), 4, 59–77, p. 61.
6 Patrick O'Brien, "Transport and economic development in Europe, 1789–1914", in Patrick O'Brien, *Railways and the economic development of Western Europe, 1830–1914* (London: Macmillan, 1983), pp. 1–27 (p. 8).
7 Mark Casson, *The World's . . .* , *op. cit.*, p. 137.
8 Gary Hawke & Jim Higgins, "Britain", In Patrick O'Brien, *Railways*, *op. cit.*, pp. 170–202 (p. 182).
9 B.R. Mitchell, *Internacional Historical Statistics: Europe 1750–1993* (London:

Macmillan, 1998), pp. 673–674. The same source is used for historical data on the extensión of networks by mid-19th century in all reviewed countries.

10 Alfonso Herranz Loncán, *Infraestructuras y crecimiento económico en España (1850–1935)* (Madrid: Fundación de los Ferrocarriles Españoles, 2008), p. 49.

11 Gary Hawke & Jim Higgins, "Britain", *op. cit.*, p. 184.

12 T.K. Derry & Trevor I. Williams, *Historia de la tecnología. Desde 1750 hasta 1900 (I)* (Madrid: Siglo XXI, 2002, 1st ed. in English, Oxford University Press, 1960), p. 426.

13 Michel Laffut, "Belgium", in Patrick O'Brien, *Railways*, *op. cit.*, pp. 203–226 (p. 205).

14 Erwin Berghaus, *Historia del Ferrocarril* (Barcelona: Ediciones Zeus, 1964, 1st ed. in German, 1960), p. 53.

15 Taken from Erwin Berghaus, *Historia . . . op. cit.*, p. 54.

16 Rainer Fremlindg, "Germany", in Patrick O'Brien, *Railways*, *op. cit.*, pp. 121–148 (p. 121).

17 Erwin Berghaus, *Historia . . . op. cit.*, p. 84.

18 Rainer Fremdling, "Germany", in Patrick O'Brien, *Railways*, *op. cit.*, p. 122.

19 Société d'Agriculture, Sciences, Art et Commerce de l'arrondissement de ST-Étienne (Loire), *Bulletin Industriel* (Saint Étienne: Imprimerie de Gaudelet, 1830), pp. 10–13.

20 François Caron, "France", in Patrick O'Brien, *Railways*, *op. cit.*, pp. 28–48 (p. 29).

21 Arthur L. Dunham, "How the first French railways were planned", *Journal of Economic History* (1941), 1(1), 12–25, p. 24.

22 François Caron, "France", *op. cit.*, p. 29.

23 Stefano Fenoaltea, "Italy", in Patrick O'Brien, *Railways*, *op. cit.*, pp. 49–121 (pp. 49–51).

24 *Ibid.*, p. 51.

25 Pere Pascual Domènech, *Los caminos de la era industrial. La construcción y financiación de la Red Ferroviaria Catalana (1843–1898)*(Barcelona: Edicions de la Universitat de Barcelona, 1999), p. 55.

26 Francisco Wais, *Historia . . .* , *op. cit.*, p. 84.

27 Diego Mateo del Peral, "Los orígenes de la política ferroviaria en Espala (1844–1877)", in Miguel Artola (dir.), Ramón Cordero, Diego Mateo & Fernando Menéndez, *Los ferrocarriles en España 1844/1943. Tomo I. El Estado y los ferrocarriles* (Madrid: Banco de España, 1978), pp. 31–159 (p. 46).

28 Francisco Wais, *Historia . . .* , *op. cit.*, p. 77.

29 *Ibid.*, p. 84.

30 Pedro Tedde Lorca, "Las compañías ferroviarias en España", in Miguel Artola (dir.), Rafael Anes & Pedro Tedde, *Los ferrocarriles en España 1844/1943. Tomo II. Los ferrocarriles y la economía* (Madrid: Servicio de Estudios del Banco de España, 1978), pp. 9–354 (p. 17).

31 Miguel Artola, "La acción del Estado", in Miguel Artola (dir.), *Tomo I.*, *op. cit.*, pp. 339–453 (pp. 344–348).

32 Pere Pascual Domènech, *Los caminos . . .* , *op. cit.*, pp. 91–94.
33 This information is based on Francisco Wais, *Historia . . .* , *op. cit.*
34 Francisco Comín Comín, Pablo Martín Aceña, Miguel Muñoz Rubio & Javier Vidal Olivares, *150 años de historia de los ferrocarriles españoles. Volumen I* (Madrid: Anaya, 1998), p. 41.
35 Miguel Artola, "Introducción", in Miguel Artola (dir.), *Tomo I.*, *op. cit.*, pp. 13–25 (pp. 24–25).
36 Diego Mateo del Peral, "Los orígenes . . . ", *op. cit.*, p. 48.
37 *Ibid.*, p. 56 (emphasis is mine).
38 Content is available in *Información parlamentaria hecha por la Comisión de Ferro-carriles nombrada por el Congreso de los Diputados en 10 de enero de 1850* (Madrid: Imprenta Nacional, 1850).
39 *Información parlamentaria . . .* , *op. cit.*, p. 161.
40 *Ibid.*, p. 19.
41 *Ibid.*, p. 162.
42 *Ibid.*, p. 162.
43 *Ibid.*, p. 163.
44 *Ibid.*, p. 164.
45 *Ibid.*, p. 165.
46 *Ibid.*, pp. 183–184.
47 *Ibid.*, p. 185.
48 *Ibid.*, p. 186.
49 *Ibid.*, p. 190.
50 *Ibid.*, pp. 209–210.
51 *Ibid.*, p. 214.
52 Diego Mateo del Peral, "Los orígenes . . . ", *op. cit.*, p. 88.
53 Comisión de ingenieros, "Ante-proyectos del Plan General de Ferro-carriles. Memoria", *Revista de Obras Públicas* (1864), 12 (17 & 18), 198–204 & 208–215 (p. 200).
54 "Ante-proyectos . . . ", *op. cit.*, p. 201.
55 *Ibid.*, p. 214.
56 *Ibid.*, pp. 201–204 y 208–214.
57 Junta Consultiva de Caminos, Canales y Puertos, "Ante-proyectos del Plan General de Ferro-carriles. Informe y ante-proyecto", *Revista de Obras Públicas*, 1864, 12 (21, 22, y 23), 246–251, 259–262, 268–273 (pp. 269–272).
58 *Memoria presentada al gobierno por la comisión especial encargada de proponer el plan general de ferrocarriles*. Taken from Diego Mateo del Peral, "Los orígenes . . . ", *op. cit.*, p. 101.
59 Diego Mateo del Peral, "Los orígenes . . . ", *op.*, *cit.*, p. 118.
60 However, the new government was not a strong supporter of the absence of State intervention in the economy, as shown in Antón Costas Comesaña, *Apogeo del liberalismo en 'La Gloriosa'. La reforma económica en el Sexenio liberal (1868–1874* (Madrid: Siglo XXI, 1988) (pp. 129–160).

61 Pelayo Clairac Sáenz, "La administración de Obras públicas en el período revolucionario", *Revista de Obras Públicas* (1871), 19 (4), 43–48, p. 44.
62 Diego Mateo del Peral, "Los orígenes . . . ", *op. cit.*, pp. 123 & 125. I follow this work (pp. 122–131) in what refers to the policy in the liberal period and the Law of 1877.
63 *Ibid.*, p. 130.
64 Antonio Gómez Mendoza, "Madrid, centro de la red de comunicaciones", *Arbor* (2001), 169, 343–358, p. 345.
65 Francisco Comín et al., *150 años* . . . , *op.*, *cit.*, p. 58.
66 Pablo Alzola y Minondo, *Las obras públicas en España: Estudio histórico* (Bilbao: Biblioteca de la Revista de Obras Públicas, 1899), p. 372. See as well Alfonso Herranz Loncán, "The Spanish Infrastructure Stock, 1845–1935", *Research in Economic History* (2005), 23, 85–129.
67 Francisco Comín et al., *150 años* . . . , *op.*, *cit.*, p. 93.
68 Gabriel Tortella Casares, *Los Orígenes del capitalismo en España: Banca, industria y ferrocarriles en el siglo XIX* (Madrid: Tecnos, 1973), pp. 168–173.
69 Alfonso Herranz Loncán, *Infraestructuras* . . . , *op. cit.*, p. 125.
70 See Alfonso Herranz Loncán, *La dotación de infraestructuras en España, 1844–1935* (Madrid: Banco de España, 2004).
71 Information published in "Lo de siempre", *Fomento de la Producción Española, Semanario de Intereses Generales*, 9 December 1876, I, 22, 404–406.
72 *Fomento de la Producción Española*, *op. cit.* p. 405.
73 The propensity to subsidies to the radial lines existed even the cases in which they were profitable, such as the Madrid–Irún line, which was among the most heavily used and profitable rail lines in the XIX century.
74 Antonio Gómez Mendoza, "Madrid, . . . ", *op. cit.*, , p. 353.
75 Gabriel Tortella Casares, *Los Orígenes* . . . *op. cit.*, and Gabriel Tortella Casares, *El desarrollo de la España contemporánea. Historia económica de los siglos XIX y XX* (Madrid: Alianza, 1994).
76 Jordi Nadal, *El fracaso de la revolución industrial en España. 1814–1913* (Barcelona: Ariel, 1975).
77 Antonio Gómez Mendoza, *Ferrocarril y cambio económico en España (1855–1913)* (Madrid: Alianza, 1982).
78 Alfonso Herranz Loncán, *Infraestructuras*, *op. cit.;* and Alfonso Herranz Loncán, "Railroad Impact in Backward Economies: Spain, 1850–1913", *Journal of Economic History* (2006), 66 (4), 853–881. According to Herranz, one of the outstanding reasons why the impact on growth was small was the dominance of political interests in the extension of railways (Alfonso Herranz Loncán, "Infrastructure investment and Spanish economic growth, 1850–1935", *Explorations in Economic History* (2007), 44 (3), 452–468).
79 Robert W. Fogel, *Railroads and American Economic Growth: Essays in Econometric History* (Baltimore: Johns Hopkins Press, 1964).
80 Francisco Comín et al., *150 años* . . . , *op. cit.*, pp. 142–145; see as well, Francisco Comín, "Comentarios en torno al ferrocarril y el crecimiento económico

español entre 1855 y 1931", *Revista de Historia Económica* (1983), 1 (1), 181–195.

81 Jordi Nadal, *El fracaso*, *op. cit.*, p. 74.

82 Rafael Izquierdo de Bartolomé, "El modelo de transporte", in Rafael Acosta España, et al. *La España de las Autonomías. Pasado, presente y futuro. Tomo I* (Madrid: Espasa-Calpe, 1981), pp. 367–470 (p. 407).

83 Ramón Cordero & Fernando Menéndez, "El sistema ferroviario español", in Miguel Artola (dir), *Tomo I*, *op. cit.*, pp. 161–338 (p. 195).

84 Mark Casson, *The World's . . .* , *op. cit.*, p. 4.

85 Ramón Cordero & Fernando Menéndez, "El sistema . . . ", *op. cit.*, p. 195.

86 Some against the radial network, such as Magí Casañas Vallés, "El ferrocarril en España, 1844–1868. Consideraciones en torno a una crisis", *Investigaciones Económicas* (1977), 4, 9–68; others in favor of that design, such as Gabriel Tortella Casares, *El desarrollo . . .* , *op. cit.*

87 Antonio Gómez Mendoza, *Ferrocarril, industria y mercado en la modernización de España* (Madrid: Espasa-Calpe, 1989), pp. 169 & 171.

88 Antonio Gómez Mendoza, "Madrid, . . . ", *op. cit.*, p. 348.

89 *Ibid.*, p. 354.

90 Adam Smith, *The Wealth of Nations*, *op. cit.*, pp. 95–96.

4 Transversal Market, Radial State (II): The First Motorways

1 Data on the extension of the network for different dates have been obtained from Rafael Izquierdo de Bartolomé, "El modelo de transporte", in Rafael Acosta España, et al. *La España de las Autonomías. Pasado, presente y futuro. Tomo I* (Madrid: Espasa-Calpe, 1981), pp. 367–470 (p. 407).

2 José I. Uriol Salcedo, *Historia de los caminos de España. Vol. II Siglos XIX y XX* (Madrid: Editorial AC, 1992), p. 25.

3 Juan Pemán Gavín, "Sobre la regulación de las carreteras en el Derecho Español: Una visión de conjunto", *Revista de Administración Pública* (1992), 129 (September–December), 117–161, p. 125.

4 Pedro García Ormaechea, "La red de carreteras españolas. Su modernización", *Revista de Obras Públicas* (1957), 105 (2906), 294–296, p. 294.

5 Alfonso Puncel Chornet, *La Autopista del Mediterráneo. Cesiones, concesiones, servicios y servidumbres* (València: Universitat de Valéncia, 1996), p. 15.

6 Pedro García Ortega, *Las concesiones administrativas de carreteras en el ordenamiento jurídico español* (Madrid: Ministerio de Obras Públicas y Urbanismo, 1979).

7 A detailed explanation of those motorway projects can be found in Teresa Navas, "Il riflesso della modernità: le autostrade spagnole, 1920–1960", *Storia urbana* (2002), XXVI (100), 27–54, pp. 45–46.

8 Details on the route design are available in Enrique Colás Arias, "Autostradas italianas", *Revista de Obras Públicas* (1925), 73 (2429), 204–207, p. 207.

9 Manuel Aguilar López, "Carreteras modernas", *Revista de Obras Públicas* (1926), 74 (2467), 524–527, p. 527.

10 Teresa Navas, "Il riflesso . . . ", *op. cit.*, p. 48.
11 José I. Uriol Salcedo, *Historia* . . . p. 258.
12 Pedro García Ormaechea, "La red de carreteras españolas . . . ", *op. cit.*, p. 295.
13 Banco Mundial, *Informe del Banco Mundial. El desarrollo económico de España* (Madrid: BIRF, 1962), p. 312.
14 Juan R. Cuadrado Roura, "La política regional de los Planes de Desarrollo (1964–1975)", in Rafael Acosta España et al. *La España de las Autonomías. Pasado, presente y futuro. Tomo I* (Madrid: Espasa-Calpe, 1981), pp. 547–608.
15 Juan R. Cuadrado Roura, "La política regional . . . ", *op. cit.*, p. 592.
16 Rafael Izquierdo de Bartolomé, "El modelo de transporte", *op. cit.* (p. 420).
17 Werner Rothengatter, "Motorways and motorway finance in Germany and Austria", *Research in Transportation Economics* (2005), 15, 75–91, p. 77.
18 Germà Bel & John Foote, "Tolls, terms and Public Interest in road concessions privatization: A comparative analysis of recent transactions in the USA and France", *Transport Reviews* (2009), 29 (3), 397–413, p. 401.
19 Werner Rothengatter, "Motorways", *op. cit.*, p. 77.
20 Marc Desportes, "Le prime autostrade francesi: resistenze e dilazioni", *Storia Urbana* (2002), XXVI (100), 55–84, p. 55.
21 Alain Fayard, David Meunier & Emile Quinet, "Motorway Provision and Management in France: Analyses and Policy Issues", *Network and Spatial Economics*, forthcoming.
22 Alain Fayard, Francesco Gaeta & Emile Quinet, "French motorways: Experience and assessment", *Research in Transportation Economics* (2005), 15, 93–105, p. 97–99.
23 Germà Bel & John Foote, "Tolls, terms and Public Interest", *op. cit.*, p. 400.
24 M. R. Buccella, "Le autovie nel sistema dei trasporti", *Giornale degli Economisti e Rivista di Statistica* (1927), LXVIII (Dicembre), 726–748, p. 745.
25 Enrique Colás Arias, "Autostradas italianas", *op. cit.*, p. 204.
26 Massimo Moraglio, "Per una storia delle autostrade italiane: Il periodo tra le due Guerre Mondiali", *Storia Urbana* (2002), XXVI (100), 11–25, p. 15.
27 Lando Bortolotti, "Origini e primordi della rete autostradale in Italia, 1922–1933", *Storia Urbana* (1992), XVI (59), 35–70 (p. 47); Lando Bortolotti & Giuseppe De Luca. *Fascismo e autostrade. Un caso di sintesi: la Firenze-mare* (Milano: Francoangeli, 1994), p. 46.
28 See a more detailed explanation in Germà Bel, "The first privatization: Selling SOEs and privatizing public monopolies in fascist Italy (1922–1925)", *Cambridge Journal of Economics*, forthcoming.
29 Massimo Moraglio, "L'autostrada Torino-Milano, 1923–1933: I progetti e la costruzione", *Storia Urbana* (1999), XXIII (86), 103–121, pp. 103–104.
30 De Luca, Giuseppe. "La costruzione della rete autostradale italiana: L'autostrada Firenze-mare, 1927–1940" *Storia Urbana* (1992), XVI (59), 71–126, p. 75.
31 Andrea Greco & Giorgio Ragazzi, "History and regulations of Italian high-

ways concessionaires", *Research in Transportation Economics* (2005), 15, 121–133, p. 121.

32 Massimo Moraglio, "Per una storia", *op. cit.*, p. 23.

33 Andrea Greco & Giorgio Ragazzi, "History . . . ", *op. cit.*, p. 122.

34 Daniel Albalate, Germà Bel & Xavier Fageda, "Privatization and regulatory reform of toll motorways in Europe", *Governance* (2009), 22 (2), 295–318, p. 300.

35 Ramón Fernández, Eduardo Molina & Fernando Nebot, "El fracaso de la política de las autopistas de peaje", *Información Comercial Española* (1983), 594, 37–54. p. 38.

36 Banco Mundial, *Informe* . . . , *op. cit.*, p. 312.

37 Montserrat Sansalvadó, *La financiación de las inversiones a largo plazo. El caso de las autopistas de peaje.* PhD Dissertation (Universitat de Barcelona, 1987), p. 22.

38 Montserrat Sansalvadó, *La financiación . . . , op. cit.*, p. 112.

39 See a theoretical economic analysis of direct tolls in Germà Bel, "Financiación de infraestructuras viarias: la economía política de los peajes", *Papeles de Economía Española* (1999), 82, 123–139, pp. 124–126.

40 José A. Gómez-Ibáñez & John R. Meyer, *Going private. The international experience with transport privatization* (Washington DC: Brookings Institution, 1993).

41 In fact, the first concessions have been very profitable, as shown in Daniel Albalate & Germà Bel, "Regulating Concessions of Toll Motorways: An Empirical Study on Fixed vs. Variable Term Contracts", *Transportation Research-A* (2009), 43(2), 219–229.

42 MOPU, *Informe sobre las Autopistas Nacionales de Peaje* (Madrid: Ministerio de Obras Públicas y Urbanismo, 1974).

43 An in-deep analysis of concessions' conditions and their impact on the Treasury is available in Germà Bel, "Financiación de infraestructuras viarias . . . ", *op. cit.*, pp. 127–130.

44 Ramón Fernández, Eduardo Molina & Fernando Nebot, "El fracaso . . . ", *op. cit.*

45 El *Plan General de Carreteras 1984–1991* was published in the Boletín Oficial de la Cortes Generales (Congreso de los Diputados), Serie E, nº. 160, 1 March 1986, pp. 1853–1882 (p. 1873).

46 *Plan General de Carreteras 1984–1991*, *op. cit.*, pp. 1864.

47 Germà Bel. *La demanda de transporte en España: Competencia intermodal sobre el ferrocarril interurbano* (Madrid: Instituto de Estudios del Transporte y las Comunicaciones IETC-, 1994).

48 Emilio Pérez Touriño, "Efectos del Plan. Realizaciones y balance socioeconómico", *Estudios de Transporte y Comunicaciones* (1994), 65 (separata), 9–27, pp. 14–15.

49 The regional government of Catalonia had been active in promoting toll motorways since the early 1980s.

50 Rafael Izquierdo, *Gestión y financiación de las infraestructuras de transporte terrestre* (Madrid: Asociación Española de la Carretera, 1997), p. 279.
51 See an updated list of toll motorway concessions in Germà Bel & Xavier Fageda, "Is a mixed funding model for the highway network sustainable over time? The Spanish case?", *Research in Transportation Economics* (2005), 15, 187–203, pp. 195–196.
52 Data on networks extensión obtained from Ministerio de Fomento, *Los transportes, las infraestructuras y los servicios postales. Informe Anual 2008*. Madrid: Ministerio de Fomento, 2009, p. 36; and Ministerio de Fomento, *Anuario Estadístico 2008* (Madrid: Ministerio de Fomento, 2009), p. 158.

5 The New Spain (I): Railway Modernization Starting from Kilometre Zero

1 Ginés De Rus & Chris Nash, *In what circumstances is investment in HSR worthwhile?* (*¿En qué circumstancias vale la pena invertir en ferrocarril de alta velocidad?*) (University of Leeds: ITS, working paper 590, 2007), p. 2.
2 Discussion based on Daniel Albalate & Germà Bel, "High-Speed Rail: Lessons for Policy Makers from Experiences Abroad", *Public Administration Review* (forthcoming).
3 Moshe Givoni, "Development and impact of the Modern High-speed Train: A Review", *Transport Reviews* (2006), 26 (5), 593–611.
4 Alain Plaud, "Les nouvelles voies ferrées à grande vitesse et l'aménagement du territoire au Japon", *Transports* (1977), 225, 387–393.
5 Mitsuhide Imashiro, "Changes in Japan's Transport Market and Privatization", *Japan Railway and Transport Review* (1997), 13, 50–53, p. 51.
6 Roger Vickerman, "High-speed rail in Europe: experience and issues for future development", *Annals of Regional Science* (1997), 31 (1), 21–38.
7 James Dunn & Anthony Perl, "Policy networks and industrial revitalization: High Speed Rail initiatives in France and Germany", *Journal of Public Policy* (1994), 14 (3), 311–343.
8 Roger Vickerman, "High-speed rail in Europe . . . ", *op. cit.*
9 A. Bonnafous, "The regional impact of the TGV", *Transportation* (1987), 14 (2), 127–137, p. 136.
10 *Ibidem*, p. 133.
11 Valérie Mannone, *L'impact régional du TGV Sud-Est* (Université de Provence, Aix-en-Provence: PhD Dissertation, 1995).
12 A. Bonnafous, "The regional . . . ", *op. cit.*, p. 132.
13 James Dunn & Anthony Perl, "Policy networks . . . ", *op. cit.*
14 Kingsley E. Haynes, "Labor markets and regional transportation improvements: the case of high-speed trains. An introduction and review", *Annals of Regional Science* (1997), 31 (1), 57–76.
15 Roger Vickerman, "High-speed rail in Europe . . . ", *op. cit.*
16 *Ibid.*, p. 28.

17 Grupo Ferrovie dello Stato, *Rete AV/AC. Analisi dei costi* (Roma: Grupo Ferrovie dello Stato, 2007).

18 Ginés de Rus y Gustavo Nombela, "Is investment in High Speed Rail socially profitable?", *Journal of Transport Economics and Policy* (2007), 41 (1), 3–23, p. 21.

19 European Commission, *Interaction between High Speed and Air Passenger Transport – Interim Report. Interim Report on the Action COST 318* (Brussels: European Commission, April 1996).

20 Huib van Essen, Olivier Bello, Jos Dings, & Robert van den Brink, *To shift or not to shift, that's the question. The environmental performance of the principal modes of freight and passenger transport in the policymaking process* (Delft: CE Delft, 2003).

21 Bert van Wee, Robert van den Brink, & Hans Nijland, "Environmental impacts of high-speed rail links in cost-benefit analyses: a case study of the Dutch Zuider Zee line", *Transportation Research D* (2003), 8 (4), 299–314.

22 Jordi Martí Hennenberg, "Un balance del tren de alta velocidad en Francia. Enseñanzas para el caso español", *Ería* (2000), 52, 131–143.

23 Alain Plaud, "Les nouvelles . . . ", *op. cit.*; Moshe Givoni, "Development . . . ", *op. cit.*; Louis S. Thompson, "High Speed Rail in the United States- Why isn't there more?, *Japan Railway and Transport Review* (1994), 3, 32–39; and Leo van den Berg & Peter Pol, *The European high-speed train-network and urban development* (Aldershot: Ashgate, 1998).

24 Kingsley E. Haynes, "Labor markets . . . ", *op. cit.*

25 Miguel Rodríguez Bugarín, Margarita Novales Ordax & Alfonso Orro Arcay, "Alta velocidad y territorio: Algunas experiencias internacionales", *Ingeniería y Territorio* (2005), 70, 4–11, p. 11.

26 A. Bonnafous, "The regional . . . ", *op. cit.*, p. 132.

27 Roger Vickerman, "High-speed rail in Europe . . . ", *op. cit.*

28 See *El País*, 15/02/2007. "España tendrá en tres años la mayor red de AVE del mundo, según Zapatero". In www.elpais.com.

29 See, for instance, minister Magdalena Álvarez in the Committee of Fomento of the Congreso de los Diputados of 29 June 2005 (*Diario de Sesiones del Congreso*, nº. 239, 29 June 2005, p. 4)

30 Guillaume Pépy, *El País, Negocios*, 7 February 2010, p. 14

31 De Rus, Ginés Concepción Román, "Análisis económico de la línea de alta velocidad Madrid-Barcelona", *Revista de Economía Aplicada* (2006), 14 (42), 35–80.

32 De Rus, Ginés & Vicente Inglada, "Cost-benefit analysis of the high-speed train in Spain", *Annals of Regional Science* (1997), 31(2), 175–188.

33 De Rus, Ginés & Concepción Román, "Análisis económico . . . ", *op. cit.*

34 In *Expansión*, 22 January 2010, data on the communication of the European Commission is provided.

35 José I. Uriol Salcedo, *Historia de los caminos de España. Vol. II Siglos XIX y XX* (Madrid: Editorial AC, 1992), p. 448.

36 Antonio Gómez Mendoza, "Del ferrocarril al AVE. ¿Los mismos errores históricos?", *Clío. Revista de Historia* (2005), 45, 44–49, p. 48.
37 Germà Bel & Carme Miralles, "Papá o mamá: ¿Ven en tren?", *El País*, 6 October 2003.

6 The New Spain (II): Airport Management from Kilometre Zero

1 Besides managing airports, AENA manages as well the air traffic control, which is subject to an ongoing process of reform.
2 See Jan Brueckner, "Airline traffic and urban economic development", *Urban Studies* (2003), 40(8), 1455–1469, and Germà Bel & Xavier Fageda, "Getting there fast: Globalization, intercontinental flights and location of headquarters», *Journal of Economic Geography* (2008), 8(4), 471–495.
3 Antonio Gómez Mendoza, "Madrid, centro de la red de comunicaciones», *Arbor* (2001), 169, 343–358 (p. 353).
4 AENA, *Los aeropuertos españoles. Su historia 1911–1996* (Madrid: Aeropuertos Españoles y Navegación Aérea, 1996), p. 51.
5 *Ibid.*, p. 57.
6 *Ibid.*, p. 65.
7 The Act was passed on 2 November 1940, and was published in the BOE (Official State Gazette) on 16 November 1940.
8 It is worth noting that the centralized model in the Scandinavian countries –especially in Finland and Norway– is due to different reasons, for they have one unique relevant airport and a variety of very small and territorially disperse airports.
9 See a more detailed analysis on the main trends of airport management models in OECD countries in Germà Bel & Xavier Fageda "Airport management and airline competition in OECD countries», in F. Fichert, Justus Haucap, & K. Rommel (eds.), *Competition Policy in Network Industry* (LIT-Verlag, 2006), pp. 81–98.
10 Michael Kerkloh, "El modelo alemán, y el caso del aeropuerto de Múnich", in Germà Bel & Xavier Fageda, eds., *Buena práctica sobre gestión aeroportuaria en Europa* (Barcelona: Fundació Catalunya-Europa, 2009), pp. 73–87 (p. 76).
11 Anne Graham, "Airport Planning and Regulation in the United Kingdom", in Clifford Winston & Ginés de Rus, eds., *Aviation Infrastructure Performance. A Study in Comparative Political Economy* (Washington DC: Brookings Institution Press, 2008), pp. 100–136.
12 Claude Terrazoni & Jean-Michel Vernhes, "El modelo francés, y el caso del aeropuerto de Tolosa", in Germà Bel & Xavier Fageda, eds., *Buena práctica sobre gestión aeroportuaria en Europa* (Barcelona: Fundació Catalunya-Europa, 2009), pp. 58–72 (p. 60).
13 *Ibid.*, p. 18.
14 Gordon Mills, "Airports users don't pay enough – and now here's privatisation", *Economic Papers* (1995), 14 (1), 73–84.

15 George Williams Romano Pagliari, "A comparative analysis of the application and use of public service obligations in air transport within the EU", *Transport Policy* (2004), 11(1), 55–66; James Nolan, Pamela Ritchie y John Rowcroft, "Small market air service and regional policy", *Journal of Transport Economics and Policy* (2005), 39(3), 363–378.
16 Andrés Ayala, *Comparecencia de la señora ministra de Fomento (Álvarez Arza) para informar sobre las líneas básicas del nuevo modelo de gestión aeroportuaria*. Diario de Sesiones del Congreso de los Diputados. Comisión de Fomento. Year 2008, nº. 177 (16 December), p. 18.
17 Magdalena Álvarez, *Comparecencia de la señora ministra . . .* , *op. cit.*, p. 22.
18 Andrés Ayala, *Comparecencia de la señora ministra . . .* , *op. cit.*, p. 30.
19 Rafael Simancas, *Comparecencia del señor ministro de Fomento (Blanco López), para informar sobre la propuesta del Gobierno de modelo de gestión aeroportuaria.* Diario de Sesiones del Congreso de los Diputados. Comisión de Fomento. Year 2010, nº. 458 (12 January), p. 19.
20 *Ibid.*, p. 21.
21 Andrés Ayala, *Comparecencia del señor ministro . . .* , *op. cit.*, p. 32.
22 Ministerio de Fomento, *Previsión de resultados económicos de los aeropuertos españoles. Ejercicio 2009. Ejercicio 2010.* Information released in the Spanish Congress on 12 january 2010, p. 3.
23 Germà Bel & Xavier Fageda, "Preventing competition because of 'solidarity': Rhetoric and reality of airport investments in Spain", *Applied Economics* (2009), 41(22), 2853–2865.
24 For instance: Germà Bel & Xavier Fageda, "Implicacions de la gestió centralitzada dels aeroports a Espanya", *Revista Econòmica de Catalunya* (2007), 55, 32–44; Germà Bel & Xavier Fageda, "La reforma del model de finançament i gestió dels aeroports a Espanya: lliçons de l'experiència internacional", *Revista Econòmica de Catalunya* (2008), 57, 11–26.
25 It is worth noting that the recent reforms implemented by the central government regarding air traffic control can reduce AENA's deficit, but to a limited extent.
26 Cuatro Vientos, Sabadell and Son Bonet have no commercial traffic.
27 European Commission, *Study on Competition Between Airports and the Application of State Aid Rules* (European Commission, Directorate-General Energy and Transport, Directorate F- Air Transport, September 2002), p. 5/33.
28 *Expansión*, "Aena es el gestor aeroportuario que más pierde con su negocio", 29 December 2009, p. 4.
29 See Germà Bel, "Las infraestructuras y los servicios de transporte en la LES", in Jesús Fernández-Villaverde, Luis Garicano & Manuel Bagüés, *La Ley de Economía Sostenible* (Madrid: FEDEA, 2010), pp. 102–105 (p. 103).
30 Juan Carlos Martín, Concepción Román & Augusto Voltes-Dorta, "A stochastic frontier analysis to estimate the relative efficiency of Spanish airports", *Journal of Productivity Analysis* (2009), 31 (3), 163–176.

Epilogue: And Now, A Spain Like France

1 Beatriz González López-Valcárcel & Patricia Barber Pérez, *Desigualdades territoriales en el Sistema Nacional de Salud (SNS) de España* (Madrid: Fundación Alternativas, Working Paper 90/2006), p. 46.

2 José Luis García Delgado, "Madrid, capital económica", *Arbor* (2001), 169 (666), 359–369, p. 361.

References

Acosta España, Rafael, et al., *La España de las Autonomías. Pasado, presente y futuro. Tomo I* (Madrid: Espasa-Calpe, 1981).

AENA, *Los aeropuertos españoles. Su historia 1911–1996* (Madrid: Aeropuertos Españoles y Navegación Aérea, 1996).

Aguilar López, Manuel, «Carreteras modernas», *Revista de Obras Públicas* (1926), 74 (2467), 524–527.

Albalate, Daniel & Germà Bel, "Regulating Concessions of Toll Motorways: An Empirical Study on Fixed vs. Variable Term Contracts", *Transportation Research-A* (2009), 43 (2), 219–229.

Albalate, Daniel & Germà Bel, "Cuando la economía no importa: Auge y esplendor de la alta velocidad en España", *Revista de Economía Aplicada* (2011), XIX (55), 171–190.

Albalate, Daniel & Germà Bel, "High-Speed Rail: Lessons for Policy Makers from Experiences Abroad", *Public Administration Review* (forthcoming).

Albalate, Daniel, Germà Bel & Xavier Fageda, "Privatization and regulatory reform of toll motorways in Europe", *Governance* (2009), 22 (2), 295–318.

Alcaide Guindo, Pablo, "Avance de las magnitudes económicas españoles en 2009 y serie provisional del Balance Económico Regional. Años 2000 a 2009", *Cuadernos de Información Económica* (2010), 214, 1–64.

Alvar Ezquerra, Alfredo, *Felipe II, la corte y Madrid en 1561* (Madrid: CSIC, 1985).

Alvar Ezquerra, Alfredo, *El nacimiento de una capital europea. Madrid entre 1561 y 1606* (Madrid: Turner Libros, 1989).

Álvarez Junco, José, *Mater Dolorosa. La idea de España en el siglo XIX* (Madrid: Taurus, 2001).

Álvarez-Nogal, Carlos & Leandro Prados de la Escosura, "The decline of Spain (1500–1850): conjectural estimates", *European Review of Economic History* (2007), 11 (3), 319–366.

Alzola y Minondo, Pablo, *Las obras públicas en España: Estudio histórico* (Bilbao: Biblioteca de la Revista de Obras Públicas, 1899).

Artola, Miguel, "Introducción", in Miguel Artola (dir.), Ramón Cordero, Diego Mateo & Fernando Menéndez, *Los ferrocarriles en España 1844/1943. Tomo I. El Estado y los ferrocarriles* (Madrid: Banco de España, 1978), pp. 13–25.

Artola, Miguel, "La acción del Estado", in Miguel Artola (dir.), Ramón Cordero, Diego Mateo & Fernando Menéndez, *Los ferrocarriles en España 1844/1943. Tomo I. El Estado y los ferrocarriles* (Madrid: Banco de España, 1978), pp. 339–453.

Artola, Miguel (dir.), Ramón Cordero, Diego Mateo & Fernando Menéndez, *Los ferrocarriles en España 1844/1943. Tomo I. El Estado y los ferrocarriles* (Madrid: Banco de España, 1978).

Artola, Miguel (dir.), Rafael Anes & Pedro Tedde, *Los ferrocarriles en España 1844/1943. Tomo II. Los ferrocarriles y la economía* (Madrid: Banco de España, 1978).

Artola, Miguel, *Los afrancesados* (Madrid: Alianza Universidad, 1989).

Astigarraga, Jesús, "Necker en España, 1780–1800", *Revista de Economía Aplicada* (2000), 8 (23), 119–141.

Aznar, José María, *Debate sobre la investidura del candidato a la Presidencia del Gobierno.* Diario de Sesiones del Congreso de los Diputados. Pleno y Diputación Permanente. Year 2000, nº. 2 (25 April).

Banco Mundial, *Informe del Banco Mundial. El desarrollo económico de España* (Madrid: BIRF, 1962).

Bel, Germà, *La demanda de transporte en España: Competencia intermodal sobre el ferrocarril interurbano* (Madrid: Instituto de Estudios del Transporte y las Comunicaciones [IETC], 1994).

Bel, Germà, "Efectos imprevistos de la política de transporte", *Revista de Economía Aplicada* (1994), 2 (6), 105–127.

Bel, Germà, "Un estudio desagregado de la demanda de transporte ferroviario interurbano" *Estudios de Transportes y Comunicaciones* (1994), 62, 69–88.

Bel, Germà, "Intermodal competition on inter-urban rail", *International Journal of Transport Economics* (1995), 22 (2), 181–198.

Bel, Germà, "Diagnóstico de algunos impactos intermodales de las autovías previstas en el PDI", *Estudios de Transportes y Comunicaciones* (1996), 71, 51–60.

Bel, Germà, "Changes in travel time across modes and its impact on the demand for inter-urban rail travel", *Transportation Research-E* (1997), 33 (1), 43–52.

Bel, Germà, "Financiación de infraestructuras viarias: la economía política de los peajes", *Papeles de Economía Española* (1999), 82, 123–139

Bel, Germà, "Infraestructures i Catalunya: alguns problemes escollits", *Revista Econòmica de Catalunya* (2002), 45, 11–25.

Bel, Germà, "Política de transporte: ¿Más recursos o mejor gestión?", *Economistas* (2007), 111, 279–284.

Bel, Germà, "La (desitjable) gestió de les infraestructures de Catalunya en el futur", *IDEES* (2009), 32, 32–37.

Bel, Germà, "Comment VIII", in Núria Bosch, Marta Espasa & Albert Solé Ollé, eds., *The political economy of inter-regional fiscal flows. Measurement, determinants and effects on country stability* (Cheltenham: Edward Elgar, 2010), pp. 320–325.

Bel, Germà, "Las infraestructuras y los servicios de transporte in la LES", in Jesús Fernández-Villaverde, Luis Garicano & Manuel Bagüés, *La Ley de Economía Sostenible* (Madrid: FEDEA, 2010), pp. 102–105.

Bel, Germà, "The first privatization: Selling SOEs and privatizing public monopolies in fascist Italy (1922–1925)", *Cambridge Journal of Economics* (forthcoming).

Bel, Germà & Xavier Fageda, "Is a mixed funding model for the highway network sustainable over time? The Spanish case?", *Research in Transportation Economics* (2005), 15, 187–203.

Bel, Germà & Xavier Fageda, "Airport management and airline competition in OECD countries", in F. Fichert, Justus Haucap, & K. Rommel (eds.), *Competition Policy in Network Industry* (LIT-Verlag, 2006), pp. 81–98.

Bel, Germà, & Xavier Fageda, *Aeroports i Poder* (Barcelona: Edicions 62, 2007).

Bel, Germà & Xavier Fageda, "Implicacions de la gestió centralitzada dels aeroports a Espanya", *Revista Econòmica de Catalunya* (2007), 55, 32–44.

Bel, Germà & Xavier Fageda, "Getting there fast: Globalization, intercontinental flights and location of headquarters", *Journal of Economic Geography* (2008), 8 (4), 471–495.

Bel, Germà & Xavier Fageda, "La reforma del model de finançament i gestió dels aeroports a Espanya: lliçons de l'experiència internacional", *Revista Econòmica de Catalunya* (2008), 57, 11–26.

Bel, Germà & Xavier Fageda, eds. *Buena práctica sobre gestión aeroportuaria en Europa* (Barcelona: Fundació Catalunya-Europa, 2009).

Bel, Germà, & Xavier Fageda, "Preventing competition because of 'solidarity': Rhetoric and reality of airport investments in Spain", *Applied Economics* (2009), 41 (22), 2853–2865.

Bel, Germà, & Xavier Fageda, "Privatization, regulation and airport pricing: An empirical analysis for Europe", *Journal of Regulatory Economics* (2010), 37 (2), 142–161.

Bel, Germà & John Foote, "Tolls, terms and Public Interest in road concessions privatization: A comparative analysis of recent transactions in the USA and France", *Transport Reviews* (2009), 29 (3), 397–413.

Berghaus, Erwin, *Historia del Ferrocarril* (Barcelona: Ediciones Zeus, 1964; 1st ed. in German, 1960).

Bonnafous, A., "The regional impact of the TGV", *Transportation* (1987), 14 (2), 127–137.

Boira, Josep Vicent, "El eje mediterráneo y las redes transeuropeas de transporte (RTE-T): Historia de un desencuentro. De la cumbre de Essen (1994) a la dimensión exterior (2006)", *Papers* (2007), 44, 44–63.

Bortolotti, Lando, "Origini e primordi della rete autostradale in Italia, 1922–1933", *Storia Urbana* (1992), XVI (59), 35–70.

Bortolotti, Lando & Giuseppe De Luca, *Fascismo e autostrade. Un caso di sintesi: la Firenze-mare* (Milano: Francoangeli, 1994).

Bosch, Núria, Marta Espasa & Albert Solé Ollé, eds., *The political economy of inter-regional fiscal flows. Measurement, determinants and effects on country stability* (Cheltenham: Edward Elgar, 2010).

Brueckner, Jan, "Airline traffic and urban economic development", *Urban Studies* (2003), 40 (8), 1455–1469.

Buccella, M.R, "Le autovie nel sistema dei trasporti", *Giornale degli Economisti e Rivista di Statistica* (1927), LXVIII (Dicembre), 726–748.

Cambridge Econometrics. *European Regional Database* (Cambridge: Cambridge Econometrics, 2008).

Caron, François, "France", in Patrick O'Brien, *Railways and the economic development of Western Europe, 1830–1914* (London: Macmillan, 1983), pp. 28–48.

Carr, Raymond. *España 1808–1939* (Oxford: Oxford University Press, 1996; Barcelona: Ariel, 1970).

Casañas Vallés, Magí, "El ferrocarril en España, 1844–1868. Consideraciones en torno a una crisis", *Investigaciones Económicas* (1977), 4, 39–68.

Casson, Mark. *The World's First Railway System* (Oxford: Oxford University Press, 2009).

Castells, Antoni, & Albert Solé-Ollé, "The regional allocation of infrastructure investment: the role of equity, efficiency and political factors", *European Economic Review* (2005), 49 (5), 1165–1205.

Clairac Sáenz, Pelayo, "La administración de obras públicas en el período revolucionario", *Revista de Obras Públicas* (1871), 19 (4), 43–48.

Colás Arias, Enrique, "Autostradas italianas", *Revista de Obras Públicas* (1925), 73 (2429), 204–207.

Comín, Francisco, "Comentarios en torno al ferrocarril y el crecimiento económico español entre 1855 y 1931", *Revista de Historia Económica* (1983), 1 (1), 181–195.

Comín Comín, Francisco, Pablo Martín Aceña, Miguel Muñoz Rubio & Javier Vidal Olivares, *150 años de historia de los ferrocarriles españoles. Volumen I* (Madrid: Anaya, 1998).

Comisión de ingenieros, "Ante-proyectos del Plan General de Ferro-carriles. Memoria.", *Revista de Obras Públicas* (1864), 12 (17 & 18), 198–204 & 208–215.

Congreso de los Diputados. *Información parlamentaria hecha por la Comisión de Ferro-carriles nombrada por el Congreso de los Diputados en 10 de enero de 1850* (Madrid: Imprenta Nacional, 1850).

Cordero, Ramón & Fernando Menéndez, "El sistema ferroviario español", in Miguel Artola (dir.), Ramón Cordero, Diego Mateo & Fernando Menéndez, *Los ferrocarriles en España 1844/1943. Tomo I. El Estado y los ferrocarriles* (Madrid: Servicio de Estudios del Banco de España, 1978), pp. 161–338.

Costas Comesaña, Antón. *Apogeo del liberalismo en "La Gloriosa". La reforma económica en el Sexenio liberal (1868–1874)* (Madrid: Siglo XXI, 1988).

Cuadrado Roura, Juan R, "La política regional de los Planes de Desarrollo (1964–1975)", in Rafael Acosta España et al. *La España de las Autonomías. Pasado, presente y futuro. Tomo I* (Madrid: Espasa-Calpe, 1981), pp. 547–608.

De Diego García, Emilio, "El ferrocarril: La Habana-Güines", *Cuadernos de Historia Moderna y Contemporánea* (1983), 4, 59–77.

De la Encina, Salvador, *Comparecencia de la señora ministra de Fomento (Álvarez Arza) para informar sobre las líneas básicas del nuevo modelo de gestión aeroportuaria*. Diario de Sesiones del Congreso de los Diputados. Comisión de Fomento. Year 2008, nº. 177 (16 December).

De la Fuente, Ángel, "Second-best redistribution through public investment: a characterization, an empirical test and an application to the case of Spain", *Regional Science and Urban Economics* (2004), 34 (5), 489–503.

De Luca, Giuseppe, "La costruzione della rete autostradale italiana: L'autostrada Firenze-mare, 1927–1940" *Storia Urbana* (1992), XVI (59), 71–126.

De Luzán, Ignacio, *Memorias literarias de París* (Madrid: Imprenta de don Gabriel Ramírez, 1751).

De Riquer i Permanyer, Borja, "Aproximación al nacionalismo español contemporáneo", *Studia Historica. Historia Contemporánea* (1994), 12, 11–29.

De Rus, Ginés & Vicente Inglada, "Cost-benefit analysis of the high-speed train in Spain", *Annals of Regional Science* (1997), 31 (2), 175–188.

De Rus, Ginés & Chris Nash, *In what circumstances is investment in HSR worthwhile?* (University of Leeds: ITS, WP 590, 2007).

De Rus, Ginés & Gustavo Nombela, "Is investment in High Speed Rail socially profitable?", *Journal of Transport Economics and Policy* (2007), 41 (1), 3–23.

De Rus, Ginés & Concepción Román, "Análisis económico de la línea de alta velocidad Madrid-Barcelona", *Revista de Economía Aplicada* (2006), 14 (42), 35–80.

Derry, T.K. & Trevor I. Williams, *Historia de la tecnología. Desde 1750 hasta 1900 (I)* (Madrid: Siglo XXI, 2002; 1st ed. in English, Oxford University Press, 1960).

Desportes, Marc, "Le prime autostrade francesi: resistenze e dilazioni", *Storia Urbana* (2002), XXVI (100), 55–84.

Dunham, Arthur L, "How the first French railways were planned", *Journal of Economic History* (1941), 1 (1), 12–25.

Dunn, James & Anthony Perl, "Policy networks and industrial revitalization: High Speed Rail initiatives in France and Germany", *Journal of Public Policy* (1994), 14 (3), 311–343.

Elliot, John H. *La España Imperial 1469–1716* (Barcelona: CL & Vicens Vives, 1996; 1st ed. in English, London: Edward Arnold Publishers, 1963).

European Commission, *Interaction between High Speed and Air Passenger Transport – Interim Report.* Interim Report on the Action COST 318 (Bruselas: European Commission, April 1996).

European Commission, *Study on Competition Between Airports and the Application of State Aid Rules* (European Commission, Directorate-General Energy and Transport Directorate F-Air Transport, September 2002).

Fayard, Alain, Francesco Gaeta & Emile Quinet, "French motorways: Experience and assessment", *Research in Transportation Economics* (2005), 15, 93–105.

Fayard, Alain, David Meunier & Emile Quinet, "Motorway Provision and Management in France: Analyses and Policy Issues", *Network and Spatial Economics* (forthcoming).

Fenoaltea, Stefano, "Italy", in Patrick O'Brien, *Railways and the economic development of Western Europe, 1830–1914* (London: Macmillan, 1983), pp. 49–121.

Fernández, Ramón, Eduardo Molina & Fernando Nebot, "El fracaso de la política de las autopistas de peaje", *Información Comercial Española* (1983), 594, 37–54.

Fernández Álvarez, Manuel. *Felipe II y su tiempo* (Madrid: Espasa Calpe, 1998; 6th ed.).

Fernández de Pinedo, Emiliano, "Coyuntura y políticas económicas", in Manuel Tuñón de Lara, dir., *Historia de España. Tomo VII, Centralismo, Ilustración y agonía del Antiguo Régimen (1715–1833)* (Barcelona: Editorial Labor, 1980), pp. 9–173.

Fernández-Villaverde, Jesús, Luis Garicano & Manuel Bagüés, *La Ley de Economía Sostenible* (Madrid: FEDEA, 2010).

Fichert, F., Justus Haucap, & K. Rommel (eds.), *Competition Policy in Network Industry* (LIT-Verlag, 2006).

Fogel, Robert W. *Railroads and American Economic Growth: Essays in Econometric History* (Baltimore: Johns Hopkins Press, 1964).

Fremdling, Rainer, "Germany", in Patrick O'Brien, *Railways and the economic development of Western Europe, 1830–1914* (London: Macmillan, 1983), pp. 121–148.

García Delgado, José Luis, "Madrid, capital económica", *Arbor* (2001), 169 (666), 359–369.

García Ormaechea, Pedro, "La red de carreteras españolas. Su modernización", *Revista de Obras Públicas* (1957), 105 (2906), 294–296.

García Ortega, Pedro. *Las concesiones administrativas de carreteras en el ordenamiento jurídico español* (Madrid: Ministerio de Obras Públicas y Urbanismo, 1979).

Gil Novales, Alberto, "Política y sociedad", in Manuel Tuñón de Lara, dir., *Historia de España. Tomo VII, Centralismo, Ilustración y agonía del Antiguo Régimen (1715–1833)* (Barcelona: Editorial Labor, 1980), pp. 175–320.

Givoni, Moshe, "Development and impact of the Modern High-speed Train: A Review", *Transport Reviews* (2006), 26 (5), 593–611.

Goerlich Gisbert, Francisco, Matilde Mas Ivars (dirs.); Joaquín Azagra Ros & Pilar Chorén Rodríguez, *La localización de la población española sobre el territorio, un siglo de cambios; un estudio basado en series homogéneas (1900–2001)* (Bilbao: Fundación BBVA, 2006).

Gómez-Ibáñez, José A. & John R. Meyer, *Going private. The international experience with transport privatization* (Washington DC: Brookings Institution, 1993).

Gómez Mendoza, Antonio, *Ferrocarril y cambio económico en España (1855–1913)* (Madrid: Alianza, 1982).

Gómez Mendoza, Antonio, *Ferrocarril, industria y mercado en la modernización de España* (Madrid: Espasa-Calpe, 1989).

Gómez Mendoza, Antonio, "Madrid, centro de la red de comunicaciones", *Arbor* (2001), 169 (666), 343–358.

Gómez Mendoza, Antonio, "Del ferrocarril al AVE. ¿Los mismos errores históricos?", *Clío. Revista de Historia* (2005), 45, 44–49.

González López-Valcárcel, Beatriz & Patricia Barber Pérez. *Desigualdades territoriales en el Sistema Nacional de Salud (SNS) de España* (Madrid: Fundación Alternativas, Working Paper 90/2006).

Graham, Anne, "Airport Planning and Regulation in the United Kingdom", in Clifford Winston & Ginés de Rus, eds., *Aviation Infrastructure Performance. A*

*Study in Comparative Political Economy (*Washington DC: Brookings Institution Press, 2008), pp. 100–136.

Greco, Andrea & Giorgio Ragazzi, "History and regulations of Italian highways concessionaires", *Research in Transportation Economics* (2005), 15, 121–133.

Grupo Ferrovie dello Stato, *Rete AV/AC. Analisi dei costi* (Roma: Grupo Ferrovie dello Stato, 2007).

Hawke, Gary & Jim Higgins, "Britain", in Patrick O'Brien, *Railways and the economic development of Western Europe, 1830–1914* (London: Macmillan, 1983), pp. 170–202.

Haynes, Kingsley E., "Labor markets and regional transportation improvements: the case of high-speed trains. An introduction and review", *Annals of Regional Science* (1997), 31 (1), 57–76.

Herranz Loncán, Alfonso, *La dotación de infraestructuras en España, 1844–1935* (Madrid: Banco de España, 2004).

Herranz Loncán, Alfonso, "The Spanish Infrastructure Stock, 1845–1935", *Research in Economic History* (2005), 23, 85–129.

Herranz Loncán, Alfonso,"Railroad Impact in Backward Economies: Spain, 1850–1913",*Journal of Economic History* (2006), 66 (4), 853–881.

Herranz Loncán, Alfonso, "Infrastructure investment and Spanish economic growth, 1850–1935", *Explorations in Economic History* (2007), 44 (3), 452–468.

Herranz Loncán, Alfonso. *Infraestructuras y crecimiento económico en España (1850–1935)* (Madrid: Fundación de los Ferrocarriles Españoles, 2008).

Imashiro, Mitsuhide, "Changes in Japan's Transport Market and Privatization", *Japan Railway and Transport Review* (1997), 13, 50–53.

Izquierdo de Bartolomé, Rafael, "El modelo de transporte", in Rafael Acosta España, et al. *La España de las Autonomías. Pasado, presente y futuro. Tomo I* (Madrid: Espasa-Calpe, 1981), pp. 367–470.

Izquierdo de Bartolomé, Rafael, *Gestión y financiación de las infraestructuras de transporte terrestre* (Madrid: Asociación Española de la Carretera, 1997).

Juliá, Santos, "Madrid, capital del Estado (1833–1993)", in Santos Juliá, David Ringrose & Cristina Segura, *Madrid. Historia de una capital* (Madrid: Alianza Editorial, 1994, ed. 2000), pp. 315–576.

Juliá, Santos, David Ringrose & Cristina Segura, *Madrid. Historia de una capital* (Madrid: Alianza Editorial, 1994, ed. 2000).

Juliana, Enric, *La deriva de España. Geografía de un país vigoroso y desorientado (*Barcelona: RBA, 2009).

Junta Consultiva de Caminos, Canales y Puertos, "Ante-proyectos del Plan General de Ferro-carriles. Informe y ante-proyecto.", *Revista de Obras Públicas* (1864), 12 (21, 22, & 23), 246–251, 259–262, 268–273.

Kemmerling, Achim, & Andreas Stephan, "The contribution of local public infrastructure to private productivity and its political economy: evidence from a panel of large German cities", *Public Choice (*2002), 113 (3/4), 403–424.

Kerkloh, Michael, "El modelo alemán, y el caso del aeropuerto de Múnich", in

Germà Bel & Xavier Fageda, eds., *Buena práctica sobre gestión aeroportuaria en Europa* (Barcelona: Fundació Catalunya-Europa, 2009), pp. 73–87.

Keynes, John Maynard, *The General theory of employment interest and Money*, 1936 (London: St. Martin's Press, 1973).

Laffut, Michel, "Belgium", in Patrick O'Brien, *Railways and the economic development of Western Europe, 1830–1914* (London: Macmillan, 1983), pp. 203–226.

Lluch, Ernest, *La Catalunya vençuda del segle XVIII. Foscors i clarors de la Il·lustració (*Barcelona: Edicions 62, 1996).

Madrazo, Santos, *El Sistema de Transportes en España, 1750–1850* (Madrid, Ediciones Turner, 1984).

Mannone, Valérie, *L'impact régional du TGV Sud-Est* (Université de Provence, Aix-en-Provence: PhD Dissertation, 1995).

Maragall, Pasqual, "Madrid se va", *El País*, 27 February 2001.

Martí Hennenberg, Jordi, "Un balance del tren de alta velocidad en Francia. Enseñanzas para el caso español", *Ería* (2000), 52, 131–143.

Martín, Juan Carlos, Concepción Román & Augusto Voltes-Dorta, "A stochastic frontier analysis to estimate the relative efficiency of Spanish airports", *Journal of Productivity Analysis* (2009), 31 (3), 163–176.

Mas Ivars, Matilde, Francisco Pérez García & Ezequiel Uriel Jiménez (dirs.), *El stock y los servicios del capital en España y su distribución territorial (1964–2005). Nueva metodología (*Bilbao: Fundación BBVA, 2007).

Mateo del Peral, Diego, "Los orígenes de la política ferroviaria en España (1844–1877)", in Miguel Artola (dir.), Ramón Cordero, Diego Mateo & Fernando Menéndez, *Los ferrocarriles en España 1844/1943. Tomo I. El Estado y los ferrocarriles (*Madrid: Servicio de Estudios del Banco de España, 1978), pp. 31–159.

Menéndez Pidal, Gonzalo, *Los caminos en la Historia de España* (Madrid: Ediciones Cultura Hispánica, 1951).

Mills, Gordon, "Airports users don't pay enough – and now here's privatisation", *Economic Papers* (1995), 14 (1), 73–84.

Ministerio de Fomento, *Los transportes, las infraestructuras y los servicios postales. Informe Anual 2008* (Madrid: Ministerio de Fomento, 2009).

Ministerio de Fomento, *Anuario Estadístico 2008* (Madrid: Ministerio de Fomento, 2009).

Ministerio de Fomento, *Previsión de resultados económicos de los aeropuertos españoles. Ejercicio 2009. Ejercicio 2010.* Information provided by the Minister in the meeting of the Public Works Committee (Spanish Congress) on 12 January 2010.

Mitchell, B.R., *Internacional Historical Statistics: Europe 1750–1993* (London: Macmillan, 1998).

MOPU, *Informe sobre las Autopistas Nacionales de Peaje (*Madrid: Ministerio de Obras Públicas y Urbanismo, 1974).

Moraglio, Massimo, "L'autostrada Torino-Milano, 1923–1933: I progetti e la costruzione", *Storia Urbana (*1999), XXIII (86), 103–121.

Moraglio, Massimo, "Per una storia delle autostrade italiane: Il periodo tra le due Guerre Mondiali", *Storia Urbana* (2002), XXVI (100), 11–25.

Nadal, Jordi, *El fracaso de la revolución industrial en España. 1814–1913* (Barcelona: Ariel, 1975).

Navas, Teresa, "Il riflesso della modernità: le autostrade spagnole, 1920–1960", *Storia urbana* (2002), XXVI (100), 27–54.

Nolan, James, Pamela Ritchie & John Rowcroft, "Small market air service and regional policy", *Journal of Transport Economics and Policy* (2005), 39 (3), 363–378.

O'Brien, Patrick, "Transport and economic development in Europe, 1789–1914", in Patrick O'Brien, *Railways and the economic development of Western Europe, 1830–1914* (London: Macmillan, 1983), pp. 1–27.

Oliver Alonso, Josep, dir. *La apertura exterior de las regiones en España* (València: Tirant lo Blanch, 2003).

Onaindía, Mario, *La construcción de la nación española* (Barcelona: Ediciones B, 2002).

Ortega y Gasset, José. *España invertebrada*, 1921 (2nd ed., Madrid: Espasa Calpe, 1967).

Pascual Domènech, Pere. *Los caminos de la era industrial. La construcción y financiación de la Red Ferroviaria Catalana (1843–1898)* (Barcelona: Edicions de la Universitat de Barcelona, 1999).

Pemán Gavín, Juan. "Sobre la regulación de las carreteras en el Derecho Español: Una visión de conjunto", *Revista de Administración Pública* (1992), 129 (September–December), 117–161.

Pérez Touriño, Emilio, "Efectos del Plan. Realizaciones y balance socioeconómico", *Estudios de Transporte y Comunicaciones* (1994), 65 (separata), 9–27.

Plaud, Alain, "Les nouvelles voies ferrées à grande vitesse et l'aménagement du territoire au Japon", *Transports* (1977), 225, 387–393.

Pujol, Jordi, *Un modelo malogrado* (Barcelona: Centre d'Estudis Jordi Pujol, 2009).

Puncel Chornet, Alfonso, *La Autopista del Mediterráneo. Cesiones, concesiones, servicios y servidumbres* (València: Universitat de València, 1996).

Ringrose, David R., *Los transportes y el estancamiento económico de España (1750–1850)* (Madrid: Editorial Tecnos, 1972; 1st ed., in English, Durham, NC: Duke University Press, 1970).

Ringrose, David R. *Madrid y la economía española, 1560–1850. Ciudad, Corte y País en el Antiguo Régimen* (Madrid: Alianza Universidad, 1985; 1st ed. in English, Berkeley: University of California Press, 1983).

Ringrose, David R, "Madrid, capital imperial (1561–1833)", in Santos Juliá, David Ringrose & Cristina Segura, *Madrid. Historia de una capital* (Madrid: Alianza Editorial, 1994, ed. 2000), pp. 153–314.

Ringrose, David R. *España, 1700–1900: el mito del fracaso* (Madrid: Alianza Editorial, 1996).

Rodríguez Bugarín, Miguel, Margarita Novales Ordax & Alfonso Orro Arcay, "Alta velocidad y territorio: Algunas experiencias internacionales", *Ingeniería y Territorio* (2005), 70, 4–11.

Rodríguez Zapatero, José Luis. *Una idea actual de España*. Speech of the Spanish Premier in the presentation of nº. 100 of the journal *La Aventura de la Historia*. Madrid, 1 February 2007.

Rothengatter, Werner, "Motorways and motorway finance in Germany and Austria", *Research in Transportation Economics* (2005), 15, 75–91.

Sànchez, Esther, "La inversió de l'Estat en infraestuctures per comunitats autònomes", *Nota d'economia. Revista d'economia catalana i de sector públic* (2006), 83/84, 51–67.

Sansalvadó, Montserrat. *La financiación de las inversiones a largo plazo. El caso de las autopistas de peaje* (PhD Dissertation, Universitat de Barcelona, 1987).

Segura, Cristina, "Madrid en la Edad Media. Génesis de una capital (873?–1561)", in Santos Juliá, David Ringrose & Cristina Segura, *Madrid. Historia de una capital* (Madrid: Alianza Editorial, 1994, ed. 2000), pp. 11–151.

Smith, Adam. *The Wealth of Nations*, 1776 (3rd ed., London: W. Strahan & T. Cadell, 1784).

Société d'Agriculture, Sciences, Art et Commerce de l'arrondissement de ST-Étienne (Loire). *Bulletin Industriel* (Saint Étienne: Imprimerie de Gaudelet, 1830).

Tedde Lorca, Pedro, "Las compañías ferroviarias en España" in Miguel Artola (dir.), Rafael Anes & Pedro Tedde, *Los ferrocarriles en España 1844/1943. Tomo II. Los ferrocarriles y la economía* (Madrid: Servicio de Estudios del Banco de España, 1978), pp. 9–354.

Terrazoni, Claude & Jean-Michel Vernhes, "El modelo francés, y el caso del aeropuerto de Tolosa", in Germà Bel & Xavier Fageda, eds., *Buena práctica sobre gestión aeroportuaria en Europa* (Barcelona: Fundació Catalunya-Europa, 2009), pp. 58–72.

Thompson, Louis S.,"High Speed Rail in the United States- Why isn't there more?", *Japan Railway and Transport Review* (1994), 3, 32–39.

Tortella Casares, Gabriel, *Los Orígenes del capitalismo en España: Banca, industria y ferrocarriles en el siglo XIX* (Madrid: Tecnos, 1973).

Tortella Casares, Gabriel, *El desarrollo de la España contemporánea. Historia económica de los siglos XIX y XX* (Madrid: Alianza, 1994).

Tuñón de Lara, Manuel, dir. *Historia de España. Tomo VII, Centralismo, Ilustración y agonía del Antiguo Régimen (1715–1833)* (Barcelona: Editorial Labor, 1980).

Turró, Mateu, "L'EURAM, porta d'Europa. Reflexions a partir del llibre blanc de les infraestructures de l'EURAM", in EURAM, *Llibre blanc de les infraestructures. Euroregió del arc mediterrani* (València: EURAM, 2010, pp. 389–434).

Uriol Salcedo, José I, "Los viajes por la posta en el siglo XVIII y en los primeros años del siglo XIX", *Revista de Obras Públicas* (1977), 124 (3151), 837–856.

Uriol Salcedo, José I, "Las carreteras y los canales de navegación en los reinados de Fernando VI y Carlos III", *Revista de Obras Públicas* (1978), 125 (3159), 533–546.

Uriol Salcedo, José I, "Las carreteras y los canales de navegación en los reinados de Fernando VI y Carlos III. Auge de la construcción de carreteras y canales. Carlos III", *Revista de Obras Públicas* (1978), 125 (3160), 625–636.

Uriol Salcedo, José I, "Las calzadas romanas y los caminos del siglo XVI", *Revista de Obras Públicas* (1985), 132 (3237), 553–563

Uriol Salcedo, José I. *Historia de los caminos de España. Vol. I Hasta el siglo XIX* (Madrid: Editorial AC, 1990).

Uriol Salcedo, José I. *Historia de los caminos de España. Vol. II Siglos XIX y XX* (Madrid: Editorial AC, 1992).

Van den Berg, Leo & Peter Pol, *The European high-speed train-network and urban development* (Aldershot: Ashgate, 1998).

Van Essen, Huib, Olivier Bello, Jos Dings, & Robert van den Brink, *To shift or not to shift, that's the question. The environmental performance of the principal modes of freight and passenger transport in the policymaking process* (Delft: CE Delft, 2003).

Van Orman Quine, Willard, "On what there is", *Review of Metaphysics* (1948), 2 (5), 21–38.

Van Wee, Bert, Robert van den Brink, & Hans Nijland, "Environmental impacts of high-speed rail links in cost-benefit analyses: a case study of the Dutch Zuider Zee line". *Transportation Research D* (2003), 8 (4), 299–314.

Vicens Vives, Jaume. *Aproximación a la Historia de España* (Barcelona: Vicens Vives, 1952; 4th ed., Barcelona: Vicens Vives, 1966).

Vickerman, Roger, "High-speed rail in Europe: experience and issues for future development", *Annals of Regional Science* (1997), 31 (1), 21–38.

Wais San Martín, Francisco, "Recuerdo a Bernardo Ward y sus caminos", *Revista de Obras Públicas* (1963), 111 (2981), 563–566.

Wais San Martín, Francisco, *Historia de los ferrocarriles españoles I* (Madrid: Fundación de los Ferrocarriles Españoles, 1987, 3rd ed.; 1st ed. 1968).

Whitehead, Alfred North, *Process and Reality* (Cambridge: Cambridge University Press, 1929).

Williams, George & Romano Pagliari, "A comparative analysis of the application and use of public service obligations in air transport within the EU", *Transport Policy* (2004), 11 (1), 55–66.

Winston, Clifford & Ginés de Rus, eds., *Aviation Infrastructure Performance. A Study in Comparative Political Economy* (Washington DC: Brookings Institution Press, 2008).

Yamano, Nohiriko, & Toru Ohkawara, "The regional allocation of public investment: efficiency or equity?", *Journal of Regional Science* (2000), 40 (2), 205–229.

Index